CW00539058

The Essen

Truth

Some titles are not available in North America.

The Essence
of Truth

On Plato's Cave Allegory and
Theaetetus

Martin Heidegger

Translated by Ted Sadler

B L O O M S B U R Y
LONDON • NEW DELHI • NEW YORK • SYDNEY

Bloomsbury Academic

An imprint of Bloomsbury Publishing Plc

50 Bedford Square	1385 Broadway
London	New York
WC1B 3DP	NY 10018
UK	USA

www.bloomsbury.com

Bloomsbury is a registered trade mark of Bloomsbury Publishing Plc

Originally published as *Vom Wesen der Wahrheit*
© Vittorio Klosterman GmbH, Frankfurt am Main, 1988

Die Herausgabe dieses Wekes wurde aus Mitteln von
INTER NATIONES, Bonn gefördert

English translation first published by Continuum in 2002
© Continuum 2002

This paperback edition first published in 2013 by Bloomsbury Academic

British Library Cataloguing-in-Publication Data
A catalogue record for this book is available from the British Library.

ISBN: PR 978-1 4725-2571-0

Library of Congress Cataloging-in-Publication Data
A catalog record for this book is available from the Library of Congress.

Typeset by Newgen Imaging Systems Pvt Ltd, Chennai, India
Printed and bound in India

Contents

Translator's Foreword

This book is a translation of *Vom Wesen der Wahrheit: zu Platons Höhleng-leichnis und Theätet*, first published in 1988 as volume 34 of Martin Heidegger's *Gesamtausgabe*. The text is based on a lecture course delivered by Heidegger at the University of Freiburg in the winter semester 1931–32. Part One of the course provides a detailed analysis of Plato's allegory of the cave in the *Republic*, while Part Two gives a similarly painstaking exegesis and interpretation of a central section of Plato's *Theaetetus*. As always with Heidegger's writings on the Greeks, the point of his interpretative method is to bring to light the original meaning of philosophical concepts, especially to free up these concepts, which in the subsequent tradition have become overlaid by secondary and even quite different meanings, to their intrinsic power. In this regard the present text must count as one of Heidegger's most important works, for nowhere else does he give a comparably thorough explanation of what is arguably the most fundamental and abiding theme of his entire philosophy, namely the difference between truth as the 'unhiddenness of beings' and truth as the 'correctness of propositions'. For Heidegger, it is by neglecting the former *primordial* concept of truth in favour of the latter *derivative* concept that Western philosophy, beginning already with Plato, took off on its 'metaphysical' course towards the bankruptcy of the present day. In the lectures here translated, Heidegger is not concerned to demonstrate this larger thesis as such, but to clarify the aforesaid *distinction* upon which it is founded. This he does through his characteristic combination of philological acumen and philosophical incisiveness, or, more precisely, by employing philological expertise *in the service of* philosophical insight.

Heidegger himself often emphasizes that the results or constituent theses of a philosophical discourse cannot be separated from its method, indeed that the latter, as precisely what makes a genuine 'showing' possible, is ultimately more important than theoretical conclusions. This applies to Plato's dialogues or the closely argued treatises of Aristotle as much as to the present lecture course by Heidegger. In the following pages the reader will encounter the 'art of going slowly' brought to the highest consummation, always for the purpose of thoroughly comprehending the matter at hand. Indeed it is Heidegger's conviction that philosophy, genuinely undertaken and carried through, subverts the impatient 'hunger for results' so characteristic of the modern age. The hunger for truth, on the other hand, which is how Heidegger understands the Platonic *eros,* eschews nothing so much as the half-digested theories of the academic tradesman, or journalist, who is always intent on 'situating' ideas within a framework of received opinion. Thus, by persevering in the present text, the reader will discover not just 'Heidegger's ideas' but a method for philosophizing in general.

Information on the origin of the German text as printed in the *Gesamtausgabe* can be found in Hermann Mörchen's Afterword to the original edition (pp. 238–41 of this volume). Here it is necessary only to underline the fact that Heidegger did not himself originally intend, let alone prepare, this lecture course for publication. The German text does not have the smoothness of a polished work, but contains many irregularities such as are to be expected from manuscripts prepared for teaching, and from transcripts of lectures. In my translation I have tried to remain faithful to this unfinished character of the German text, at the same time giving due attention to readability.

The longer Greek quotations from Plato are translated by Heidegger immediately afterwards in the text, and I have translated his translations, only occasionally making concessions for the sake of fluent reading. I have throughout consulted standard English translations of Plato. The many shorter quotations of Greek words and phrases are also either translated or paraphrased by Heidegger in the adjacent portion of text and should present no problem for the reader; the Greek-English glossary at the end of the volume may help with the central and most frequently recurring Greek words. As for Heidegger's German, which includes many complex and unusual constructions, I have sometimes placed the original in square brackets immediately after my translation. In general, however, I have restricted this practice to philosophically operative expressions, and to words whose etymological interrelations

Heidegger is seeking to highlight. An English-German glossary has also been provided, which, while not an infallible guide (given necessary variations in rendering the same German word), should answer most queries as to what word of Heidegger is being translated at any particular point.

A few translational matters require specific comment:

1 The standard English translation of 'Wesen' as 'essence' has been retained throughout. It should be noted, however, that in contexts relating to truth and the human being Heidegger does not intend 'Wesen' in the sense of the Latin 'essentia', which refers to the 'what-ness' or 'essential nature' of a thing. Instead, in such contexts Heidegger wants the original *verbal* meaning of 'Wesen' to come to the fore; thus the 'essence of truth' does not refer to anything static, but to an 'occurrence' within which the human being is *actively* situated.

2 The German word 'Dasein', which normally means 'existence', but in Heidegger most often means the 'way of being' (ontological character) of the human being, has usually been left untranslated. This is now common practice in English translations of Heidegger.

3 'Sein' has been rendered as 'being' and not as 'Being'; the difference between the nominalization of the verb 'to be' on the one hand, and 'being' in the sense of thing or entity ('Seiende') on the other hand, is in every case clear from the context. Another standard practice I have adopted (in most cases) is the pluralized rendering of 'das Seiende' as 'the beings' or 'beings'. Especially difficult or noteworthy occurrences of 'Sein', 'Seiende' and their cognates have been placed in square brackets immediately following my translation.

I have inserted a small number of footnotes giving English translations (and sources) of Heidegger's Greek quotations, e.g. from Parmenides and Democritus. Where Heidegger discusses, in Part Two, Schleiermacher's German translation of specific words of Plato, I have given, for comparison, the English translations of Fowler and Cornford. My footnotes are marked by 'Trans.'; otherwise all footnotes are from the editor of the German edition (see Afterword), who, in addition to providing philological and bibliographical information, sometimes puts supplementary material from Heidegger at the bottom of the page.

Everything in square brackets stems from Heidegger; this occurs most often in his translation of Platonic passages. The approximate page numbering of the German edition appears at the bottom of the page in square brackets.

For her expert assistance in checking and commenting on this translation I would like to thank Dr Marnie Hanlon. Valuable comments have also been received from Professor Parvis Emad and Professor F.-W. von Herrmann.

Ted Sadler
August 2001

Preliminary Considerations

§ 1. The Questionworthiness of Our 'Self-Evident' Preconceptions Concerning 'Essence' and 'Truth'

We wish to consider the *essence of truth*.

'Truth': what is that? The answer to the question 'what is that?' brings us to the 'essence' of a thing. 'Table': what is that? 'Mountain', 'ocean', 'plant'; in each case the question 'what is that?' asks about the 'essence' of these things. We ask – and yet we already *know* them! Indeed, *must* we not know them, in order afterward to ask, and even to give an answer, about *what* they are?

What, for example, is a table? Just what makes it what it is, what applies to *everything* that is a table. What all actual and possible tables have in common is the *universal*, the 'essence': what something is 'in general'.

But we discover what is universal to *all* only by comparing *particular* things and observing the sameness of what they have in common. We already *know* particular tables, and all kinds of particular things, when we ask about their 'essence'. Thus too in the case of our question 'what is truth?' (As will be shown in the following, this 'thus' may be our *undoing*.)

What is the 'essence' of truth? We know particular truths; e.g. that $2 + 1 = 3$, that the earth revolves around the sun, that autumn is followed by winter, that the World War began in early August 1914, that Kant is a philosopher, that it is noisy on the street outside, that this lecture room is heated, that there is a light on here, and so on. These are 'particular truths'; we call them this because they contain 'something true'. And *wherein* is the true 'contained'? What is it which so to speak 'bears' this truth? It is the *propositions* we just enunciated. Each particular proposition is true, is 'something true', 'a truth'. We now ask: what is truth as such and in general? What makes each of these propositions true? Just this: that *what* they say corresponds with the facts *about which* they say something. Therefore the being-true of the proposition means such correspondence. What then *is* truth? Truth is *correspondence.* Such correspondence obtains because the proposition is directed to the facts and states of affairs *about which* it says something. Truth is *correctness* [*Richtig-keit*]. So truth is *correspondence, grounded in correctness, between proposition and thing.*

We thus encounter something rather peculiar: not only do we know particular truths, but we also already know what truth *is.* Therefore we already *know* the essence of truth. It is not just that we know accidentally and incidentally, as well as particular truths, *also* the essence of truth, but clearly we must *necessarily* already know the essence. For how otherwise could we know how to respond to the request to name truths? We could not otherwise bring forward what is stated and claim it *as* a truth.

In this way we know the *essence* of truth, what it is, i.e. correspondence, correctness in the sense of directedness-to . . . We also know that by the 'essence' of a thing we mean the universal, and we know what essence is as essence: essence-hood, that which makes essence what it is. Why then do we still *inquire* into the essence of truth and make this question the topic of a long series of lectures? Especially since what we have stated about essence is quite obvious and comprehensible to anyone?

Something is 'intelligible' to us if we understand it,[1] i.e. if we can set ourselves before the thing and have its measure, if we can survey and comprehend it in its basic structure. Is what we have just called 'self-evident' (truth as correspondence and correctness, essence as the universal, the what-being) really *intelligible*?

1. We said that *correspondence* is the essence of truth. The proposition corresponds with that about which it speaks. 'Here in the room a light is on.' That about which something is said in this proposition, that *towards which* it is directed, must already be *given*

as the measure for the proposition, for how otherwise could the proposition be directed towards it? So we must already know what and how the thing is about which we speak. We know that a light is on here. Such knowing [*Wissen*] can only arise from knowledge [*Erkenntnis*], and knowledge grasps the true, for false knowledge is no knowledge at all. And what *is* the true? The true is *what is known.* It is just what corresponds with the facts. The proposition corresponds with what is known in knowledge; thus with what is true. The true? So does the correspondence of the proposition amount to correspondence with something corresponding? A fine definition! Truth is correspondence with a correspondence, the latter itself corresponds with a correspondence, and so forth. And the *first* correspondence to which we revert? Must what is given first of all *resemble* something given, therefore itself be necessarily a correspondence? What creeps in between here, and why? Since everything is discussed in a groundless and formal way, we obtain nothing at all intelligible with the concept of truth as correspondence. What presents itself as self-evident is utterly obscure.

2. We said that what is true is the *proposition.* But we also call 'true' a thing or a human being. We say 'true gold', 'a true friend'. What does 'true' mean *here?* What does true gold correspond with, if being-true means correspondence? With a proposition perhaps? Clearly not. 'True' is at any rate ambiguous. How does it happen that, as well as propositions, we also call things and human beings 'true'? Does 'true' mean something different as applied to propositions and to things? What then is the *proper* meaning of 'true' – that which applies to propositions or that which applies to things? Or does *neither* of these two meanings have priority over the other? But do we then have a common *derivation* from *another* meaning of 'true' which is not expressed in the concept of truth as correspondence?

Truth as correspondence (characteristic of the proposition) is thus ambiguous, insufficiently delimited in itself or determined in its origins. It is therefore not intelligible, its self-evidence is illusory.

3. The *essence* of truth, we said, is that which determines particular truths *in general*, in respect of *what* they *are.* We called 'essence' the universal, the what-being. We proceeded by clarifying this concept of essence in terms of what we mean by the essence of a table. Now clearly the essence of 'table' as such, and of 'truth' as such, are quite

incomparable in terms of content, but is the *essence-hood* of essence also different in the two cases? Or is the essence-character of the essence of table and the essence- character of the essence of truth *the same*? Are truths like tables, which just stand around, such that one can ask about them in the same way? Was our procedure justified when, without further ado, we transposed our conception of the essence of table, chair and letter-box (*the* question of essence we direct at *things*) on to our conception of the essence of *truth?*

Even if we grant that the essence-hood of essence is in both cases the same and gives the general what-being of a thing, what do we understand by what-being, what does *being* [*Sein*] mean there? Do we really understand that? We do not. We speak in such a self-evident fashion about essence, the question of essence, the concept of essence, and thus too about the essence of truth, yet at bottom what we are asking about remains unintelligible.

4. In outlining the essence of table and of truth it was indicated that not only do we know particular tables and truths, but also, in so far as we know them *as such* (precisely as what they are) we already know them in their essence, indeed that we must already know this essence *in advance* in order to recognize anything encountered *as* table, *as* mountain, *as* truth. What are we to make of this peculiarity of essence, that it *must* already be known in advance? What kind of necessity is this? Why is it so? Is it an accident, simply a fact that we register and submit to? Do we understand the essence-hood of essence if we stand helplessly before this peculiarity? Not at all. Essence and essence-hood are also in this respect unintelligible.

5. But even assuming what we proposed concerning the essence of truth, namely correspondence between proposition and fact, and concerning essence as what-being (as the same, i.e. the universal governing all particulars), even assuming all that is quite intelligible and lacking in anything unintelligible, may we take this *self-evidence* without further ado as the foundation for our investigation, as vouching for itself and as something secure and true? How do we know that what is understood in this way is really *secured*? How do we know that what is self-evident really *is* so and is *true*? How do we know that the self-evidence of something – assuming that this does obtain – is a *guarantee* for the truth of the relevant thing or proposition? Is *that* also self-evident? How much has been self-evident and obvious to us

humans and yet later turned out to be illusory, the opposite of truth and sound knowledge! Thus our appeal to self-evidence as the guarantee of truth is ungrounded and unintelligible.

6. Something that is 'of itself' evident or intelligible is called this because it 'enters into us' with no doing on our own part. It is self-evident *to us*, *we* find it so. Who are we then? How is it that we come to regard ourselves as the court of appeal for deciding what is or is not self-evident? That we apparently do not need to add anything for the self-evidence to be accepted by us: does that prove that we cannot, and that we really must not, add anything? We, as we exist in our daily problems and pleasures, we who are now occupied with the question concerning the essence of truth (because it appears on the register of lectures), are *we,* and what is self-evident to *us,* the ultimate and primary criterion? Do we in the least understand why that must be so, and indeed, why that cannot be so? We humans, do we know who we are and who or what *the human* is? Do we know whether in general, within which limits, and with which deficiencies, the self-evident can and may be a standard for human beings? Who *tells* us who the human being is? Is this not all completely unintelligible?

We began by defining the essence of truth as correspondence and correctness. This seemed self-evident, and therefore binding. Now, already after a few crude steps, this self-evidence has emerged as thoroughly incomprehensible: the concept of the essence of *truth* in two respects (1 and 2), the concept of the *essence-hood* of essence in two respects (3 and 4), the appeal to *self-evidence* as the measure and guarantee of secure knowledge again in two respects (5 and 6). The seemingly self-evident has become incomprehensible. But this means, in so far as we want to linger over and further examine this incomprehensibility, that it has become *worthy of questioning.* We must first of all ask how it comes about that we quite naturally move and feel comfortable within such self-evidences. How is it that the apparently self-evident turns out, upon closer examination, to be understood least? Answer: because it is too close to us and because we proceed in this way with everything close. We take care, for example, that this and that is in order, that we come here with pen and exercise book, and that our propositions, if possible, correspond with what we intend and talk about. We know that truth belongs in a certain way to our daily affairs, and we know quite naturally what this means. It lies so close to us that we have no distance from it, and therefore no possibility of having an overall view of it and comprehending it.

So the first thing must be to distance ourselves from this self-evidence, to step back from it so that what we so readily conceive as truth can be left standing and resting in itself. But *where* are we to step back to, *from where* are we to observe the self-evident? From what has earlier been *said* about all this, back to the way in which truth was *earlier* conceived; therefore by looking around in the *history* of the concept of truth! Yes: but is that not a useless undertaking, to dig up earlier opinions about things and go into them at length? Is this fruitless business, notwithstanding all the enthusiasm surrounding it, not ultimately a flight from what is today required of us? Are these safe promenades in the old gardens of earlier conceptions and doctrines not a comfortable avoidance of responsibility in face of the demands of the day, a diversionary spiritual luxury to which we no longer have any right (today least of all)?[2]

§ 2. History of the Concept of Truth: Not Historical Confirmation of Preconceptions, But Return to the Originary Greek Experience of ἀλήθεια (Unhiddenness)

But let us for a moment accede to the wish for historical orientation! How was what we self-evidently referred to as the essence of truth, and as the essence of essence, *previously* conceived? In the Middle Ages and later the definition was: *veritas est adaequatio rei et intellectus sive enuntiationis,* truth is the bringing of the thought or proposition into alignment with the thing, i.e. into correspondence with the latter, *commensuratio,* the measuring up to, or the measuring against, something. And how was essence conceived? As *quidditas,* as what-ness, the what-being of a thing – its genus: the universality of the genus.

And how were the concepts of truth and essence conceived still earlier, in antiquity? Truth was there defined as ὁμοίωσις (ὁμοίωμα) τῶν παθημάτων τῆς ψυχῆς καὶ τῶν πραγμάτων (*adaequatio*, equivalence, correspondence with the things) and essence as τὸ τί ἐστιν *(quidditas*, what-being), as γένος (the universal of the species).

What do we conclude from these definitions, which are found in the Middle Ages with Thomas Aquinas (*Quaestiones de veritate*, qu. I art. 1) and in antiquity with Aristotle (*On Interpretation*, Ch. 1, 16 a)? It is remarkable that what we ourselves took as self-evident concerning the essence of truth already counted as such so long ago. Historical reflection *confirms* precisely what is also self-evident to us; indeed this confirmation ultimately gives the self-evidence its *justification*, as opposed to the incomprehensibility which we thought to find. So it happens that today as well one calls on the Middle Ages and Aristotle for the thesis that truth has the character of the proposition, of thought and knowledge.

What did we seek from this 'historical reflection'? To obtain a *distance* from what we take as self-evident, from what lies all too close to us. And now, through a demonstration of its noble antiquity, we are even more bound to this self-evidence! What inner power of proof and validity this conception of the essence of truth must possess, that it could endure for over two thousand years through all the changes of philosophical standpoints and systems!

What then can it mean if we bring forward doubts and find something incomprehensible in this self-evidence? And again: what does the attempt at distancing ourselves from the present through historical reflection lead to? To this: that what is current today is confirmed as itself ancient!

But have we really *enacted* the historical reflection? Did we really *go* back? Beginning from our present definition of truth, we looked for the way it had earlier been conceived, and we found it was the *same*. Is this historical reflection, or is it just an historical recording of earlier concepts and names? Have we really gone back to what *happened* at the beginning of Western philosophy, and to what is perhaps *still* happening? No. May we then wonder that we encountered the past only as the present and not as itself, which might perhaps be something quite different? May we wonder that we did not attain detachment and distance from the present? Perhaps historical reflection is quite different to reporting on the past and fleeing from the present?

But even if that were so: is the present not so corrupt that in the end it is worthwhile fleeing from it, really fleeing, in order that one should not be destroyed on account of it, thus in the end to be in a position to truly overcome it? For in *genuine* historical reflection we take just that distance from the present which allows us room to leap out beyond our own present, i.e. to treat it just as every present as present deserves to be treated, namely as something to be *overcome*. Genuine historical return is the decisive beginning of authentic *futurity*. No one has ever leapt out over themselves from and at the place where they presently stand.[3] And what happens when we do not learn to understand this, everyone knows.

In the end it is *historical* return which brings us into what is actually happening *today*. In the end it is also only a self-evident and therefore doubtful everyday opinion which takes history as something 'past'.

But what is it about historical *return*? Instead of speaking about it in general terms, we want to attempt it, or in any case a step thereto (we are only concerned with the history of philosophy).

Let us leave aside the indicated long-standing definition of the essence of truth and ask how at the beginning of Western philosophy truth was conceived, i.e. how the *Greeks* understood what we call 'truth'. What *word* did they have for this? The Greek word for truth – one can hardly remind oneself of this too often – is ἀλήθεια, *unhiddenness* [*Unverborgenheit*]. Something true is ἀληθές, unhidden. What do we glean first of all from this word?

We discover two things:

1. The Greeks understood what *we* call the true, as the un-hidden, as what is no longer hidden, as what is *without* hiddenness, as what has been torn away from hiddenness [*Verborgenheit*] and, as it were, been robbed of its hiddenness. For the Greeks, therefore, the true is something which no longer possesses something else, namely hiddenness, and is freed from this. Therefore the Greek expression for truth, in both its semantic structure and its morphology, has a fundamentally different content to our German word 'Wahrheit' [truth], as also to the Latin expression Veritas'. The Greek expression is *privative*. The meaning-structure and word- formation of ἀλήθεια are analogous to the German word 'Unschuld' [*innocence*] in its contrast with 'Schuld'

[*guilt*], where the negative word presents the positive (to be free from guilt) and the positive word presents the negative (guilt as deficiency). So, for the Greeks, *truth* too is privative.

It is curious that 'true' means what something *no longer* has. We could let this stand as a curiosity and remain at the practical level!

2. Initially, the meaning of the Greek word for truth, unhiddenness, has nothing to do with *assertion* and *that* factual contexture in terms of which the essence of truth is usually explained, i.e. with correctness and correspondence. To be hidden and unhidden means something quite different to correspondence, measuring up, directedness towards . . . Truth as unhiddenness and truth as correctness are quite different things; they arise from quite different fundamental experiences and cannot at all be equated.[4]

This rough indication of the *meaning* of the Greek word for truth already suffices to show that, so far as we understand this word, at one stroke we have cut ourselves loose from the normal concept of truth. But from this nothing much can be concluded. On the contrary, we must beware of reading too much out of the analysis and meaning of a word, instead of going into the actual *substance* of the matter. To what fruitless discussions and fateful errors have the daring artifices of etymology led! Especially when we consider (in relation to the present case) that the substantive essence of truth was already conceived by the Greeks in the sense of a ὁμοίωσις (alignment, correspondence). So we should not give too much, indeed any significance whatever, to the discussion of mere word-meaning – least of all to support the claim that originally and in ancient times the essence of truth was understood quite differently to the manner which has since become usual.

We should not, to be sure, proceed in this way. But we have become suspicious: the Greek word for truth *means* something quite different to 'correctness'! Although we do not want to fixate on a mere word-meaning, we must still bear in mind that the word for truth, ἀ-λήθεια, does not stand for some arbitrary and irrelevant thing, but is a word for what man wants and seeks in the ground of his essence, a word, therefore, for something ultimate and primary. And could the word for this be unimportant, its formation accidental, especially when it shows the peculiarity to which we have drawn attention? Instead, must not this word, if it is a word for what constitutes the ground of human Dasein, derive from a primordial experience of world and self? Is ἀλήθεια then not a basic and primal word?

Who would dispute that! But just for this reason we must demand to be shown *whether* and *how* the word arises from the fundamental experience of ancient man. If *there was* such a fundamental experience, what *testifies* to this? If the 'true' for the Greeks means the unhidden, that which is free from hiddenness, then the experience of the true as unhidden must also involve experience of the *hidden* in its hiddenness.

What then do the Greeks call ἀληθές; (unhidden, true)? Not assertions, not sentences and not knowledge, but the beings [*das Seiende*] themselves, the totality of nature: the human world and the work of God. When Aristotle says (*Metaphysics* 983 b) that philosophizing is directed περὶ τῆς ἀληθείας 'to truth', he does not mean that philosophy must put forward correct and valid propositions, but that philosophy seeks beings in their unhiddenness as beings. Accordingly, beings must previously, and also simultaneously, be experienced in their hiddenness, i.e. as concealing themselves. The fundamental experience of hiddenness is obviously the ground from which the *seeking after* unhiddenness arises. Only if beings are previously experienced in their hiddenness and self-concealment, if the hiddenness of beings encompasses man and besets him in a fundamental way, only then is it necessary and possible for man to set about wresting beings from hiddenness and bringing them into unhiddenness, thus also placing himself within the unhiddenness of beings.

Now do we have some witness from antiquity for this fundamental experience of beings as hidden and self-concealing? Fortunately we do, and indeed from one of the greatest and oldest philosophers of the ancient world, from *Heraclitus*. The important saying of Heraclitus has been passed down: [ἡ] φύσις . . . κρύπτεσθαι φιλεῖ.[5] The holding sway of beings, i.e. beings in their being, loves to conceal itself. Several things are to be found in this saying, ἡ φύσις, 'nature': that does not mean the *region* of beings which is today the object of natural-scientific research, but the holding sway of beings, *all* beings: human history, the processes of nature, divine happenings. Beings as such, i.e. in what they are as beings, *holds sway*. κρύπτεσθαι φιλεῖ: Heraclitus does not say that beings as a matter of fact hide themselves from time to time, but φιλεῖ: they *love* to hide themselves. It is their proper innermost drive to remain hidden, and if brought out of hiddenness, to return to it. We cannot discuss here how this saying of Heraclitus relates to his fundamental conception of being. The godhead builds the world playfully, countless times, and always as something different.

It suffices that this saying of Heraclitus expresses *the* fundamental experience *in* which and *from* which is awoken an insight into the essence of truth as the unhiddenness of beings. This saying is as old as Western philosophy itself, giving expression to *that* fundamental experience and orientation of ancient man from which philosophy begins; ἀ-λήθεια, unhiddenness, into which philosophy seeks to bring the hidden, is nothing arbitrary, and is especially not a property of a proposition or sentence, nor is it a so-called 'value'. It is rather that reality, that occurrence [*Geschehen*], into which only *that* path (ἡ ὁδός) leads of which another of the oldest philosophers likewise says: 'it runs outside the ordinary path of men', ἀπ᾿ ἀνθρώπων ἐκτὸς πάτου ἐστίν (Parmenides, Fr. 1, 27).

Yet another reservation occurs to us. We can admit that this saying of Heraclitus, and the word ἀλήθεια, are ancient, and belong to the period of the beginning of Western philosophy; but doesn't this show that we need not pay much attention to them? For 'the beginning' is still 'primitive', awkward and unclear, half or fully 'poetical'. Philosophy has in the meantime progressed and become science, yet at a very early stage it thoroughly abandoned the idea of unhiddenness. It is indeed true that the idea of unhiddenness was given up. But is it really the case that the beginning is primitive, half-baked, groping, and unclear? Or is the beginning what is greatest? Not always, to be sure. In everything inessential and without purpose the beginning is what can be and is overcome; therefore in the inessential there is progress. In the essential, however, where philosophy belongs, the beginning can never be overcome. Not only not overcome: it can no longer be attained. In the essential, the beginning is the unattainable and greatest, and it is precisely because *we* can no longer grasp anything of this, that with us everything is so decayed, laughable, without order, and full of ignorance. Today, people regard it as a mark of superiority to philosophize without this beginning. Philosophy has its own law; what people think about it is something else.

Already we are no longer confronted by a simple word (ἀλήθεια) and its dictionary meaning, but by what the word refers to: the reality from which and into which this word was first spoken and formed. To be sure, we have some *intimation* (on the basis of Heraclitus' saying) that something must have happened with man; a history which initially appears as just an arbitrary series of events. On no account should we interpret what has been said to mean that the fundamental experience of the hiddenness of beings is a 'personal experience', which the philosopher then expresses in a poem or proposition. We mean that with man himself something *occurred* which is greater and more primordial than his usual activity; an occurrence and a history to which we must return, and which we *must* reenact if we want to grasp something of the essence of truth.[6]

But are we equipped for this return? What do we already *have*? The word ἀλήθεια, its (perhaps strange) meaning, and the saying of Heraclitus. This is not much; and if we seek further witnesses, we quickly convince ourselves of the scantiness of our sources for the oldest Greek philosophy. Is not such a return therefore uncertain and indefinite?

One thing is certain, namely that what has been transmitted and preserved of the authentic material of Presocratic philosophy is small in comparison with the extent of Plato's and Aristotle's works. So one is easily tempted to think that the older and oldest philosophers, because they are unquestionably superior to Plato and Aristotle, must have written at least as much, or even more. But perhaps the reverse is true. Human beings write and talk all the more, the less they have anything essential to say. This is clear today.

Already the saying of Heraclitus suffices to show that the Greek word for truth, 'unhiddenness', is nothing accidental. Such evidence does not become more convincing through further enumeration of cases.

The return to the Greek beginnings of Western philosophy is difficult not because our sources are scanty, but because our Dasein is impoverished, because it does not measure up to the claim and power of the little which *has* been transmitted. For even where we have a great deal, as with Plato and Aristotle – what have we made out of this? A perhaps distinguished but nevertheless groundless scholarship, and a diligent but rather tasteless enthusiasm. Or one thinks it is actually preferable no longer to know anything whatever about it.

How are we supposed to initiate this return? Should we not return to the past through what is closer to us, by passing through what is more recent? Do not Plato and Aristotle treat the essence of truth more comprehensively, from more points of view, and more reflectively? Could we not come to more certain conclusions about earlier philosophy by taking our lead from these later thinkers? This seems to be possible, and to a certain degree we want to pursue this method, but for different reasons. Not because, in order to compensate for scanty witnesses, we hope to make retrospective conclusions, but because in Aristotle and Plato we can see how the indicated fundamental experience has already begun to be ineffective, so that the fundamental stance [*Grundhaltung*] expressed in the basic meaning of the word ἀλήθεια is re-formed in a way which prepares for what we alluded to earlier: the common conception of the essence of truth, which apparently has nothing more to do with ἀλήθεια. Unhiddenness becomes correctness, a development of the concept which later led to pseudo-problems, and had to do so, because everything gets uprooted.

What we wish to examine first of all is neither ἀλήθεια in its primordiality, nor truth as correctness (ὁμοίωσις) in its simple self-evidence, but their characteristic intertwinedness. We want to see how these two concepts have become entangled with each other. This transition itself, of ἀλήθεια *qua* unhiddenness to truth *qua* correctness, is an *occurrence*, indeed nothing less than *the* occurrence wherein, already at the beginning of its history, Western philosophy takes off on an erroneous and fateful course.

In order to further investigate this *transition* from truth as unhiddenness to truth as correctness (their characteristic intertwining), we wish to consider a reflection of Plato's treating of ἀλήθεια – not in the sense of concern for definition and conceptual analysis, but by presenting a story. I am referring to the allegory of the cave at the beginning of Book VII of the work which bears the title Πολιτεία, and which we miscomprehendingly translate into German as 'Der Staat' ('The Republic').

We are halting now at an intermediate point, with Plato, in order to see how already in the classical time of ancient philosophy the double-meaning of the concept of truth is formed, but without the intertwinings and inner connections being seen.

In the following interpretation, we deliberately leave unconsidered the precise placement of this allegory within the dialogue. To begin with we leave aside all discussion concerning the dialogue as a whole. What is crucial about the allegory is that it can stand entirely on its own, so we can consider it by itself without in any way minimizing its content or meaning.

We speak of an 'allegory', also of 'sensory image' [*Sinn-Bild*], of a sort that provides a hint or due. The image is never intended to stand for itself alone, but indicates *that* something is to be *understood,* providing a *clue* as to *what* this is. The image provides a hint – it leads into the intelligible, into a region of intelligibility (the dimension within which something is understood), into a *sense* (hence sensory image). However, it is important to bear in mind: *what* is to be understood is not a sense, but rather an *occurrence*. 'Sense' [*Sinn*] says only: it is a matter of something intelligible. What is understood is never *itself* sense; we do not understand something *as* sense, but always only 'in the sense of'. Sense is never the *topic* of understanding.

The presentation of an allegory, of a sensory image, is therefore nothing else than a clue for seeing (a provision of a clue through something which is presented sensuously). Such a clue *leads* us to what simple description, be it ever so accurate and rigorous, can never grasp. There is thus an inner necessity to the fact that when Plato wants to say something fundamental and essential in philosophy, he always speaks in an allegory and places us before a sensory image. Not that he is unsure about what he is speaking of; on the contrary, he is *quite sure* that it cannot be described or proved. In all genuine philosophy there is something in the face of which all description and proof, however brilliantly scientific, fails and sinks down into empty business. This fact alone, that Plato speaks of ἀλήθεια in an allegory, gives us the crucial clue as to where we must search, and where we must stand, if we want to come closer to the essence of truth. This indescribable and unprovable something, however, is crucial – and to come to this is what the whole effort of philosophizing is about.[7]

We thus close our introductory remarks. Whether you are to understand our interpretation does not depend on whether you have a poor or non-existent understanding of Greek, also not on whether you have much or little understanding of philosophical doctrines, but only on whether you have yourselves experienced, or are ready to experience, a necessity to be *here* now – whether, in this allegory, something unavoidable speaks in and *to* you. Without this all science remains mere outward show and all philosophy a façade.

Notes

1 Cf. below p. 45.

2 See Supplement 1.

3 Cf. below § 15.

4 Precisely 'correctness' is necessary, but simultaneously in the possibility of *derailing* and free-floating.

5 Heraclitus Fr. 123, in *The Presocratic Philosophers,* ed. G. S. Kirk, J. E. Raven and M. Schofield, Cambridge: Cambridge University Press, 1983 p. 192, translated in this volume as The real constitution is accustomed to hide itself'. [Trans.].

6 See Supplement 2.

7 The un-sayable [*das Un-sagbare*]; silence, language.

PART ONE

The Clue to the 'Essence' of Αλhθeia Interpretation of the Allegory of the Cave in Plato's *Politeia*

1

The Four Stages of the Occurrence of Truth

We shall now treat the allegory of the cave in Plato's Πολιτεία (Book VII, 514 a–517 a), understanding it as a clue to the essence of unhiddenness (ἀλήθεια). We divide the text into four sections (A–D), corresponding to the *four stages* of the occurrence as depicted in the allegory.

We proceed with the interpretation by clarifying each stage in turn, at the same time recognizing that the individual stages are not the essential matter, which is rather the *transitions* from one stage to another, that is, the *whole path* consisting of these transitions. When the first stage has been discussed, therefore, we cannot put it aside as something over and done with, but we must draw it into the transition and thus take it over into all the succeeding transitions. We do not understand the first stage at all until we grasp it from the second, and, strictly speaking, from the final stage.

Plato introduces the allegory by having Socrates enter into conversation with Glaucon and recount it to him. We could easily follow the common practice and briefly summarize the content of the allegory, likewise attaching a short explanation, without, however, being touched by anything essential, and without following up the clue to the decisive question. This usual hackneyed way of proceeding would not assist us at all. If we wish to avoid this the first thing we must do is to give ourselves totally over to the text. Only in this way are we perhaps also moved by the power of Plato's presentation – which in understanding philosophy is not at all incidental, not at all an aesthetic addition.

At each point I give the Greek text first,[1] then the translation, which can only be an aid.

A. The First Stage (514 a 2–515 c 3): the Situation of Man in the Underground Cave

(We pass over the first sentence, to which we shall return at the end.)

… ἰδὲ γὰρ ἀνθρώπους οἷον ἐν καταγείῳ οἰκήσει σπηλαιώδει, ἀναπεπτα μένην πρὸς τὸ φῶς τὴν εἴσοδον ἐχούσῃ μακρὰν παρὰ πᾶν τὸ σπήλαιον, ἐν ταύτῃ ἐκ παίδων ὄντας ἐν δεσμοῖς καὶ τὰ σκέλη καὶ τοὺς αὐχένας, ὥστε μένειν τε αὐτοὺς εἴς τε τὸ πρόσθεν μόνον ὁρᾶν, κύκλῳ δὲ τὰς κεφαλὰς ὑπὸ τοῦ δεσμοῦ ἀδυνάτους περιάγειν, φῶς τε αὐτοῖς πυρὸς ἄνωθεν καὶ πόρρωθεν καόμενον ὄπισθεν αὐτῶν, μεταξὺ δὲ τοῦ πυρὸς καὶ τῶν δεσμωτῶν ἐπάνω ὁδόν, παρ᾽ ἣν ἰδὲ τειχίον παρῳκοδομημένον, ὥσπερ τοῖς θαυματοποιοῖς πρὸ τῶν ἀνθρπων πρόκειται τὰ παραφάγματα, ὑπὲρ ὧν τὰ θαύματα δεικνύασιν.

Ὁρῶ, ἔφη.

"Ορα τοίνυν παρὰ τοῦτο τὸ τειχίον φέροντας ἀνθρώπους σκεύη τε παντοδαπὰ ὑπερέχοντα τοῦ τειχίον καὶ ἀνδριάντας καὶ ἄλλα ζῷα λίθινά τε καὶ ξύλινα καί παυτοῖα εἰργασμένα, οἷον εἰκὸς τοὺς μὲν φθελλομένους, τοὺς δὲ σιλῶντας τῶν παραφεπόντων.

Ἄτοπον, ἔφη, λέλεις εἰκόνα καὶ δεσμώτας ἀτόπους.

Ὁμοίους ἡμῖν, ἦν δ᾽ ἐγώ τοὺς γὰρ τοιούτους πρῶτον μὲν ἑαντῶν τε καὶ ἀλλήλων οἴει ἄν τι ἑωρακέναι ἄλλο πλὴν τὰς σκιὰς τὰς ὑπὸ τοῦ πυρὸς εἰς τὸ καταντικρὺ αὐτῶν τοῦ σπηλαίου προσπιπτούσας;

Πῶς γάρ, ἔφη, εἰ ἀκινήτους γε τὰς κεφαλὰς ἔχειν ἠναγκασμένοι εἶεν διὰ βίου;

Τί δὲ τῶν παρακερομένων; οὐ ταὐτὸν τοῦτο;

Τί μήν;

Εἰ οὖν διαλέγεσθαι οἷοί τ᾽ εἶεν πρὸς ἀλλήους οὐ ταὐτὰ ἡγῇ ἂν τὰ ὄντα αὐτοὺς νομίζειν ὀνομάζειν ἅπερ ὁρῶεν;

Ἀνάγκη.

Τί δ᾽ εἰ καὶ ἠχὼ τό δεσμωτήριον ἐκ τοῦ καταντικρὺ ἔχοι; ὁπότε τις τῶν παριόντων φθέγξαιτο, οἴει ἂν ἄλλο τι αὐτοὺς ἡγεῖσθαι τὸ φθελλόμενον ἢ τὴν παρτοῦσαν σκίαν;

Μὰ Δί᾽ οὐκ ἔγωγ᾽, ἔφη.

'Picture people dwelling in an underground chamber like a cave, with a long entrance open to the light on its entire width. In this chamber people are shackled at their legs and necks from childhood, so that they remain in the same spot, and look only at what is in front of them, at what is present before them. Because of their shackles they are unable to turn their heads. However, light reaches them from behind, from a fire burning higher up and at a distance. Between the fire and the prisoners, behind their backs, runs a path along which a small wall has been built, like the screen at puppet shows between the exhibitors and their audience, and above which they, the puppeteers, show their artistry.'

'I see,' he says [Glaucon].

'Imagine further that there are people carrying all sorts of things along behind the screen, projecting above it, including figures of men and animals made of stone and wood, and all sorts of other man-made artefacts. Naturally, some of these people would be talking among themselves, and others would be silent.'

'A peculiar picture you have drawn, and peculiar prisoners!'

'They are very much like us! Now tell me, do you think such people could see anything, whether on their own account or with the help of their fellows, except the shadows thrown by the fire on the wall of the cave opposite them?'

'How could they see anything else if they were prevented all their lives from moving their heads?'

'And what about the things carried about behind them? Does not the same apply (that they see only shadows)?'

'How could it be otherwise?'

'Now if they were able to talk with one another about what they see, don't you think they would take this for real beings?'

'Inevitably.'

'And if the wall of their prison opposite them reflected sound, don't you think that they would suppose, whenever one of the passers-by on the road spoke, that the voice belonged to the shadow passing before them?'

'Of course, by Zeus!'

What is this first stage of the allegory steering towards, this description of the situation of the prisoners in the cave? We can learn this without difficulty from the final sentence, which is meant as a decisive summary:

Παντάπασι δή, ἦν δ᾽ ἐγώ, οἱ τοιοῦτοι οὐκ ἂν ἄλλο τι νομίζολεν τὸ ἀληθὲς ἢ τὰς τῶν σκευαστῶν σκιάς.

Πολλὴ ἀνάλκη, ἔφη.

'And so in every way they would take to shadows of the artefacts for the un-hidden [*das Un-verborgene*]?'

'Inevitably.'

§ 3. The Unhidden in the Cave: the Shadows

The situation of human beings is described in order to show what people in *such* a position take as the *unhidden*, the true. What is ultimately symbolized is τὸ ἀληθές. We must now trace out more clearly the individual features of this image, gathering together everything to do with the unhidden.

1. However strange this situation remains, and however peculiar these people, in this situation too man already has τὸ ἀληθές, the unhidden. Plato does not say *an* unhidden but *the* unhidden. This means that man, from childhood on and already in his nature, is set

before the unhidden. *What* this is in each case, what in particular cases presents itself as unhidden, is another question. Even in this strange situation in the cave, the human being is not sealed off from everything else as a simple I, but is πρὸς τὸ πρόσθεν, directed to what is *before* him: τὸ ἀληθές. It belongs to being human – this is already indicated at the beginning of the allegory – to stand in the unhidden, or as we say, in the true, in the truth. Being human means, and may the situation be ever so peculiar, not only, but among other things: *to comport oneself to the unhidden.*

2. And just for this reason the question can be raised (by whom?) as to *what*, in this situation, is unhidden to man. Answer: what is immediately before him, without any doing on his part, as it gives itself; here therefore the *shadows* of things which are cast on the wall in front of him by the light of the fire behind. Yet this description of the unhidden requires a more precise determination.

3. The prisoners do indeed *see* the shadows but not *as* shadows of something. When we say that, to them, the shadows are the un-hidden, this is ambiguous and already says *too much*. It is only we, privy to the whole situation, who call what the prisoners face 'shadows'. Why couldn't they say this themselves? Because they do not know anything about a fire which gives off a glow, and in whose luminosity something like shadows can first of all be cast. Thus, when (under 2) we said it could be asked '*what* that is' which is unhidden there, this is not a question the prisoners themselves could raise. For the essence of their being is such that, to them, precisely *this* unhidden before them *suffices* – so much so indeed that they also do not know *that* it suffices. They are entirely given over to what they *immediately* encounter.

4. Plato expressly remarks: φῶς δὲ αὐτοῖς πυρὸς ἄνωθεν καὶ πόρρωθεν καόμενον ὄπισθεν αὐτῶν. There is indeed *brightness*, 'light', inside the cave, but from behind. The prisoners have no relationship to light *as* light, for neither do they see the fire that casts the light. Here, and for the understanding of the whole allegory, it is necessary to understand the difference between πῦρ, fire (the source of light), and φῶς, illumination (to which there corresponds in Latin: *lux* and *lumen*). 'Light' is ambiguous: 1) the candle that burns, the source of brightness; 2) light, the opposite of dark. The cave-dwellers have no relationship to light, they are completely unfamiliar with the distinction between light and dark. Thus they also do not understand things like shadows, which

(through brightness) are cast by another body. All this, things that cast shadows, fire that makes shadows possible, is ὄπισθεν, behind their backs, as distinct from τὸ πρόσθεν, what they see before them. Only the latter is unhidden; the former remains hidden. Here, therefore, being human *also* means, among other things: to stand within the *hidden,* to be surrounded by the hidden (within the unhidden to comport oneself to this; at the same time to be surrounded by the hidden, so much so that also the unhidden is not at all understood *as* such).

5. The cave-dwellers do not consider what they have before them as unhidden to be a semblance of something else. Instead, they would not hesitate to acknowledge what is before them as τὰ ὄντα, as *beings* (assuming that they could talk among themselves about what is given).[2] In other words, man straightforwardly takes whatever presents itself before him as un-hidden, to be beings; indeed man is nothing else but *the* being that comports itself to what it takes as beings (an animal, plant, even less a stone, never comports itself to beings).

But the comportment of these prisoners to the unhidden is so distinctive that as yet we have not sufficiently grasped it. Something else is required:

6. The prisoners see only shadows of themselves and their fellow prisoners, they see only what is set over against them. They have no relationship to themselves at all. They do not know any I-myself or any you-yourself. In the condition described they are entirely ensnared in what lies before them. Plato calls what they have before them τὸ ἀληθές, the *unhidden.* But we must now add that this unhidden is not encountered by the prisoners *as* unhidden. The prisoners know the distinction between hiddenness and unhiddenness *as* such just as little as they know the distinction between shadows and things that cast shadows, or the distinction between light and dark. This absence of the distinction makes the cave- dwellers, as we say, 'utterly removed' [*ganz weg*], ensnared by and in something, shackled. But as we see, even to this condition of shackled- ness, even to this complete removedness, there belongs, in the end, unhiddenness, light, beings.

It is therefore not surprising that Glaucon, to whom this allegory is recounted, finds it ἄτοπον: something having no place within the ordinary, something extra-ordinary that is peculiar and removed from anything everyday and normal (the obvious, hearsay, gossip). And yet, Socrates assures us, the allegory depicts precisely the everyday situation of man, who, in so far as he does not possess any standard *other* than everydayness, cannot see its strangeness. How this provides a clue to the essence of the truth of everydayness will be shown later. Perhaps we have an intimation of this, without being able to see the details.

In so far as the first stage, taken on its own account, is the stage of an allegory, a sensory image, this already provides us with a clue, admittedly not one that itself amounts to insight into the *essence* of unhiddenness, but a clue *that* somehow in this situation there is unhiddenness. This means only that the unhiddenness of something, *to which* man comports himself, belongs to the being of man (as an *indication* of his situation). Just *how* this unhiddenness is to be comprehended in its essence remains obscure. We do not obtain a view of the *essence* of man. For us, it is firstly a matter of seeing *that* and *how*, from the very beginning, ἀλήθεια stands in the centre.

To this purpose we can in the first place collect together everything which, in this situation, shows itself *simultaneously* with ἀληθές. We want to enumerate all the essential moments having a role in the remarkable fact that these human beings, however peculiar their situation may be, have the unhidden, or, as we inappropriately say, the true, before them. These moments are:

1 τὸ ἀληθές, the unhidden;

2 σκιαί, shadows;

3 δεσμῶται, prisoners: the human condition of being shackled;

4 πῦρ and φῶς, fire and light: brightness;

5 the prisoners have no relationship to the light and to the things, ὄπισθεν, which remain hidden behind them;

6 the prisoners have no relationship to themselves and each other; they see only shadows of themselves;

7 the unhidden is taken straightforwardly for beings, τὰ ὄντα;

8 there is no distinction between hidden and unhidden, shadows and real things, light and dark.

Are all these only accidental moments, which we refer to just for a more vivid depiction of the situation, or are they constitutive elements as it were, which have a role in building up the essence of ἀληθές, truth as unhiddenness? Are all these elements bound together by an inner connection? Indeed, is the *unity* of this interconnection, that which holds everything together, nothing else but ἀληθές, unhiddenness?

But before we put this question, let us place ourselves once again in the situation of the prisoners, which basically is not difficult to do. If we restrict ourselves to the first stage, *submitting* to it so to speak, we see no such interconnection, indeed we do not even recognize the enumerated individual moments; instead, caught up in our misapprehension, we see only what is played off on the wall. The latter is, as it were, the whole world. The condition of misapprehension is indicated by the fact that the prisoners, in their situation, could not describe what we are *now* able to see. Indeed, the prisoners do not even know that they are in a 'situation'. When questioned, they always talk about shadows, which, however, they do not know *as* shadows. They know their way around their own proper abode, and are not to be dissuaded from what they recognize straightforwardly as beings. They would regard any such presumption as perverse. But what they take as beings is still called (this cannot be said too often) τὸ ἀληθές, and there is nothing here about resemblance, correctness, or correspondence.

B. The Second Stage (515 c 4–515 e 5): a 'Liberation' of Man within the Cave

Σκόπει δή, ἦν δ' ἐγώ, αὐτῶν λύσιν τε καὶ ἴασιν τῶν τε δεσμῶν καὶ τῆς ἀφροσύνης, οἵα τις ἂν εἴη φύσει,[3] εἰ τοιάδε συμβαίνοι αὐτοῖς· ὁπότε τις λυθείη καὶ ἀναγκάζοιτο ἐξαίφνης ἀνίστασθαί τε καὶ περιάγειν τὸν αὐχένα καὶ βαδίζειν καὶ πρὸς τὸ φῶς ἀναβλέπειν, πάντα δὲ ταῦτα ποιῶν ἀλγοῖ τε καὶ διὰ τὰς μαρμαρυγὰς ἀδυνατοῖ καθορᾶν ἐκεῖνα ὧν τότε τὰς σκιὰς ἑώρα, τί ἂν οἴει εἰπεῖν, εἴ τις αὐτῷ λέγοι ὅτι τότε μὲν ἑώρα φλυαρίας, νῦν δὲ μᾶλλόν τι ἐγγυτέρω τοῦ ὄντος καὶ πρὸς μᾶλλον ὄντα τετραμμένος ὀρθότερον βλέποι καὶ δὴ καὶ ἕκαστον τῶν παριόντων δεικνὺς αὐτῷ ἀναγκάζοι ἐρωτῶν ἀποκρίνεσθαι ὅτι ἔστιν; οὐκ οἴει αὐτὸν ἀπορεῖν τε ἂν καὶ ἡγεῖσθαι τὰ τότε ὁρώμενα ἀληθέστερα ἢ τὰ νῦν δεικνύμενα;

Πολύ γ', ἔφη.

Οὐκοῦν κἂν εἰ πρὸς αὐτὸ τὸ φῶς ἀναγκάςοι αὐτὸν βλέπειν, ἀλγεῖν τε ἂν τὰ ὄμματα καὶ φεύγειν ἀποστρεφόμενον πρὸς ἐκεῖνα ἃ δύναται καθορᾶν, καὶ νομίζειν ταῦτα τῷ ὄντι σαφέστερα τῶν δεικνυμένων;

Οὕτως ἔφν.

'Now imagine what would happen if the prisoners were released from their shackles and cured of their delusions. Consider what would necessarily happen if the following were to occur. Suppose one of them were unshackled and compelled to suddenly stand up, turn his head, and look and walk towards the light; but all this would be painful, and because of the flickering brightness he would be too dazzled to see properly the things whose shadows he used to see. What do you think he would say if he were told that what he used to see was so much empty nonsense, and that he was now nearer to beings and turned towards more beingful beings, so seeing more correctly? And if he were compelled to say what each of the passing objects was [τί ἐστιν] when it was shown to him? Don't you think he would be at a loss, and think that what he used to see was more unhidden than what was now being shown to him?'

'Absolutely.'

'And if he were made to look directly into the light, would this not hurt his eyes, and would he not turn back and retreat to the things which he had the power to see, thinking that these [the shadows] were in fact clearer [more visible] than the things now being shown to him?'

'Yes.'

§ 4. New Features of ἀλήθεια Revealed by the Unsuccessful Attempt at Liberation

In the second stage something *happens* to one of the prisoners: his shackles are removed. What does this lead to, i.e. what necessarily belongs to it? Plato emphasizes specifically: οἵα τις εἴη φύσει, 'what thereby [with this unshackling] necessarily occurs'. What Plato wants to bring to light is the φύσις of man. As with the first stage, he says again at the end of the second stage: ἡγεῖσθαι αὐτὸν τὰ τότε ὁρώμενα ἀληθέστεπα ἢ τὰ νῦν δεικνύμενα, the unshackled prisoner 'would hold what he formerly saw [the shadows] to be more unhidden than the things now being shown to him [the things in the light itself]'. Once again this is clearly all about ἀληθές.

In the second stage, therefore, something happens which has to do with *unhiddenness*. We saw in the first stage that ἀληθές comes forth together with other elements of the situation, but we did not grasp their interconnections. But now, when something happens with ἀληθές, when this itself comes to life, it must become clear if and how, with this event, its connections also change, i.e. these connections must themselves emerge. In respect of the second stage we therefore ask whether the connections between the (previously only listed) elements, which presumably belong to ἀληθές,[4] become clearer, and whether thereby ἀληθές itself, the essence of unhiddenness, becomes clearer.

We answer by again outlining the features of the image presented by Plato, grasping the second stage precisely as second, thus in its relationship to the first, which in this way is itself further illuminated.

1. We encounter ἀληθές not only (as in the first stage) in general terms, but now the talk is of ἀληθέστερα (in pure linguistic terms a comparative), of what is *more unhidden*. The unhidden can therefore be *more* or *less* unhidden. This does not mean more or less in numerical terms (that *more* shadows are unhidden), but that the *things themselves* are more unhidden, the things which the now unshackled prisoner, as he turns around, is supposed to see. Unhiddenness, therefore, has gradations and levels. 'Truth' and 'true' is not something in itself, such that for everyone it is in every aspect unchangeable and common. It is not the case that everyone, without further ado, has the same right and same strength to every truth. And every truth has its *time*. In the end it is a sign of education to withhold certain truths from knowledge and to keep silent about them. Truth and truth is not simply the same.

2. The progression from the first stage to the second involves a second differentiation. It is a *transition*. In so far as what was initially seen (the shadows) are left behind and the freed prisoner turns away from them, a divorce occurs between what was first *seen* and what is now *shown* (the text makes the sharp distinction: τὰ τότε ὁρώμενα – τὰ

νῦν δεικνύμενα). The unhidden separates out: there the *shadows*, here the *things*. Two species of the unhidden, but connected by the fact that each is accessible (manifest).

3. But these two (shadows and real things), that now separate out from each other, are assessed differently. The former prisoner holds the shadows, i.e. what immediately shows itself, τὰ τότε ὁρώμενα ἀληθέστερα, to be more true, more unhidden, more clear, more present. On the other hand, he who removes the shackles says that what is now revealed, τὰ νῦν δεικνύμευα, the things themselves and the human beings, are μᾶλλον ὄντα, *are* to a greater degree [*mehr seiend*], are *more beingful* [*seiender*] beings. What *is* admits of *degrees*! Being and being is not necessarily the same. And not only is the assessment of what was previously seen, and what is now shown, different, but the way in which the assessment *is made* also differs: there the previously seen is *more unhidden*, while here what is now shown is *the more beingful*. There more unhiddenness, here more being. Do both belong together? Clearly. For what is called unhidden *is* the beings and is taken as such (cf. the first stage). The more the unhidden is unhidden, the closer do we come to beings (μᾶλλον ἐγγυτέρω τοῦ ὄντος). So coming closer to beings goes together with the heightening of unhiddenness and vice versa. *Closeness* to beings, i.e. the being-with what is there [*das Da-bei-sein des Da-seins*], the inner proximity or distance of being-human to beings, the *degree* of the unhiddenness of beings, and the *heightening* of beings themselves as beings – these three are intertwined. Above all we must be clear that beings separate out into those that are more and those that are less *beingful.* There are 'beings that are more beingful'. Closeness and distance to beings changes the beings themselves.

4. The proximity to beings, as this is claimed for the second stage, has still another characteristic result: ὁ πρὸς μᾶλλον ὄντα τετραμμένος ὀρθότερου βλέπει. 'Whoever [like the former prisoner] is turned towards more beingful beings [towards what is more beingful than something else, thus to more genuine beings] sees more *correctly.*' Thus ὀρθός, ὀρθότης, 'correctness' [*Richtigkeit*] crops up, and indeed in the comparative, in an intensification: there are *gradations*. The correctness of seeing and viewing things, and thus of definition and assertion, is *grounded* in the particular manner of orientation and proximity to beings, i.e. in the *way* in which beings are in each case unhidden. Truth

as correctness is grounded in truth as unhiddenness. We now see for the first time, albeit only roughly, a *connection* between the two forms of essence (concepts of truth), which at the beginning we only considered separately and stood alongside one another. Truth as correctness of assertion is quite impossible without truth as the unhiddenness of beings. For that to which the assertion must direct itself, in order to be correct, must already be unhidden. So if one takes the essence of truth exclusively as correctness of assertion, one betrays a complete lack of understanding. Not only does one stand before a *derivative* concept of truth, but, because one does not see the origin of this derivative concept, one calls upon a half-measure, which does not become full by everyone going along with it. On the other hand, one will only be able to grasp the *essence* and specific *necessity* of this derivative form of truth, truth as correctness,[5] if truth *qua* unhiddenness is explained and its necessity grounded; that is, if one can clarify both the origin and the derivation. This is indicated by Plato's clear and simple statement: whoever is turned towards the more beingful beings, sees and talks more correctly'. This is a decisive step towards solving the problem of the relationship between the two concepts of truth.

5. But, as stated, *what* the more true and the more beingful is, has not yet been settled. On the contrary, judgements and estimations run counter to one another. Why is this so? What kind of standard does the prisoner employ in wanting to return to the shadows and in claiming *them* as the more unhidden? There in the cave, turned to the shadows, he has no inkling of what will happen when he must see in the light; he has no pain in his eyes, and above all, there amidst the shadows he moves within that which, ἃ δύναται, he is capable of, which demands no great effort of him, and happens of its own accord so to speak. There amidst the shadows, in his shackles, he finds his familiar ground, where no exertion is required, where he is unhindered, where nothing recoils upon him, where there is no confusion, and where everyone is in agreement. The main standard for his estimation of higher or lower unhiddenness is preservation of the undisturbedness of his ordinary activities, without being set out to any kind of reflection, demand, or command.

6. On the other hand, what does turning around to the things themselves *require*? Release from the shackles; but this is only the *beginning* of emancipation. What is supposed to eventuate is a turning

around to the light. This liberation fails; it does not come to fulfilment. Proof: he who has been unshackled wants to go back to his former situation! For what reason? Why does this attempted liberation fail?

7. Since the unshackling, the standing up, the turning around, the looking into the light, all happen *suddenly* (ἐξαίφνης), this freeing (λύδις) cannot become an ἴασις τῆς ἀφροσύνης, a healing from *delusion*. ἀφροσύνη, which is how Plato describes the situation of the prisoners, is the counter-concept to φρόνησις, σωφροσύνη. φρόνησις is Plato's word for knowledge in general, i.e. for grasping the true, for circumspection and insight in relation to world and self, the unity of both. I emphasize this because with Aristotle the concept of φρόνησις is developed quite differently, and in particular is narrowed down. Where φρόνησις is lacking, where everything, world and self, is shadow-like, there is no relationship to the *genuinely* true and unhidden, ἀφροσύνη is the absence of circumspection and insight, where man is in every respect removed from truth, where he has no familiarity with the world and no insight into himself. There, man is lacking something. He is sick, and healing is necessary. But healing presupposes the correct diagnosis of the illness. This does not occur through release from the shackles. The released prisoner does not recognize what he previously saw *as* shadows. Instead, he is simply removed from what he formerly saw and placed before things glimmering in the light. For him, these latter can only be things which are somehow different from what he formerly saw. Through this bare difference there arises nothing but confusion. What is shown to him does not take on any clarity and definiteness. For this reason he wants to return to his shackles.

8. Removal of the shackles is thus not genuine emancipation, for it remains external and fails to penetrate to man in his ownmost self. The circumstances of the prisoner change, but his inner condition, his willing [*Wollen*], does not. The released prisoner does indeed will, but he wills to return to his shackles. Thus willing, he wills not-willing: he does not want to be involved himself. He avoids and shrinks back from the demand to fully give up his previous situation. He is also a long way from understanding that man truly *is* only in so far as he demands this of himself.

The second stage ends with this thwarted emancipation. The emancipation fails because the one to be freed does not understand it.

Liberation is only genuine when he who is liberated thereby becomes free for himself, i.e. comes to stand in the ground of his essence.

We repeat our guiding question: what does the second stage say about ἀλήθεια? Do we experience anything positive about the essence of truth as unhiddenness? Have we made any progress beyond what was shown in the first stage, namely that various other moments go together with ἀληθές? Do we already see an inner connection between these?

In the second stage what happens is a failure, namely that he who has been unshackled fails to encounter unhiddenness as such. He does not come to it. But does not Plato say that the prisoners are set before the unhidden, before ἀληθές from childhood on? Certainly, but not before the unhidden *as* unhidden. They do not know that and how the unhidden, to which they are delivered over, as such *is,* that such a thing as unhiddenness *occurs.* This occurrence of unhiddenness is not present for the former prisoner, for he cannot distinguish between shadows and things, between their *respective kinds* of unhiddenness. To be sure, the difference between shadows and things announces itself, but the former prisoner does not *enact* this difference, cannot grasp it as such, cannot bring the distinguished things into *relationship.* But the difference occurs in the *enactment* of the differentiation. To bring the differentiation to enactment would be being-human [*Menschsein*], existing [*Existieren*].

Why is it that the difference only *announces* itself? This we cannot immediately say. We can only see that the first attempt at emancipation fails. From this we can only conclude that the occurrence and existence of unhiddenness as such is connected with the *liberation* of man, more precisely with the *success* of liberation, i.e. with genuine *being-tree.* And we can suspect something else, namely that the success of liberation must lie in the opposite direction to its failure. The failure is shown in wanting to go back to the shackles, *away from the light.* The opposite direction, in which liberation attains its goal, is therefore a matter of moving *towards* the light, of becoming free as facing the light. In this turning around towards the light, beings are to become more beingful, the unhidden more unhidden!

It is clear, therefore, that the essence of truth as unhiddenness belongs in the context of freedom, light, and beings, more precisely in the being- free of man, the looking into the light, and comportment to beings. Freedom, light, beings, unhiddenness: these are not related to one another like isolated things. But what is the *interconnection* that we are seeking? The second stage has not yet shown this, but it becomes visible in the third stage of the allegory. Is there an answer?

C. The Third Stage (515 e 5–516 e 2): the Genuine Liberation of Man to the Primordial Light

Εἰ δέ, ἦν δ' ἐγώ, ἐντεῦθεν ἕλκοι τις αὐτὸν βίᾳ διὰ τραχείας τῆς ἀναβάσεως καὶ ἀνάντους, καὶ μὴ ἀνείη πρίν ἐξελκύσειεν εἰς τὸ τοῦ ἡλίου φῶς, ἆρα οὐχὶ ὀδυνᾶσθαί τε ἂν καὶ ἀγανακτεῖν ἑλκόμενον, καὶ ἐπειδὴ πρὸς τὸ φῶς ἔλθοι, αὐγῆς ἂν ἔχοντα τὰ ὄμματα μεστὰ ὁρᾶν οὐδ' ἂν ἓν δύνασθαι τῶν νῦν λεγομένων ἀληθῶν

Οὐ γὰρ ἄν, ἔφη, ἐξαίφνης γε.

Συνηθείας δὴ οἶμαι δέοιτ' ἄν, εἰ μέλλοι τὰ ἄνω ὄψεσθαι. καὶ πρῶτον μὲν τὰς σκιὰς ἂν ῥᾷστα καθορῷ, καὶ μετὰ τοῦτο ἐν τοῖς ὕδασυ τά τε τῶν ἀνθρώπων καὶ τὰ τῶν ἄλλων εἴδωλα, ὕστερον δὲ αὐτά. ἐκ δὲ τούτων τὰ ἐν τῷ οὐρανῷ καὶ αὐτὸν τὸν οὐρανὸν νύκτωρ ἂν ῥᾷον θεάσαιτο, προσβλέπων τὸ τῶν ἄστρων τε καὶ σελήνης φως, ἢ μεθ' ἡμέραν τὸν ἥλιόν τε καὶ τὸ τοῦ ἡλίου.

Πῶς δ' οὔ;

Τελευταῖον δὴ οἶμαι τὸν ἥλιον, οὐκ ἐν ὕδασιν οὐδ' ἐν ἀλλοτρίᾳ ἕδρα φαντάσματα αὐτοῦ, αλλ' αὐτὸν καθ' αὑτὸν ἐν τῇ αὑτοῦ χώρᾳ δύναρτ' ἂν κατιδεῖν καὶ θεάσασθαι οἷός ἐστιν.

'Αναλκαῖον, ἔφη.

Καὶ μετὰ ταῦτ' ἂν ἤδη συλλογίζοιτο περὶ αὐτοῦ ὅτι οὗτος ὁ τάς τε ὥρας παρέχων καὶ ἐνιαντοὺς καὶ πάντα ἐπιτροπεύων τὰ ἐν τῷ ὁρωμένῳ τόπῳ καὶ ἐκείνων ὧν σφεῖς ἑώρων τρόπον τινὰ πάντων αἴτιος.

Δῆλον, ἔφη ὅτι ἐπὶ ταῦτα ἂν μετ' ἐκεῖνα ἔλθοι.

Τί οὖν; ἀναμιμνησκόμενον αὐτὸν τῆς πρώτης οἰκήσεως καὶ τῆς
ἐκεῖ σοφίας καὶ τῶν τότε συνδεσμωτῶν οὐκ ἂν οἴει αὐτὸν μὲν
εὐδαιμονίζειν τῆς μεταβολῆς, τοὺς δὲ ἐλεεῖν;

Καὶ μάλα.

Τιμαὶ δὲ καὶ ἔπαινοι εἴ τινες αὐτοῖς ἦσαν τότε παρ' ἀλλήλων
καὶ γέρα τῷ ὀξύτατα καθορῶντι τὰ παριόντα, καὶ μνημονεύοντι
μάλιστα ὅσα πρότερα αὐτῶν καὶ ὕστερα εἰώθει καὶ ἅμα πορεύεσθαι,
καὶ ἐκ τούτων δὴ δυνατώτατα ἀπομαντενομένῳ τὸ μέλλον ἥξειν,
δοκεῖς ἂν αὐτὸν ἐπιθυμητικῶς αὐτῶν ἔχειν καὶ ζηλοῦν τοὺς παρ'
ἐκείνοις τιμωμένους τε καὶ ἐνδυναστεύοντας, ἢ τὸ τοῦ Ὁμήρου
ἂν πεπονθέναι καὶ σφόδρα "ἐπάρουρον ἐόντα θητευέμεν ἄλλῳ
ἀνδρὶ παρ' ἀκλήρῳ" καὶ ὁτιοῦν ἂν πεπονθέναι μᾶλλον ἢ 'κεῖνά τε
δοξάζειν καὶ ἐκείνως ζῆν;

Οὕτως ἔφη, ἔγωγε οἶμαι, πᾶν μᾶλλον πεπονθέναι ἂν δέξασθαι ἢ
ςῆν ἐλείνως.

'And if he were forcibly dragged up the steep and rugged ascent of
the cave and not let go till he had been dragged out into the sunlight,
would he not experience pain, and so struggle against this? And
would he not, as soon as he emerged into the light, his eyes dazzled,
be unable to see any of the things he was now told were unhidden?'

'No, at least not at first.'

'He would need, I believe, to first become accustomed to the light
before he could see things in the upper world. First he would find it
easier to look at shadows, next at the reflections of men and other
objects in water, and later on at the things themselves. After that
he would find it easier to observe the sky at night and the heavenly
dome, and to look at the light of the moon and stars rather than at
the sun and its light by day.'

'Of course.'

'Finally, I believe, he would be able to look directly at the sun itself,
and gaze at it as it is in itself, without using reflections in water or any
other medium.'

'Necessarily.'

'Later on he would come to the conclusion that it is the sun which produces the changing seasons and years and controls everything in the visible world, and that it was also at bottom responsible for what he and his fellow prisoners used to see in the cave.'

'That is the **next** conclusion he would obviously reach.'

'And when he remembered his first home, and what passed for wisdom there, and his fellow prisoners, don't you think he would feel himself fortunate on account of his change of circumstance, and be sorry for them?'

'Very much so.'

'And if the cave-dwellers had established, down there in the cave, certain prizes and distinctions for those who were most keen-sighted in seeing the passing shadows, and who were best able to remember what came before, and after, and simultaneously with what, thus best able to predict future appearances in the shadow-world, will our released prisoner hanker after these prizes or envy this power or honour? Won't he be more likely to feel, as Homer says, that he would far rather be 'a serf in the house of some landless man'.[6] Would he not rather put up with anything, than take truth as they do and live like them?'

'Yes, I believe he would prefer anything to a life like theirs.'

§ 5. The Ascent of Man from the Cave Towards the Light of the Sun

The third stage is described at greater length than the others. The occurrence described by Plato now arrives at its goal. Genuine liberation is not just release from shackles within the cave, but is an exit from the cave into the light of day, i.e. to the sun, completely away from the artificial light of the cave.

The first thing to be noticed, compared with the previous stage, is that no more mention is made of the thwarted liberation. There is no new attempt of this kind, not because it is incomplete, but because it is not a liberation at all. It is essential that we properly understand this total abandonment of the first attempt, which means understanding the nature of the transition between the second and third stages. That the first attempt at liberation is no longer taken up, is shown above all by the fact that Plato simply passes over the light and fire within the cave. Looking into the light, when it is only a light, does not suffice: light and light is not the same. Therefore our heading: the *genuine* liberation of man to the *primordial* light.

a) Levels of Unhiddenness outside the Cave

This transition also leads to ἀληθές: τὰ νῦν λεγόμενα ἀληθή – to what 'from now on' (in the condition of freedom) is 'said to be the unhidden'. Since in *every* stage ἀληθές is mentioned at a decisive point, we can no longer be in any doubt that the allegory as a *whole* predominantly treats of ἀλήθεια. However, we do not yet know why. To know this would be to at once understand its essence. Initially, we see only that the true, the unhidden, is different depending on the circumstance and position of man. So we must first, without recourse to what was referred to as 'unhidden' in the first two stages, analyse what is *now* spoken of as the unhidden. What most characteristically occurs here?

1. The transition to what is now (outside the cave, in the condition of freedom) unhidden happens βίᾳ (with force). Liberation, in the sense of turning around towards the light of the sun, is *violent*. Attaining what is now unhidden involves violence, thus ἀγανακτεῖν, resistance, such that the one to be freed is forced up along a rugged path. The ascent demands work and exertion, causing strain and suffering.

2. Neither release from the shackles, nor mere exit from the cave, is enough. What is also unavoidable is the συνήθεια: as distinct from the kind of liberation in the second stage, there occurs a sudden ripping loose, followed by, outside the cave, a *slow adaptation*, not so much to the things as to illumination and light itself. At first the eyes are dazzled by the brilliance of the sunlight; only slowly do they unaccustom themselves to darkness. Despite the illumination, indeed because of the illumination, the released prisoner initially sees nothing at all of what is now unhidden in the light, and claimed to be unhidden.

3. This adaptation of vision from darkness to light occurs in various stages. At first, the vision which loves darkness and shadows searches for everything outside the cave which is most closely related to darkness, for what *here too* does not give the things themselves, but only shadows

or reflections. After this, vision arrives at the things themselves, but then the released prisoner still sees better by night, where vision slowly grows accustomed to the illuminated things – the smooth light, the unblinding light of the stars and the moon. When he gets used to this, he is able to see things by day in the light of the sun, then the light itself. Finally he is able to see the sun as what *gives* the light, as what gives *time,* as what *rules over* everything, and which is the ground even of what is seen in the *cave,* of the shadows and the light and the fire.

4. The genuine liberation does not only depend on an act of violence, but requires persistence and courage to endure the individual stages of adaptation to the light, the strident courage that can also wait, that is not deterred by reversals, that knows that, in all genuine becoming and growing, no stage can be leapt over, that empty busy-ness is just as useless and disastrous as blind enthusiasm.

5. He who in his ownmost self has adapted in this way, secures for himself, by becoming free for the light, i.e. through familiarity with and towards light, a new standpoint. No longer does he want to go back, for he now sees through the shadowy character of his whole cave-existence, of the hustle and bustle which there prevails, and of the honours which are there conferred.

All this is clear *in the picture* presented. But what does this picture *point* to? The purpose of the allegory is not stated. What are we to *understand* concerning this stay of the released prisoner outside the cave, if indeed cave-existence stands for the everyday activity and business of man, thus precisely what takes place in the sunlight?

At a later point (517 b ff.), Plato himself gives the interpretation of the whole allegory. The cave, he says, is the earth under the heavenly dome (remember that the Greeks conceived the earth as a flat disk over which the heavens are vaulted, so that man actually does move about within a cave). The fire in the cave is the sun, the light of the fire is the sunlight. The shadows are beings, the things we see under the sky and with which we commonly have dealings. We, the prisoners, are bound to self-evidence, and to people who are guided only by this. What is outside the cave, over and above this, τὰ ἄνω, is the place of the ideas, a ὑπερουράνιος τόπος, over the vault of the heavens (above the vault of the cave). And the sun that shines outside the cave symbolizes the highest idea, the ἰδέα τοῦ ἀλαθοῦ, which one hardly dares to view directly: μόγις ὁρᾶσθαι (517b).

b) Four Questions Concerning the Visible Connections of ἀλήθεια in the Occurrence of Liberation

Does this Platonic elucidation allow us to *understand* the essence of ἀλήθεια? Do we thereby obtain an insight into what necessarily *occurs* in the everyday existence of human beings? Do we, in addition, comprehend what occurs with or to *one* of these human beings? Do we understand that *to which* man can be freed in this violent way, and how he is supposed to adapt in order to arrive at the unhiddenness of beings? Ideas, the idea of the good: what does this mean? What do ideas have to do with truth and with everything else we have encountered concerning ἀλήθεια and freedom, light, beings, gradations of being?

However clearly the allegory may be presented, however simple and clear the Platonic interpretation may appear – do we understand much, or even a little, of all this? It does not help to ask how Plato himself interprets the allegory. We find only that he redescribes the situation, i.e. he explains the position of the freed prisoner by saying that his *location* is over the heavens, that in this location there are ideas, and among these a highest idea. What all this means we do not know. Initially we understand nothing at all, especially when we consider that it is a story about something that happens with *man*. With man? Who is that? We ourselves and *only* we, every self in so far as, through Plato, it is now placed before this allegory and *lets* itself be placed before this *occurrence.* Therefore *not* those who are now listening to a lecture by Heidegger. After a few weeks they will already have had enough and so will disappear just as they have come. But supposing one sits here until the final session of the semester – would that prove that one has allowed oneself to be *placed* before this allegory? No, and least of all can this be proven through an examination. It therefore cannot be proven at all – but *authenticated*, yes! How, and before whom, and when and where and how far: that is known only by each individual. This is what the mysterious 'effect' of a philosophy consists in – when it is effective at all.

Initially we understand nothing at all, and for this reason we *ask*. We ask firstly (not only with respect to the third stage, but also with respect to the previous stages): what is this allegory *saying*? What does it mean for man, i.e. for our Dasein and its relation to truth as unhiddenness?

Unhiddenness in connection with freedom, light, being, ideas, the highest idea of the good? As many questions as there are words!

We attempt to get our bearings here by singling out and clarifying the indicated connections and the phenomena to which they refer. We pose four questions:

1   What is the interrelation between idea and light? (§ 6)
2   What is the interrelation between light and freedom? (§ 7)
3   What is the interrelation between freedom and beings? (§ 8)
4   What is the essence of truth in the sense of unhiddenness as it emerges from the unity of these interrelations? (§ 9)

By answering these four questions, and thus presenting an interpretation of the third stage, we attempt to feel our way forward to the essence of truth as unhiddenness. As you can see, for the moment we deliberately leave aside any discussion of the highest idea (the idea of the good). Plato too does not discuss the highest idea more closely within the allegory itself, because he has already treated it at length in the closing part of Book VI. Later, after the complete interpretation of the allegory, we shall return to the relation between ἀλήθεια and ἰδέα τοῦ ἀγαθοῦ, not in the sense of a mere addition but in order to gain an overview of the whole problem of truth and to orient ourselves at this pinnacle of Platonic philosophy (this is nothing else but the struggle between the two concepts of truth). From here we also first obtain the ground for the further questions raised by the Platonic definition of the essence of truth as ἀλήθεια, that is, for the debate with Plato himself and thus with the whole Western tradition.[7]

§ 6. Idea and Light

To the *first question*: what is the interrelation between idea and light? To begin with: what does 'idea' refer to?

We have already said that we must always retain the preceding stages in view; so now it is important to look more closely at the first stage.

Led along by the apron strings of the everyday, we are forced into what is ordinary and accepted. In such a situation, which looks to us like freedom, we experience only beings. How can we say 'only'? What is supposed to be still *lacking*, where we soberly behave according to the business of the day, as functionaries, as it were, of the present situation, not dreaming, not falling into outlandish plans and unrealizable wishes, but just pursuing the everyday and contributing to its endurance? Can we do *more* than to *hold* to beings, to what is actual? Yet in the allegory Plato describes precisely these beings, the everyday, as shadows, therefore indicating that the beings around us, however much we take them as such, are *not* the genuine *truth* of beings, not the beings in their unhiddenness. But is there then *something else* over and above the beings?

a) The Seeing of What-Being

To be sure, the beings we encounter in our everyday life might not encompass everything that is visible and that is. There might exist things we do not yet know and shall never know. But these unknown beings, just because we do not know them, are not for this reason different to what *is* known to us. Instead, according to Plato's symbolism, they *also* must be counted amongst the shadows, namely those which have not yet passed across the wall, those which will show themselves only in the future, those which are predicted and discussed in advance. Yes indeed. But Plato does not say that we should come to know *more* shadows. Rather, what we should come to know is something *different* from the beings which daily occupy us, i.e. just what the person (the prisoner) who is restricted to the existing things in their infinite variety is *not able* to see. And what is this? The historical interpretation says: it is the *ideas.*

Nowadays, we have long become suspicious of ideas'; we find them interesting only in gossip about 'ideology'. Ἰδέα is what gives itself, what is there for and in ἰδεῖν, in seeing. To seeing there corresponds what is seen, what is sighted. Yet *what kind of* seeing is this, in which ideas come into view? Obviously it cannot be the seeing of our bodily eyes, for with the latter we see precisely the beings that Plato calls shadows. Ideas are supposed to be *other* than these beings.

But not so fast. Do we *see* beings with our bodily eyes? Doubtless we do! I do indeed see this book. And when someone who does not know his way around this lecture room is looking for the exit, we say to him 'see the door here', and he 'sees' the door. *With what* does he see the door? What kind of question is this? With his eyes, of course, and not with his ears!

With his eyes? Let us make the attempt! We want to see this book here 'with our eyes'. We don't need to try this, we already do it! What are we supposed to still *want* here? I see the book. This is the simplest thing in the world.

Do we *see* the book with our eyes? *What* do we see with our eyes? This is easier to answer if we consider what we hear with our ears. In both cases, seeing and hearing, we hold ourselves in a perception, we register something that is presented to us. We hear tones, sounds, we see colours, coloured things. We can also see glowing, sparkling, glittering, illumination, brightness and darkness. Certainly, but we also see *more*, such as the form of this desk, of this door. We thus see spatial forms (figures) *with our eyes.*

Yet here we must already ask if spatial form is something *specifically* visible, whether we can encounter it *only* as something visible. Clearly not, because we can also perceive spatial forms, e.g. the surface of this desk, by *touching*. On the other hand, one colour cannot be distinguished from another by ever so fine a touching. We certainly cannot touch brilliance and illumination. Extended things can be touched as well as seen. Likewise, not only can we see movement, but we can hear it, e.g. the approach of a car or its moving off into the distance. Movement and moving things are not *specifically* visible. Seeing with the eyes in every case provides colour and brightness: something visible that is *only* accessible by sight, that we sense *here.* Seeing with the faculty of sight is a sight-sensation. Such a sensation of colour we call a colour-sensation.

Again we ask: do we see with our eyes, which now means: do we *sense* [*empfinden*] the book? What the eyes give, conveyed to us as a sensory something, is the reddish brown book-cover, the greyish white pattern, the black inscription. How does this happen? Do we sense the book-cover, the pattern, the inscription, *with our eyes*? Is there, just like the sensation of red, also the sensation of book-cover? No. What is sensed with our eyes is not the book, but the reddish brown, greyish white, black, and so forth. The book can no more be 'seen' than it can be heard and smelt. And yet we quite naturally *say* 'we see the book'. Clearly, seeing and seeing is not the same. More precisely, seeing is a perceiving [*Vernehmen*] 'with' the eyes; but what 'with the eyes' means is ambiguous. *Firstly* it could mean that what sees, what gives the visible, *are* the eyes. Thus understood, we cannot say that 'our eyes' see colours, but, strictly speaking, we must say *with* our eyes, meaning that they assist us. So we come to the *second* meaning: with the assistance of our eyes, *by means of them*, we perceive something, and so 'see' it, for example a book.

Strictly speaking the eye does not yet sense the colour. With sensation too the eye is only the organ into which the faculty of sensation is built, but it is not this faculty itself. The eye as instrument strictly *sees* nothing at all; at best the *sense of sight* [*Gesichtssinn*] does this with the *help* of the eyes. The sense of sight 'sees' *colours* in the manner of sensation [*Empfinden*}, but never anything like a book; only through the sense of sight do we 'see' a book. Here 'seeing' means perceiving something, a perceiving in which the sense of sight, but not it alone, is involved, and in which this is not even the *genuine* perceiver. When we say that 'we see the book', we use 'see' in a meaning which *goes beyond* perceiving the object by means of the sense of sight with the help of our eyes. However sharp and highly developed our tools for seeing, however excellent our sense of sight, we can never see a book through our sense of sight. We would never see anything like a book were we not able to see in another *more primordial* sense. To this latter kind of 'seeing' there belongs an *understanding* [*Verstehen*] of what it *is* that one encounters: book, door, house, tree. We *recognize* the thing as a book. This recognition registers the look that is given to us: of the book, table, door. We see *what* the thing is from the way it *looks:* we *see* its what-being. 'Seeing' is now a *perceiving*; of something, to be sure, namely this as a book, but no longer through our eyes and sense of sight; it is a looking whose object does not have the character of colour, an object that cannot be attained through any constellation of colours, an object that is no longer sensory at all. And yet we *see* (perceivo), in the sense that we comport ourselves to what is presented to us.

When we so naturally say 'we see the book', we use 'see' in a meaning that is quite obvious and normal, and about which we become suspicious only when someone makes us pay closer attention. The latter is precisely what Plato did with his discovery of the so-called 'ideas'. This discovery was not some far-flung speculation on the part of Plato, but relates to what everyone sees and grasps in comportment to beings. Plato just pointed this out with previously unknown power and assurance. For what we see there, a 'book', is clearly something different to 'black', 'hard', 'soft' etc. What is sighted in this seeing is the ἰδέα, the εἶδος. 'Idea' is therefore the *look* [*Anblick*] of something *as* something. It is through these looks that individual things *present* themselves as this and that, as *being-present*. Presence [*Anwesenheit*] for the Greeks is παρουσία, shortened as οὐσία, and means *being*. That something *is* means that it is present [*es ist anwesend*], or better: that it *presences* [*west an*] in the present [*Gegenwart*]. The look, ἰδέα, thus gives *what* something presences *as,* i.e. what a thing *is*, its *being*.

According to Aristotle this is the δευτέρα οὐσία, but the πρώτη is what is *more* present, the καθ᾽ ἕκαστον.[8]

We said: according to Plato there is, over and above the particular things (the shadows), *something else,* namely the ideas. If we have carefully followed the above considerations, something must have dawned on us. At least until a few moments ago, we ourselves belonged to those who thought they saw only the various particular things: book, door, house. We did not suspect that in order to see this book, door, and so forth, we must already understand what 'book' and 'door' mean. Understanding what such things mean is nothing else but the seeing of the look, the ἰδέα. In the idea we see *what* every being is and *how* it is, in short the *being* of beings [*das Sein des Seienden*].

This seeing of the ἰδέα Plato also calls νοεῖν, perceiving, or νοῦς, reason in the strict sense: the capacity to perceive.

Plato now grasps the νοεῖν of Parmenides[9] as the ἰδεῖν of the ἰδέα, of the ἀγαθόν, ἐπέκεινα τῆς οὐσίας. Kant too says clearly and unambiguously that 'reason' is the 'faculty of ideas',[10] although he uses 'idea' in a broadened Platonic and also in a restricted sense.

The seeing of the idea, i.e. the understanding of what-being and how-being, in short of *being,* first allows beings to be recognized *as* the beings they are. We never see beings with our bodily eyes unless we are also seeing 'ideas'. The prisoners in the cave see only shadow-beings and think that these are all *there are;* they know nothing of being, of the understanding of being. Therefore they must *remove* themselves from the shadow-beings. They must make an *ascent*, taking leave from the cave and everything in the lower region – also from the fire in the cave (from the actual sun, which is itself just the image of a being) – for the light and brightness of day, for the 'ideas'. But what has idea and the essence of idea got to do with *light?* Only now do we really come to our first question.

b) The Essence of Brightness: Transparency

'Light': what is this? And what does it stand for in the allegory? I have already indicated that we must distinguish πῦρ and φῶς, fire and light, thus the *bearer* of light (φωσφόρος), i.e. the stuff that is illuminated, from light and illumination itself. Once again: light, φῶς, *lumen*, is not the *source* of light, but is *brightness*. But what is that – brightness?

With light and brightness we come again into the region of seeing, of the visible. What is visible through optical sensation are colours, glimmerings, brightness and darkness. Yet what *is* this brightness, light, darkness? Certainly not a thing, neither a property of any kind of thing. Brightness, light: this is nothing which can be grasped hold of; it is something *intangible*, almost like nothingness and the void.[11]

To be sure, the physical theory of light does provide an answer: Newton's corpuscular theory, Huygens' theory of waves, Faraday's electromagnetic theory of light! But these theories no longer grasp light in its connection with looking (our immediate looking comportment), but simply as one natural process among others: 'correct' and yet untrue, because a quite inappropriate frame of reference is brought to bear.

Yet let us look closely! Do brightness and darkness stand *alongside* colour and brilliance, such that they *too* can be experienced through our sense of sight? Or? We can clarify this by considering what happens when we close our eyes (in sleep) and then open them again: first of all, *before* we see anything colourful and brilliant, we establish whether it is bright or dark. We could not see colourful or brilliant things at all if we did not already see brightness and darkness. Brightness and darkness are seen 'first', not necessarily in the sense that we grasp them as such and pay attention to them, but in the sense of 'in the first place'. Brightness and darkness must be seen from the outset if colourful and brilliant things are to be seen. Within the realm of the visible, brightness and darkness are not at the same level as colour and brilliance but possess a priority: they are the *conditions of the possibility* of experiencing the visible in the narrower sense.

But do we thereby know what brightness, light, and darkness *are*? Brightness and darkness are first and originary; they cannot be explained in terms of anything else. But we do not thereby come to a conception of the *essential* nature of brightness and darkness. Brightness and darkness are visible, are seen 'in the first place'. But how is what is visible to be defined? For colour is also something visible. So when we refer to visibility, the visible as such is not yet characterized. We must ask what brightness and darkness are in themselves. What does brightness *mean* and what does it *accomplish*'?

'Brightness' [*Helle*] comes from 'reverberate' or 'echo' [*hallen*] and is originally a character of tone or *sound*, that is, the opposite of 'dull'. Brightness, therefore, is not at all originally a character of the visible, but was transferred over in language *to* the visible, to the field where light plays a role. So we speak of a 'bright sunny day'. But such linguistic transferences from the realm of the audible to that of the visible are never accidental, and generally indicate an early power and wisdom of language – although we freely admit that we have only a very inadequate and superficial knowledge of the essence of language. If the meaning of 'bright' is transferred to the visible and made equivalent to 'lit up', 'brightness' made equivalent to 'light', this can only happen on the basis of an essential kinship between the two phenomena, such that brightness as reverberation has something essential in common with light as illumination. The bright tone or sound, which is further intensified in shrillness (e.g. the nightingale) is what *penetrates:* it not only spreads itself out, but it forces itself through. What is dull or sluggish stays back as it were, is not able to force itself through. Brightness has the character of going-through. The same thing is shown in a different way with light and the 'light of day'. Light also has the character of going-through, and it is this character, as distinct from the staying-back of darkness, which allows the meaning of 'brightness' to be transferred from the audible to the visible. Brightness is that *through which* we see. More precisely, light is not only what penetrates through, but is what *permits* penetration, namely in seeing and viewing. Light is the *transparent* [*das Durchsichtige*] that spreads out, opens, lets-through. The *essence* of light and brightness is to be transparent.

But this characterization, it immediately emerges, is insufficient. It is first necessary to distinguish the way in which e.g. a sheet of glass (even coloured glass) is transparent, from the transparency of light. Comparing the two kinds of letting-through will allow us to more accurately determine the essence of light as what lets-through.

We call glass transparent, even when it is coloured (e.g. a window pane), and likewise water. The question is whether brightness (light) is transparent in the same sense. Evidently not, and not only because brightness is not graspable in the way a sheet of glass or a body of water are, but because the transparency of glass and water, and of everything similar, already *presupposes* brightness. These kinds of things are only transparent in light; only in light can anything be seen through them. Sight in general, and thus also the sight that penetrates, is first made possible by light. Light (brightness) too is transparent, but in a stricter sense: as the genuinely originally transparent. We see two things: light first lets the object through *to be viewed* as something visible, and also lets- through the view *to* the visible object. Light is what *lets-through.* Brightness is visibility, the opening and spreading out of the open. Thus we have defined the genuine essence of brightness: it allows things to show themselves for viewing, it offers a look [*Anblick*] for seeing [*Sehen*] in the narrower meaning of perceiving through the sense of sight.

Correspondingly with the dark. This is only a limit case of brightness and thus still has the character of a kind of brightness: a brightness that *no longer* lets anything through, that *takes away* visibility from things, that *fails* to make visible. It is what does not let-through, but in a quite specific sense, different, for example, to the way a wooden wall is untransparent, does not let-through. A wooden or brick wall cannot fail in making visible, for in no sense can it secure visibility; it is untransparent in quite a different way to that of darkness. To indicate just *one* aspect of this difference: for a wall to be spoken of as untransparent, as not letting-through (for someone), light must already be assumed as present, while on the other hand, the not letting-through of the dark consists precisely in the *absence* of light (brightness) and in this alone. The dark is untransparent because it is itself a kind of letting-through. The wall is untransparent because it is not any kind of letting-through (for sight). Only that can fail which also has the possibility of securing. The dark fails to make visible because it can also secure sight: in the dark we see the stars.

c) The Fundamental Accomplishment of the Idea: Letting-through the Being of Beings

Our guiding question is: what is the connection between *idea* and light? Why are the ideas depicted through brightness? We have attempted to clarify both the essence of idea and the essence of light. What are the consequences for establishing the connection between the two?

What emerged as the essence of light and brightness, namely letting-through for seeing, is precisely the basic accomplishment of the idea. The essence of light is letting-through for sight. If light, as in the allegory, is meant in a *transferred* sense (likewise transparency, of brightness *and* sheet of glass), *seeing* must correspondingly be meant in a transferred sense (in the usual sense of seeing the book): the seeing of *beings* (book, house, chair). What is seen in and as the idea is, outside the allegory, the *being* (the what-being and how-being) of beings. Ἰδέα is what is sighted in advance, what gets perceived in advance and lets beings through as the *interpretation* of 'being'. The idea allows us to see a being as what it is, lets the being *come* to us so to speak. We *see* first of all from *being,* through the understanding of *what* a particular thing is. Through its what-being the being shows itself as this and this. Only where being, the what-being of things, is understood, is there a letting-through of beings. Being, the idea, is what lets-through: the *light.* What the idea accomplishes is given in the fundamental nature of light.

So the connection between light and the idea is clear. We see a being as a book only when we understand its sense of being in the light of its what-being, of the 'idea'. We start to understand why from the beginning of the allegory the comportment of man towards beings is bound up with light and fire. Thus we also say 'it dawns on me' [*mir geht ein Licht auf*]; we do not mean that for the first time we become aware of something, but that we now *genuinely* know what we have all along known, namely what something *is.*

But this does not explain why precisely light and seeing (ἰδέα) are taken up in relation to the understanding of *being.* Perhaps this has something to do with the *avoiding* of ἀλήθεια.

If there were no light at all in the cave, the prisoners would not even see shadows. But they do not *know* anything about the light which is already in their sight, just as little as someone who sees a book knows that he already sees something more than, and different from, what he can sense with his eyes, i.e. that he must already *understand* what 'book' as such means.

Thus we come to our *second* question: the interrelation between *freedom* and light.

§ 7. Light and Freedom. Freedom as Bond to the Illuminating

No less essential than what has just been discussed is the story of the prisoner's release from his shackles: the phenomenon of *freedom*. The allegory, i.e. the whole story as we have followed it, provides clues as to how freedom should be understood. The second and third stages show that it is not only a matter of removing the shackles, i.e. of freedom *from* something. Such freedom is simply getting loose, and as such is something negative. Unshackledness has no content in itself. He who has just been unshackled becomes insecure and helpless, is no longer able to cope; he even regards those who are still shackled as possessing an advantage in terms of this negative freedom. By wanting to return to his shackles, he who is only negatively free betrays what he authentically wants but does not understand: the 'positive' which genuine freedom offers him, i.e. support and certainty, peace and solidity. This is what genuine positive freedom offers; it is not only freedom *from* but freedom *for.* Comportment to what *gives* freedom (the light) is itself a *becoming* free. Genuine becoming free is a projective *binding of oneself* – not a simple release from shackles, but a binding of oneself for oneself, such that one remains always bound in advance, such that every subsequent activity can first of all become free and be free.

This positive liberation to genuine being-free is shown in the allegory by what happens after the removal of the shackles: an ascent into the light of day. To become free now means to see in the light, or more precisely, to gradually adapt from darkness to brightness, from what is visible *in* the brightness to brightness and light itself, such that the view becomes an *illuminating view* [*Lichtblick*]. What this means we shall discuss later.

First we ask what light has to do with genuine freedom. Does the connection with light perhaps make being-free *more free?* What *is it* about the light? The light illuminates, spreads itself out as brightness. More precisely, we say that the light *lights up.* 'The night is lit up as bright as day' (Schiller[12]). The night is illuminated, brightened; what does that mean? The dark is lit up. We speak of a 'forest clearing' [*Waldlichtung*]; that means a place which is *free* from trees, which *gives* free access for going through and looking through. *Lighting up* therefore means making-free, giving- free. Light lights up, makes-free, provides a way through. The dark bars the way, does *not* allow things to show themselves, conceals them. That the dark becomes lit up means: it goes over into light, the dark is *made* to give-free.

The light lights up. Thus to see in light means to comport myself in advance to what gives-free. What gives-free is the freeing, free-making. To see in light means to become free for what makes-free, to which I comport myself. In this comportment I am able to be *authentically* free, i.e. I can acquire power by *binding* myself to what lets-through. Such binding is not loss of power, but a taking into one's possession. This explains the interrelation between light and freedom.

§ 8. Freedom and Beings. The Illuminating View as Projection of Being (Exemplified by Nature, History, Art and Poetry)

Now to the *third question*: what is the interrelation between freedom and *being*?

Becoming free means binding oneself to what is genuinely illuminating, to what makes-free and lets-through, 'the light'. But the light symbolizes the idea. The idea contains and gives being. Seeing the ideas means understanding the what-being and how-being, the *being* of beings. Becoming free for the light means to let a light come on,[13] to understand being and essence, and thus to experience beings as such. The understanding of being gives-free beings themselves as such; only in this understanding can beings be beings. Beings in any possible region can only be encountered, can only come closer or recede, because of the freedom that gives-free. Therefore the essence of freedom, briefly stated, is the *illuminating view*: to allow, in advance, a light to come on, and to bind oneself to this. Only from and in freedom (its essence understood as we have developed it) do beings become more beingful, because being this or that. Becoming free means understanding being as such, which understanding first of all lets beings *as* beings *be*. Whether beings become more beingful or less beingful is therefore up to the freedom of man.[14] Freedom is measured according to the primordiality, breadth, and decisiveness of the binding, i.e. this *individual* grasping himself as *being-there* [*Da-sein*], set back into the isolation and thrownness of his historical past and future. The more primordial the binding, the greater proximity to beings.

Understanding, as we said earlier,[15] means being able to stand before something, to have an overview of it, to see its blueprint. To understand *being* means to project in advance the essential lawfulness and the essential construction of beings. Becoming free for beings, seeing-in-the-light, means to enact the *projection of being* [*Seinsentwurf*], so that a look (picture) of beings is projected and held up in advance, so that in viewing this look one can relate to beings as such. *How* such freedom as pre-modelling projection of being first allows us to come closer to beings, we shall briefly clarify by three fundamentally different examples.

1. What was the *discovery of nature* at the beginning of the modern period, in the works of Galileo, Kepler, and Newton, actually grounded in? Not, as people usually think, in the introduction of experimentation. The ancients too 'experimented' in their investigations of nature. Also incorrect is the common view that, instead of hidden qualities of things (Scholasticism), quantitative relations were now sought out and determined. For the ancients and medievals likewise measured and counted. It was not a matter of mathematization itself but of what this presupposes. What was decisive, what actually happened, is that a projection was made which *delineated* in advance what was henceforth to be *understood* as nature and natural process: a spatio-temporally determined totality of movement of masspoints. In principle, despite all progress and transformation, this projection of nature has not changed to the present day. Only after this delineation, in the light of this concept of nature, could nature be interrogated with respect to its lawfulness and its particular processes, and be put to the test, as it were, through experiment. Admittedly, whether this discovery of 'nature', and what followed from it, came closer to or more removed from *nature*, is a question which natural science is itself quite unable to decide upon. It is a question in itself whether beings become more beingful through this science, or whether something intervenes between the beings and the knowers by virtue of which the relationship to beings is crushed,

the instinct for the essence of nature driven out, and the instinct for the essence of man suffocated.

As stated, this projection has remained essentially the same until the present day. But something has indeed changed. Not so much substantive possibilities or radical changes in method. First and foremost, the projection has forfeited its original essential character of *liberation*. This is evident from the fact that the beings which are today the object of theoretical physics are not made *more beingful* through this science, but just the reverse: we see this from the poverty of what today calls itself philosophy of nature. Enough – whatever our philosophical estimation of natural science and its history, this penetration into nature happened on the basis of, and along the path of, a paradigmatic projection of the being of these beings, the beings of nature.

2. Something analogous can be shown from our second example, the science of the *history* of man and his works. A man of the stature of Jacob Burckhardt was not a great and genuine historian, instead of merely a scholar, on account of his conscientious mastery of sources, nor because he found a manuscript somewhere, but because of his projective essential view of the fate, greatness, and misery of man, of the conditions and limits of human action, in short, because of his anticipatory understanding of the *occurrence* we call history, of the *being* of these particular beings. This essential view illuminated research of so-called facts which others had described long before him.

To be sure, one hears it said from all sides today, that through the progress of science there has arisen such a great mass of materials and information that no individual can any longer form a synthesis. But this talk about synthesis shows a lack of understanding. It is not at all a matter of a summarizing synthetic description! Moreover, this whole argument twists things around wrongly. That the material has grown so extensive, and progress has been so great, is not the reason for the impossibility of a real relationship to history, but on the contrary is already the consequence of the long-standing inner impoverishment and powerlessness of human Dasein, precisely of the incapacity to understand the *occurrence* of history, of the incapacity to be historical in a fundamental sense instead of busying oneself with historicism or vulgar 'sociology'. Of course, it would be a misunderstanding to think that historical knowledge requires no effort. Quite the contrary! The question is only where it sets to work, and of who has, or may assume, the right to work historically.

3. Yet another example leads quite out of the region of science here considered, but all the better reveals the inner power of human understanding of being, the illuminating view. I refer to *art* and in particular to *poetry*.

The essence of art is not the expression of any 'lived experience' [*Erlebnis*], and does not consist in an artist expressing his 'soul-life' such that, as Spengler thinks, later ages have to inquire about how art reflects the cultural soul of an historical period. Neither does it consist in the artist depicting reality more accurately and more precisely, or producing something that gives pleasure to others, enjoyment of a higher or lower type. Rather, the artist possesses essential insight for the possible, for bringing out the inner possibilities of beings, thus for making man see what it really is with which he so blindly busies himself. What is essential in the discovery of reality happened and happens not through science, but through primordial philosophy, as well as through great poetry and its projections (Homer, Virgil, Dante, Shakespeare, Goethe). Poetry makes beings more beingful. Poetry, not just any old writing! But in order to understand what the work of art and poetry as such are, the philosopher must first cease to think of the problem of art in aesthetic terms.

From these examples it should be clear how freedom as self-binding to the anticipatory projection of being (the 'idea', the essential conception of beings) first makes possible a relationship to beings; in the allegory, how the illuminating view, the seeing-in-the-light, first opens and frees the look for beings.[16] On the basis of the indicated connections between idea and light, light and freedom, freedom and beings, we now take up the question concerning the nature of ἀλήθεια.

§ 9. The Question Concerning the Essence of Truth as Unhiddenness

We thus come to the fourth and decisive question: to what extent does the unity of these three moments of *one* total context allow us to grasp the *essence* of truth as unhiddenness?

We said that we wanted to *feel our way forward* to the essence of truth as unhiddenness.[17] This meant: we are dispensing with a *definition*. Perhaps a definition is precisely what is least suitable for grasping an essence. It is not a matter of capturing this essence in *sentences* (or in a *single* sentence) that we can repeat and pass on. The sentence as such says least of all. Instead, it is a matter of feeling our way, of asking if, and how, unhiddenness *consists in,* and has its origins in, the unity of the indicated connections. Pursuing this method of inquiry, we encounter three things.

a) Gradations of Unhiddenness. The Ideas as the Primordially Unhidden and Most Beingful of Beings

We begin by asking what the third stage expressly says about ἀλήθεια.

At the beginning the talk is of τὰ νῦν λεγόμενα ἀληθῆ. The more precise context has in the meantime revealed that what is *now* spoken of as the unhidden (τὰ ἀληθῆ) is the idea (indeed ideas in the plural). The 'now' is emphasized: as distinct from the first and second stages (τὰ τότε ὁρώμενα). Looking back, we can see that every stage has its own characteristic unhiddenness:

in the first: the shadows, as objects encountered within the cave,

in the second: what is perceivable in the first (inauthentic) liberation within the cave,

in the third: what is perceivable only by means of a second (authentic) liberation and thorough re-adaptation, what makes possible light, illumination, visibility, i.e. the ideas.

From one stage to another we see a heightening. The second stage at any rate, in comparison with the first, is described as ἀληθέστερον, more unhidden. The question arises: does what is reached in the third stage amount to *one* further heightening of unhiddenness, which *still others* could follow, or is this the highest level, the level of the genuinely and primarily unhidden? We asserted the latter. For understanding everything which follows, it is necessary that this statement be justified.

We must designate what was attained in the third stage τὰ ἀληθέστατα, the most unhidden, even though the latter term does not appear at this point in the text. Plato does not use the *term* ἀληθέστατα. He does not assert a distinction of grades, but says only τὰ νῦν λεγόμενα ἀληθῆ. He says this deliberately, in order to maintain the tension for the inner task of the third stage, which is to demonstrate that what is now unhidden is the genuinely unhidden. To this purpose Plato uses (admittedly not here, but most often) the expression. ἀληθινόν This cannot be translated, but can be clarified by an analogy: ξύλον (wood) and ξύλινον (wooden, consisting of wood). ἀληθινόν is that unhidden which consists of unadulterated unhiddenness so to speak: it is pure unhiddenness, unhiddenness itself and nothing besides; it is the most unhidden, it is where unhiddenness authentically resides. We must now show more precisely how this is applicable to the *ideas*.

The ideas are the most unhidden, the essentially unhidden, the primordially unhidden, because the unhiddenness of beings *originates* in them. In the first, and especially in the second stage, we already encountered a necessary ordering between ἀληθές and ὄν, ἀληθέστερα and μᾶλλον ὄντα. What is unhidden in the first stage, although shadow-like, is already in a certain sense ὄν, something of which the prisoners quite spontaneously say that it *is*. Correspondingly in the second stage, τὰ ἀληθέστερα, to which comparative there corresponds more-being, μᾶλλον ὄντα. Thus too in the third stage there must correspond to what is 'now unhidden' a being which is *most beingful* [*das Seiendste*]. Both (more- being and most-being) are asserted of what is revealed in and for seeing, the εἶδος; (what-being, τί ἐστιν): the *genuinely unhidden* must also be what *genuinely is*. What has most being is the most unhidden. In fact, in precisely the most decisive passages Plato uses a characteristic expression. He calls the ideas τὸ ὄντως ὄν, the being which has being [*das seiendlich Seiende*] – the being which is *in the way* that only beings can *be: being.* To this ὄντως ὄν there corresponds ἀληθινόν.

We must now demonstrate this more precisely from Plato himself. We shall limit ourselves to two passages, which serve to clarify, from a new angle, what was previously said.

In Book VI of the Πολιτεία (490 a 8 ff.; the passage will occupy us again later), Plato treats the question of what kind of person the φιλομαθής is, i.e. the person who has the drive to learn and become a knower, to achieve genuine knowledge, indeed ὁ ὄντως φιλομαθής, the person who has the drive to really learn. Of this person it is said:

ὅτι πρός τό ὂν πεθνκὼς εἴη ἀμιλλᾶσθαι ὅ γε ὄντως φιλομαθής, καὶ οὐκ ἐπιμένοι ἐπὶ τοῖς δοξαζομένοις, εἶναι πολλοῖς ἑκάστοις ἀλλ᾽ ἴοι καὶ οὐκ ἀμβλύνοιτο οὐδ᾽ ἀπολήλοι τοῦ ἔρωτος, πρὶν αὐτοῦ ὅ ἐστιν[18] ἑκάστου τῆς φύσεως ἅψασθαι ᾧ προσήκει ψυχῆς ἐφάπτεσθαι τοῦ τοιούτου – προσήκει δὲ συλλενεῖ – ᾧ πλησιάσας καὶ μιγεὶς τῷ ὄντι ὄντως, γεννήσας νοῦν καὶ ἀλήθειαν, γυοίη τε καὶ ἀληθῶς ζώη καὶ τρέφοιτο καὶ οὕτω λήοι ὠδῖνος, πρὶν δ᾽ οὔ;

'He is the kind of person who in his very essence is eager for beings as such and will not rest content with the various particulars which opinion takes for beings, who instead goes forward without allowing himself to be blinded and does not weaken in his desire [ἔρως] his innermost drive, till he has grasped the what-being of each thing as it is, ὅ ἐστιν in the whole, and does this with the faculty of the soul fitted to do so, that is, with the faculty having the same source as the ἰδέα. Seeing with this faculty of the soul, he who truly strives for knowledge approaches and unites with beingful beings, the ὄντως ὄν. In so far as he brings about genuine perceiving, comprehending and unhiddenness, he will truly know and truly exist and find nourishment, and so free himself from travail [i.e. of suffering in general].'

I can only interpret this passage as far as is required by our context.

He who is genuinely hungry for knowledge (who genuinely wants to know) is concerned with beings themselves and not at all with what are commonly held as such; he is concerned with the ὅ ἐστιν, with the what-being of beings, their essence, the 'ideas', the beingful beings. The ideas are therefore the *most beingful* beings – image, look, εἶδος.

But the question remains: is this most beingful being, as we maintain, also conceived by Plato as *the most unhidden,* the ἀληθινόν? The answer is given in another dialogue of Plato, the *Sophist* (240 a 7-b 4), and in a context with which we are already to some extent familiar, i.e. the question of what we understand by image, εἴδωλον. In εἴδωλον there is contained εἶδος, the visible; not actually a *look,* but something which *looks like* a look, i.e., what we have already encountered as shadows, reflections and so forth. The individual things as εἴδωλα are only *images* of εἶδος, or, put the other way around, the εἶδος is the what-being, the genuine being of the εἴδωλον. It is now asked quite generally: what *is* such an image?

Τί δῆτα, ὦ ξένε, εἴδωλον ἂν φαῖμεν εἶναι πλήν γε τὸ πρὸς τὰλνθινὸν ἀφωμοιωμένον ἕτερον τοιοῦτον;

Ἕτερον δέ λέγεις τοιοῦτον ἀλνθιόν, ἢ ἐπὶ τίνι τὸ τοιοῦτον εἶπες;

Οὐδαμῶς ἀληοινόν γε, ἀλλ᾽ ἐοικὸς μέν.

Ἆρα τὸ ἀλνθινὸν ὄντως ὂν λέγων;

Οὕτως.

'What will we call the image except what resembles the actual unhidden, thus another such thing, ἕτερον τολοῦτον?'

An image (look) of something is what resembles the *genuinely* unhidden, which latter we call the original. It is then asked:

'Another *such,* namely another which is *genuinely* unhidden: is that what you mean? Or how do you understand the τοιοῦτον?'

'No, not that. The image is not at all a second unhidden, but it looks like the unhidden.'

Then you understand the genuinely unhidden, ἀληθινόν, in the sense of the ὄντως ὄν, as the beingful being, as what genuinely is?'

'Yes. That is so.'

The εἴδωλον is indeed also an ἀληθές, but not ἀληθινόν. Not everything visible is ἀληθινόν, but only τὸ ὄντως ὄν is this. It is therefore clear that the 'most beingful beings', the ideas, are also described as the most unhidden unhidden (what is unhidden now in the third stage, τὰ νῦν λεγόμενα ἀληθῆ).

How are we to understand this *double* character of the ideas, that they are the most unhidden *and* the most beingful? What do we conclude about the essence of the ideas and its connection with the essence of truth as such? The most unhidden: this superlative means that the ideas are the primary unhidden. They stand at the forefront of everything unhidden, they play the leading role, they prepare in advance for the others. In what way? The ideas are the most beingful beings, and what is most beingful in beings, what actually constitutes beings, is their *being.* But being, as we have seen, is what first of all *lets beings through.* The ideas prepare the way. Light allows what was previously concealed to become visible. The ideas remove hiddenness. The unhiddenness of beings arises from being, from the ideas, from ἀληθινόν. What is most disclosive opens up, and what is most illuminative lights up. The ideas allow unhiddenness to arise along with beings; they are the *primordially* unhidden, unhiddenness in the primordial originary sense. This is what the superlative means.

b) The Ideas as What Is Sighted by a Pre-modelling Perceiving within the Occurrence of Unhiddenness

Why did we say (secondly) that the ideas allow unhiddenness to arise along *with* them? Is anything *else* involved in this *co*-origination? Indeed! We have already seen that ἀληθές and the ideas are *interrelated* with light and freedom.

Why then do we say that the ideas originate *along with* unhiddenness? If the ideas are what lets-through, are they unable to bring about visibility on their *own account*? What might ideas be 'in themselves'? ἰδέα is what is sighted. What is sighted *is* so only in *seeing* and *for* seeing. An unsighted sighted is like a round square or wooden iron. 'Ideas': we must at last be serious with this Platonic term for being. 'Being sighted' is not something else in addition, an additional predicate, something which occasionally happens to the ideas. Instead, it is what characterizes them *as such.* The ideas are so called because they are primarily understood as visible. Something can be sighted in the strict sense only through seeing and looking. We must be strict here, for this is a passage where our interpretation goes beyond Plato; more precisely, where Plato, for quite fundamental reasons, could not go further (cf. the *Theaetetus*), with the consequence that the whole problem of ideas was forced along a false track. The problem of ideas can only be posed anew by grasping it from the primordial *unity* of what is perceived on the one hand, and what does the perceiving on the other hand.

But what kind of looking (perceiving) is this? It is not a staring at something present, not a simple finding of something and receiving of something into our vision, but a looking in the sense of per-ceiving [*Er-blickens*]. This means first *forming* what is looked at *through* the looking and *in* the looking, i.e. forming in advance, modelling. This pre-modelling perceiving of being, of essence, is already *bound* to what is projected in such a projection.

At the origin of the unhiddenness of beings, i.e. at being's letting-through of beings, the perceiving is no less involved than what is perceived in perceiving – the ideas. *Together* these constitute unhiddenness, meaning they are nothing 'in themselves', they are never *objects.* The ideas, as what is sighted, *are* (if we can speak in this way at all) only *in* this perceiving seeing; they have an essential connection with perceiving. The ideas, therefore, are not present but somehow hidden objects which one could lure out through a kind of hocus-pocus. Just as little do they carry around *subjects*, i.e. are they something subjective in the sense of being constituted and thought-up by subjects (humans, as we know them). They are neither things, objective, nor are they thought-up, subjective. *What* they are, *how* they are, indeed *if* they 'are' at all, is still undecided. From this you could make an approximate measure of the progress of philosophy. But there is no progress in philosophy. The question is undecided not because the answer has not yet been found, but because the question has not yet been asked seriously and in a way that measures up to antiquity, i.e. because it has not yet been sufficiently interrogated in its ground. Instead, one or the other of two familiar possibilities has been prematurely seized upon. Either the ideas as objective (and since one does not know *where* they are, one eventually arrives at 'validity' and 'value'), or as subjective, perhaps just a fiction, a phantasm, a mere 'as if'. One knows nothing except subjects and objects, and especially one does not know that precisely this distinction between subject and object, this distinction from which philosophy has so long been nourished, is the most questionable thing of all. In view of this completely confused situation within the most central problem of philosophy, it was a valuable and genuine step when the ideas were made creative thoughts of the absolute spirit, in Christian terms, of God, for example with Augustine. Admittedly, this was not a philosophical solution but an avoidance of the problem. Yet it provided genuine philosophical impetus, which surfaces again and again in the great philosophers, finally in grand style with Hegel.

For now we must leave hanging the questions of what and how the ideas *are*, and of whether we may even ask about them in this way. As what is sighted by a pre-modelling perceiving, the ideas are neither objectively present nor subjectively produced. Both, what is sighted as such, and the perceiving, *together* belong to the origination of unhiddenness, that is, to the *occurrence* of truth.

c) Deconcealment as the Fundamental Occurrence of the Ex-istence of Man

When unhiddenness occurs, hiddenness and concealing are overcome and removed. The removal of concealment, that which acts against concealing, we shall henceforth call de-concealing [*Ent-bergen*]. The characteristic perceiving of the idea, this projecting, is deconcealing [*ist entbergend*]. At first this appears to be just another word. This perceiving as premodelling binding of oneself to being, which is the proper meaning of liberation, deconceals not in an incidental sense, but this looking-into-the-light has the essential character of deconcealing and is nothing else but this. To be deconcealing is the innermost accomplishment of liberation. It is *care* [*Sorge*] itself: becoming-free as binding oneself to the ideas, as letting *being* give the lead. Therefore becoming-free, this perceiving of the ideas, this understanding-in-advance of being and the essence of things, has the *character of deconcealing* [*ist entbergsam*], i.e. deconcealing belongs to the inner drive of this seeing. Deconcealing is the innermost nature of looking-into-the-light.

What we call *deconcealment* [*Entbergsamkeit*] is that which, in its fundamental accomplishment, primordially carries, unfolds and brings together the oft-mentioned phenomena of perceiving, viewing, light and freedom. What we describe in this way is the unity of perceiving, which in a sense first creates the perceivable in its innermost connection. The unhiddenness of beings happens in and through deconcealment. It is a projecting- opening order [*entwerfendend-eröffnender Auftrag*] that calls for decision. The *essence* of unhiddenness is deconcealment.

This latter proposition, if taken as a definition, would very likely be laughed at by the common understanding. Unhiddenness as deconcealment: this is like saying that obeying is following, that silence is reticence – a simple switching of words!

Where and how *is* this deconcealment? We see it as an *occurrence* – something that happens 'with *man*'. A daring thesis! The essence of truth *qua* ἀλήθεια (unhiddenness) is deconcealment, therefore located in man himself: this means that truth is reduced to something *merely* human and so annihilated. Truth is usually regarded as something that man *seeks* in order to bind himself to it *normatively*, i.e. as something *over* him. How then can the essence of truth be something human? Where is the man who has best secured the truth and through whom it is best demonstrated? Would *he* then become the norm? What is man, such that he could become the measure of *everything*? Can the essence of truth be given over to man? We are all too familiar with the unreliability of human beings – swaying reeds in the wind! Does the essence of truth depend on such beings? We immediately rebel against the idea that the essence of truth can be located in a human occurrence. This resistance is natural and obvious to everyone, which is why philosophy has always used such considerations to protect itself against so-called relativism.

But it must eventually be asked if this bad relativism is not just the apple from a branch whose roots have long ago become rotten, so that it doesn't mean anything in particular to refer to relativism, but testifies (e.g. in what is today known as the sociology of knowledge) to a miscomprehension of the problem.

When we say that the essence of unhiddenness as deconcealment is a human occurrence, that truth is in essence something human, and when one so naturally struggles against the 'humanization' of the essence of truth, everything depends on what 'human' means here. What concept of 'human' does one unreflectively assume? Does one know without further ado what man is, in order to be able to decide that truth could not be anything human? One acts as if the essence of man is the most self-evident thing in the world. However, assuming that we do not know this so easily, assuming that even the way we have to *ask* about the essence of man is very questionable – who can tell us what and who man is? Is answering this question a matter of any old inspiration? We do not mean man as we proximally know him, as he runs around and is pleased to comport himself now in this way, now in that. From where are we to take the concept of man, and how are we to justify ourselves against the objection of an attempted humanization of the essence of truth?

However, we would have poorly understood the earlier interpretation of the cave allegory if we had not already learnt where the concept of man is supposed to come from. For this allegory gives precisely the history in which man comes to himself as a being in the midst of beings. And in the history of man's essence it is precisely the occurrence of unhiddenness, i.e. of deconcealment, that is decisive. We first get to know what man is from the essence of unhiddenness; the essence of truth is what first allows the essence of man to be grasped. When we said that precisely this essence of truth is an occurrence which happens to man, this means that the man whose liberation is depicted in the allegory is *set out into* the truth [*in die Wahrheit ver-setzt*]. That is the mode of his *existence* [*Existenz*], the fundamental occurrence of his Dasein. Primordial unhiddenness is projective de-concealing as an occurrence happening 'in man', i.e. in his *history.* Truth is neither somewhere *over* man (as validity in itself), nor is it in man as a psychical subject, but man is *'in' the truth.* Truth is something greater than man. The latter is in the truth only if, and only in so far as, he masters his nature, holds himself within the unhiddenness of beings, and comports himself to this unhiddenness.

But the question is what truth *itself* is. The first step towards understanding this *question* is the insight that man comes to himself, and finds the *ground* of his Dasein, in that event of deconcealment which constitutes the unhiddenness of beings.

There is something further we discover from the allegory, namely that what man is cannot simply be read off from the living beings running around on this planet. Rather, we can only ask about this when man himself somehow *comes to be* what he *can* be, whether it be this or that. The only way in which we can really understand man is as a being bound to his own possibilities, bound in a way that itself frees the space within which he pursues his own being in this or that manner.

What man is cannot be established within the cave. It can only be experienced through participation in the whole history of liberation. We saw that βία, violence, belongs to this liberation: man must use a kind of violence to be able to ask about himself. Knowledge of what man is does not fall into anybody's lap, but man must first place himself in question, must *comport* himself to himself as that being *who is asked about,* and who, in this asking, becomes uneasy. The question of man's essence can be put only by man coming to a decision on himself, i.e. on the powers that carry and define him and on his relation to these; in brief, by man *becoming* what he *can* be. We understand the question 'what is man?' as asking about *who* we are in so far as we *are*. We are only what we have the power to entrust ourselves to be.

Who then *is* this man of the cave allegory? Not man in general and as such, but that particular being which comports itself to beings as the unhidden, and thereby becomes unhidden to itself. But the unhiddenness of beings, in which this being stands and holds itself, happens in the projective perceiving of being, or in Platonic terms, in the ideas. This projective perceiving occurs as liberation of its essence *to itself*. Man is that being which understands being and *exists* on the basis of this understanding, i.e. among other things, comports itself to beings as the unhidden. 'Exist' [*Existieren*] and 'being-there' [*Dasein*] are not used here in a vague faded sense, to mean happening [*Vorkommen*] and being present, but in a quite definite and adequately grounded sense; *ex-sistere, ex-sistens:* to stand out into the unhiddenness of beings, to be *given over* [*ausgesetzt*] to beings in their totality, thus to the confrontation between itself and beings, not closed in upon itself like plants, nor restricted like animals in their environment, nor simply occurring like a stone. How this is more concretely to be understood has been explained with sufficient clarity in my various publications, at any rate sufficiently to make discussion possible. Only by entering into the dangerous region of philosophy is it possible for man to realize his nature as transcending himself into the unhiddenness of beings. Man apart from philosophy is something else.

Understanding the cave allegory means grasping the history of human essence, which means grasping *oneself* in one's ownmost history. This demands, when we begin to philosophize at any rate, putting out of action diverse concepts and non-concepts of man, irrespective of their obviousness or currency. At the same time it means understanding what the clarification of the essence of ἀλήθεια implies for knowledge of human essence.

The proposition that man is the being who exists in the perceiving of being has its own truth, which is quite distinctive and different from such truths as 2 + 1 = 3, that the weather is good, or that the essence of a table consists in its being an object of use. The truth of the statement about the essence of man can never be scientifically proven. It cannot be established by reference to facts, nor can it be derived from principles in a formal-logical manner. This is not a deficiency, especially when one realizes that what is essential always remains unprovable, or more precisely, lies outside the sphere of provability and unprovability. What is provable (in the sense of formal-logical reckoning, detached from the fundamental decision and stance of human existence) is already dubious in respect of essentiality. Nor is the proposition about man's essence a matter of 'belief', i.e. something to be accepted simply on authority. If one took it thus, one would not understand it at all. The truth of this statement (precisely because it says something philosophical) can only be philosophically (as I say) enkindled and appropriated, that is, only when the questioning that understands being in the questionability of beings in the whole takes its standpoint from a fundamental decision, from a fundamental stance towards being and towards its limit in nothingness.

What this means is not a matter for further *talking*, but rather for *doing.* It should be said, however, that even to make a beginning with philosophy one must have rid oneself of the illusion that man could pose, let alone solve a problem, *without* some standpoint. The desire to philosophize from the standpoint of standpointlessness, as a purportedly genuine and superior objectivity, is either childish, or, as is usually the case, disingenuous. The hiddenness of the matter itself, i.e. of the being of beings, only gives way to an *attack* which has an unambiguously human starting point and path. Not freedom from any standpoint (something fantastic), but the right choice of standpoint, the courage to a standpoint, the setting in action of a standpoint and the holding out within it, is the task; a task, admittedly, which can only be enacted *in* philosophical work, not prior to it and not subsequently.

We seek the essence of truth as the unhiddenness of beings in deconcealment, as a deconcealing *occurrence* upon whose ground man exists. This is what first *determines* the essence of man, that is, of man properly understood and as treated in the cave allegory. Man is the being that understands being and exists on the basis of this understanding.

We are thus at our goal. The allegory of the cave has given us *one* answer to the question concerning the essence of truth, an answer which proceeds essentially from the meaning of ἀ-λήθεια. Yet the occurrence depicted in the allegory has *a fourth* stage, indeed a very remarkable one. The ascent does not proceed upwards, to something still higher, but *backwards*.

D. The Fourth Stage (516 e 3–517 a 6): the Freed Prisoner's Return to the Cave

Καὶ τόδε δὴ ἐννόηδον, ἦν δ᾽ ἐγώ. εἰ πάλιν ὁ τοιοῦτος καταβὰς εἰς τὸν αὐτὸν θᾶκον καθίζοιτο, ἆρ᾽, οὐ σκότους ἂν ἀνάπλεως σχοίη τοὺς ὀφθαλμούς, ἐξαίφνης ἥκων ἐκ τοῦ ἡλίου;

Καὶ μάλα γ᾽, ἔφη.

Τὰς δὲ δὴ δκιὰς ἐκείνας πάλιν εἰ δέοι αὐτὸν γνωματεύοτα διαμιλλᾶσθαι τοῖς ἀεὶ δεσμώταις ἐκείνοις, ἐν ᾧ ἀμβλυώττει, πρὶν καταστῆναι τὰ ὄμματα, οὗτος δ᾽ ὁ χρόνος μὴ πάνυ ὀλίγος εἴη συνηθείας, ἆρ᾽ οὐ γέλωτ᾽ ἂν παράσχοι, καὶ λέγοιτο ἂν περὶ αὐτοῦ ὡς ἀναβὰς ἄνω διεφθαρμένος ἥκει τὰ ὄμματα, καὶ ὅτι οὐκ ἄξιον οὐδὲ πειρᾶσθαι ἄνω ἰέναι; καὶ τὸν ἐπιχειροῦντα λύειν τε καὶ ἀνάγειν, εἴ πως ἐν ταῖς χερσὶ δύναιντο λαβεῖν καὶ ἀποκτείνειν, ἀποκτεινύναι ἄν;

Σφόδρα γ᾽, ἔφη.

'What do you think would happen if the released prisoner went back to sit in his old seat in the cave? Would not his eyes become full of darkness, because he had come in suddenly out of the sunlight?'

'Certainly.'

'And if he again had to compete with the prisoners who were still shackled in giving opinions about the shadows, while he was still blinded and before his eyes got used to the dark – a process that would take some time – wouldn't he likely be set out to mockery? And wouldn't they say that he had only come back down to regain his eyesight, and that the ascent was not worth even attempting. And if anyone tried to release them [the prisoners] and lead them up, wouldn't they kill him if they could lay hands on him?'

'Certainly.'

§ 10. The φιλόσοφος as Liberator of the Prisoners. His Act of Violence, His Endangerment and Death

What is happening here? There is no longer an ascent, but rather a turning back. We turn back around to where we previously were, to what we already know. The fourth stage does not introduce anything new. We can easily establish this if we keep to the clues that guided our characterization of the previous stages. We asked first about the ἀληθές and the moments that accompany it: light, freedom, beings, idea. None of this now appears. There is no longer any mention of ἀληθές and ἀλήθεια. Why so? The essence of truth, ἀλήθεια, is indeed clarified at the end of the third stage. If we consider all this, then we shall seriously doubt whether this final stage is an integral part of the allegory. To be sure, it is the final stage in the sense that it provides a conclusion that adorns the whole, but it does not contribute to its essential content.

So it appears, if we take what is presented externally and in relation to tangible results. But by proceeding in this way we have already forgotten that it is an occurrence of *man* which is treated. If we pay due attention to the fact that something is peculiar here, that the allegory as a whole treats of an *occurrence* and that this occurrence now involves a *reversal* we shall again ask what is actually happening. If we pay careful attention, and once again survey what is finally presented, we become suspicious. How does this occurrence end? With the prospect of *death*! Nothing was previously said about this. If the fate of death is not something unimportant in the occurrence of man, then we must see what is here finally presented as something *more* than a harmless addition or poetically painted conclusion. We must therefore attempt, just as with the previous stages, to bring out essential features.

1. The allegory as a whole ends with the fateful prospect of being killed, the most radical ejection from the human historical community. Whose death is treated? It is not a matter of death in general, but of death as the fate of him who seeks to release the prisoners, the death of *the liberator*. Hitherto he was not treated at all. We knew only, from the third stage, that liberation must happen βίᾳ, with violence. We interpreted this to mean that the liberator must be a violent person.

2. Now we see that the liberator is ὁ τοιοῦτος, someone who has become free in that he looks into the light, has the illuminating view, and thus has a surer footing in the ground of human-historical Dasein. Only then does he gain power to the violence he must employ in liberation. This violence is no blind caprice, but is the dragging of the others out into that light which already fills and binds his own view. This violence is also not some kind of crudity, but is tact of the highest rigour, that rigour of the spirit to which he, the liberator, has already obligated himself.

3. Who is this one who liberates? We know only that he is someone who, having ascended from the cave, sees the ideas, who stands towards the light and thus 'in the light'. Plato calls such a person a φιλόσοφος. So Plato says in the *Sophist* (254 a 8–b 1):

Ὁ δέ γε φιλόσοφς, τῇ τοῦ ὄντος ἀεὶ διὰ λογισμῶν προσκείμενος ἰδέα, διὰ τὸ λαμπρὸν αὖ τῆς χώρας οὐδαμῶς εὐπετὴς ὀφθῆναι· τὰ γὰρ τῆς τῶν πολλῶν ψυχῆς ὄμματα καρτερεῖν πρὸς τὸ θεῖον ἀφορῶντα ἀδύνατα.

The philosopher is someone concerned with perceiving and constantly thinking [*be-denkend*] the being of beings. Owing to the brightness of the place where he stands it is never easy to see him; for the seeing of the soul of the majority is unable to withstand looking at the godly.'

The Greek word φιηόσοφος is put together from σοφός and φίλος. A σοφός is someone who understands something, who has reliable knowledge in a particular area, who understands the matter at hand and who enacts an ultimate decision and law-giving, φίλος is friend, φιλόσοφος someone whose Dasein is determined through φιλοσοφία: not someone who pursues 'philosophy' as a matter of general 'education', but someone for whom philosophy is the basic character of the being of man and who, in advance of his age, creates this being, lets it originate, drives it forward. The philosopher is someone possessed of the drive and inner necessity to understand beings in the whole, φιλοσοφία, φιλοσοφεῖν does not mean science (research within a delimited region of beings and with a restricted problematic), nor is it primary and fundamental science, but is an openness to the questioning of being and essence, a wanting to *get to the bottom* of beings and of being as such. In short, the philosopher is the friend of being.

It is therefore a very crude error, and a sign of the most elementary misunderstanding of philosophy, when one seeks to make philosophy norm-giving for one or another science, e.g. mathematics or biology. Sciences *can* arise from philosophy, but this is not *necessary.* The sciences *can* serve philosophy, but philosophy does *not necessarily need* their service. The sciences first get their ground, dignity, and entitlements from philosophy. This sounds strange, because nowadays we estimate the sciences according to their technical utility and success. The sciences are themselves only a form of technology, a means of professional qualification. It is *for this reason* that they are promoted and maintained, and it is for this reason that the decision on what science can be is no longer made by universities, but by associations of philologists and similar organizations. This already indicates an ending, something ripe for disappearing.

But closer reflection on what is presented in the fourth stage tells us more.

4. As liberator of the prisoners, the philosopher exposes himself to the fate of death in the cave. Notice that this is death *in the cave,* at the hands of cave-dwellers who are not even masters of themselves. Plato obviously wants to remind us of the death of Socrates. One will therefore say that this connection between the philosopher and death is only a singular occurrence, that this fate does not *necessarily* belong to philosophy. Otherwise, and on the whole, philosophers have fared very well, for they sit undisturbed in their homes and occupy themselves with beautiful things. Today, philosophy (assuming there were such a thing) would be a perfectly safe occupation. In any case people no longer get killed. But from this, from the absence of any such danger, we may conclude only that no one any longer ventures so far, thus that there are no longer philosophers. But let us leave this question of whether or not philosophers exist today. The matter cannot in any case be decided by discussions in magazines and newspapers or on radio; it is quite outside any decision in the public realm.

There is something further we must reflect upon. Must the killing by the cave-prisoners necessarily result, as it did with Socrates' cup of hemlock, in a physical death? Is this not also *symbolic*? Is the process of physical death the hard thing? Not rather the actual (*actual,* I say) constant presence of death before one *during* existence? And again, not just death in the physical sense of dying, but the forfeiture and rendering powerless of one's own essence? No philosopher has been able to avoid the fate of *this* death in the cave. That the philosopher is delivered over to death in the cave means that philosophy is powerless within the region of prevailing self-evidences. Only in so far as these themselves change can philosophy have its say. Today, in the event that philosophers did exist, this fate would be more threatening than ever. The poisoning would be far more poisonous, because more concealed and devious. The poisoning would happen not through visible external damage, not through attack and struggle such that the possibility of real resistance would remain, the possibility of measuring strength, thus of liberation and heightening of power. The poisoning would happen by becoming interested in the cave- philosophers, such that everyone says to one another that these philosophers must be read, such that one hands out prizes and honours within the cave, such that one gradually creates a newspaper and magazine fame for the philosopher, and admires him. Today, the poisoning would consist in the philosopher being pushed into the circle of those who are interesting and about whom one writes and gossips, those in whom, within a few years, certainly no one will any longer be interested. For one can interest oneself only in something new, and only as long as others do so too. The philosopher would in this way be quietly killed, made harmless and unthreatening. While still alive he would die his own death in the cave. And he must put up with this. He would misunderstand himself and his task were he to withdraw from the cave. Being-free, being a liberator, is to act together in history with those to whom one belongs in one's nature. He must remain in the cave with the prisoners, and with those who count down there as philosophers. Neither may he withdraw into an ironic superiority, for in this way he would still participate in his own poisoning. Only by becoming master of such ironic superiority would he be able to die a *genuine* death in the cave.

Plato attained this high level of existence in his old age. Kant bore something of this highest freedom in himself. Poison and weapons for death are indeed ready today. But the philosopher is lacking, because today there can at best be more or less good sophists, who at best prepare the way for the philosopher who will come. However, we do not want to lose ourselves in a psychology of philosophy, but to grasp the inner task of philosophizing through the fate of the one who philosophizes.

5. We experience at the same time *how* the liberator liberates. He does not liberate by conversing with the cave-dwellers in the language, and with the aims and intentions, of the cave, but by laying hold of them violently and dragging them away. He does not try to persuade the cave-dwellers by reference to norms, grounds and proofs. In that way, as Plato says, he would only make himself laughable. Within the cave, it would be said that his assertions fail to correspond to what everyone down there agrees upon as correct. One would say of him that he is one-sided, and that, wherever he may come from, he represents an arbitrary and accidental standpoint. Presumably, indeed certainly, they would have, down there in the cave, a 'sociology of knowledge' with whose assistance they could explain how he operates with 'worldview' presuppositions contradicting and disturbing what is agreed upon within the cave. There in the cave, the only thing that matters (as Plato indeed describes it) is who is the cleverest, who can most quickly work out where all the shadows, among them philosophy, belong, i.e. in which discipline and under which type of received philosophy. Down there they don't want to know anything of philosophy, e.g. of the philosophy of Kant, but at best they take an interest in the Kant *Association*. The philosopher will not himself challenge this all too obligatory cave-chatter, but will leave it to itself, instead immediately seizing hold of *one* person (or a few) and pull him out, attempting to lead him on the long journey out of the cave.

The philosopher must remain solitary, because this is what he *is* according to his nature. His solitude is not to be *admired*. Isolation is nothing to be wished for as such. Just for this reason must the philosopher, always in decisive moments, be there [*da sein*] and not give way. He will not misunderstand solitude in external fashion, as withdrawal and letting things go their own way.

§ 11. The Fulfilment of the Fate of Philosophizing as an Occurrence of ἀλήθεια: Separation and Togetherness of the Manifest and the Hidden (Being and Illusion)

Surveying the five points, the fourth stage provides us with *more* to reflect upon than we originally suspected. It tells us something we did not previously know, although the first and second stages also treated of the sojourn within the cave. We now see that it is not simply a matter of a second sojourn, but of *a return* from the sunlight. But even this way of conceiving the fourth stage is not accurate. It is not just the reappearance of someone who had previously been in the cave, but of his return as a *liberator.* What is treated, the essential content of the allegory, is the *occurrence* of the liberated one and of the liberation itself.

This *is* a content, certainly, but does it belong essentially to the previous stages, to the occurrence of *unhiddenness*? What happens at the end, as we have just interpreted it, still does not justify our taking this as a *fourth stage.* This is because our division of the stages depends on highlighting the respective transitions from *one* ἀληθές to another, or more precisely, to ever higher stages through to the highest, for we are claiming the occurrence of ἀλήθεια (unhiddenness, deconcealing) as the genuine content of the allegory. But the fourth stage, while containing valuable information on philosophers, no longer speaks of ἀλήθεια! So there remains only this: either what we took as the fourth stage does not qualify as one at all, or our characterization of the earlier stages was inexact, such that ἀλήθεια is *not* at the centre of the whole story and was instead insinuated by us quite inappropriately, artificially, and violently. This is the great difficulty now confronting our interpretation, especially since Plato himself does not give any division into stages, with numbers or the like.

In view of the fact that it no longer treats tangibly of ἀληθές, the easiest solution would be to let the fourth stage drop out, and this in spite of its valuable hints on the nature of philosophy. But we are prevented from doing this when we recall that the philosopher is not first discussed in the fourth stage, but that this history of liberation to the light, of ascent to the ideas, is nothing but the path of the philosophizing individual into philosophy. It is even more difficult to strike out ἀλήθεια as central for the first three stages. What are we to do?

There remains one solution, which is not a last resort but the most necessary path along which we must proceed. We must ask whether, from the fact that the fourth stage no longer *explicitly* treats of ἀλήθεια, light, beings, ideas, it may be concluded that ἀλήθεια is no longer the theme and centre of the occurrence. True, ἀλήθεια is no longer *spoken of,* but we have not yet *examined* the section. Precisely the most essential part of the story has not been discussed and comprehended. We can only decide about whether the fourth stage belongs to the previous stages when we have become clear about whether, without ἀλήθεια being spoken of, this is nevertheless what is *treated,* and indeed in a definite central sense.

What then does happen? The liberated one returns to the cave with an eye for *being.* He is supposed *to be* in the cave. This means that he who has been filled with the illuminating view for the being of beings will make known to the cave-dwellers his thoughts on what *they,* down there, take for beings. He can only do this if he remains true to himself in his liberated stance. He will report what he sees in the cave from the standpoint of his view of essence. What does he *perceive* in this way? He understands the *being* of beings; in perceiving the idea he therefore knows what belongs to a being and to its unhiddenness. He can therefore decide whether something, e.g. the sun, is a being, or whether it is only a reflection in water; he can decide whether something is shadow or real thing. On the basis of his view of essence, he knows in advance, before he returns to the cave, what 'shadows' mean, and upon what their possibility is grounded. Only because he already knows this is he able, returning to the cave, to demostrate that the unhidden now showing itself upon the wall is caused by the fire in the cave, that this unhidden is shadow. With his view of essence he can now see what happens in the cave for what it is. He is now able, for the first time, to comprehend the *situation* of the prisoners, to understand why they do not recognize the shadows *as* shadows, and why they take them instead for the beings to which they must comport themselves. Therefore he will not be disturbed when the cave-dwellers laugh at him and his words, and when they, adopting a superior attitude, make cheap objections to him. On the contrary he will remain firm, putting up with the fact that the cave-dwellers despise him. He will even go over to the attack and will lay hold of one of them to try to make him see the light in the cave. He will not deny that the cave-dwellers comport themselves to something unhidden, but he will try to show them that this unhidden is such that, precisely in its showing, the beings hide themselves. He will attempt to make them understand that something does indeed show itself on the wall, but only *looks like* beings, without *being* so, that here on the wall there occurs instead a constant *concealing* of beings; and that they themselves, the prisoners, are utterly carried along and dazzled by this.

What happens, then? A conflict between different basic standpoints, each with its own historical origin, a confrontation involving beings and illusion, what is manifest and what is covered up. But beings and what *seems* to be are not simply juxtaposed. Instead, they are *set over against each other,* because both do raise and *can* raise the *claim* to unhiddenness.

This antagonism between what is manifest and what is covered up, shows that the matter at issue is not the mere existence of unhiddenness as such. On the contrary, unhiddenness, the self-showing of the shadows, will cleave more firmly to itself without knowing that it is a *concealing,* without knowing that the manifestness of beings occurs only through the *overcoming* of concealing. Truth, therefore, is not just unhiddenness of beings such that the previous hiddenness is done away with, but the manifestness of beings is in itself necessarily an overcoming of a concealment. Concealment belongs *essentially* to unhiddenness, *like the valley belongs to the mountain.*

But why are we going over all this again? Surely we have heard enough of this during the interpretation of the first and second stages! No. It is only *now* that we understand why we could interpret the first and second stages as we did, such that we always had to inquire back and had to say *too much* compared with what the prisoners have before them. Only now do we understand that the liberation which occurs from the first through to the third stages already presupposes a *being*-free; that the one who does the freeing is not just any arbitrary kind of person.

There is something else that we now understand. Whoever comes out of the cave only to lose himself in the 'appearing' [*Scheinen*] of the ideas would not truly understand these, i.e. he would not perceive the ideas as letting-through, as setting beings free, as wrenching beings from hiddenness and overcoming their concealment. He would regard the ideas themselves as just beings of a higher order. Deconcealment would not *occur* at all.

It is clear from this that liberation does not achieve its final goal merely by ascent to the sun. Freedom is not *just* a matter of being unshackled, nor just a matter of being free *for* the light. Rather, genuine freedom means *to be a liberator* from the dark. The descent back into the cave is not some subsequent diversion on the part of those who have become free, perhaps undertaken from curiosity about how cave life looks from above, but is the only manner through which freedom is genuinely *realized.*

Truth, in other words, is not something one abidingly possesses, and whose enjoyment we put aside at some point in order to instruct or lecture other people, but unhiddenness *occurs* only in the *history* of permanent freeing. History, however, is always a matter of the unique task posed by fate in a determinate practical situation, not of free-floating discussion. The liberated one will go into the cave and give his views on what, down there, is taken as beings and the unhidden. The freed one has a view only for essence. The liberator is the bearer of a *differentiation.* Since he can distinguish between beings and being, he insists on a *divorce* between beings and what appears to be, between the unhidden and what (like the shadows) conceals itself precisely in its self-showing. He insists, therefore, on the divorce between being and appearing to be, truth and untruth. At the same time, with this divorce, there arises their *co-belonging.* Only on the basis of the divorce between the true and the untrue does it become clear that the essence of truth as unhiddenness consists in the overcoming of concealing, meaning that unhiddenness contains an essential *connection* with hiddenness and concealing. This means that ἀλήθεια is not just the manifestness of beings, but (we can now more clearly understand the *alpha privatum)* is in itself a setting-apart. Thus the section we have been discussing does indeed speak of truth, in respect of its essential relatedness to concealing and the concealed. Untruth *belongs* to the essence of truth.

Deconcealment, the overcoming of concealment, happens only through a primordial struggle against hiddenness. A *primordial* struggle (not just polemic) is the kind of struggle which first *creates* its enemy and assists its enemy to the *most incisive antagonism.* Unhiddenness is not simply one river bank and hiddenness the other, but the essence of truth as deconcealment is the bridge, or better, is the *bridging over* of each *towards* and *against* the other.

But is all this really to be found in the fourth stage? Or have we violently inserted it? Plato does not speak anywhere of hiddenness, the word does not occur here at all. Nor is there any extensive treatment of the shadows as illusion [*Schein*]. Could it be that Plato was unaware that untruth is opposed to truth? Not only did he know this, but the great dialogues he wrote immediately after the *Republic* have nothing else but un-truth as their theme.

But untruth is surely the *opposite* of truth!? Certainly. But *this* untruth: can we simply call this *hiddenness*? The hiddenness of beings is not yet untruth *qua* falsity, incorrectness. It does not follow from the fact that I do not know something, from the fact that something is hidden and unknown to me, that I know something false, untrue! Hiddenness and concealing are ambiguous here. On the other hand we see that the shadows or appearances, which are just the opposite of true beings, by their own nature show and announce themselves, i.e. they are manifest, unhidden. What is peculiar here is that the hidden is not without further ado the false – while illusion, the false, is always and necessarily something unhidden, therefore in *this* sense true. How does all this fit together?

The essence of ἀλήθεια is not clarified, so that we come to suspect that Plato does not yet grasp it, or no longer grasps it, in a *primordial* manner. Yet was it *previously* grasped in such a way?

In what kind of labyrinth do we find ourselves! It remains this way today. We see in any case that even if Plato had treated expressly of shadows and illusion in the fourth stage, unhiddenness would not have been grasped in its full essence. But if hiddenness is not grasped primordially and totally, then *un*-hiddenness certainly cannot be grasped. And yet Plato treats of ἀλήθεια in its antagonism to illusion! This can only mean that the cave allegory does indeed treat of ἀλήθεια, but not such that this comes to light in its *primordiality* and essence, i.e. in its *antagonism*, characteristic of φύσις (being), to the κρύπτεσθαι φιλεῖ, thus to hiddenness as such and not just to the false, not just to illusion. If this is so, however, then in Plato the fundamental experience from which the word ἀ-λήθεια arose is already disappearing. The word and its semantic power is already on the road to impoverishment and trivialization.

How could we venture such a weighty assertion? However, before we can decide about this suspicion, we must first bring our whole interpretation of the cave allegory to the conclusion demanded by its content, i.e. we must take up the question of how the idea of the good relates to the essence of truth, and what it means for Plato in general.

We have not yet come far enough to decide the question, for we have omitted the discussion of the highest idea, ἰδέα τοῦ ἀγαθοῦ, which is precisely the culmination of liberation outside the cave. Perhaps only by answering the question of the relationship between the idea of the good and ἀλήθεια shall we be able to decide how Plato understands ἀλήθεια, whether in terms of the fundamental experience belonging to this basic word, or in a different way.

Notes

1   *Platonis Opera*, recogn. Ioannes Burnet, Oxonii: Clarendon, 2nd edition 1905–10, Vol. 4.

2   διαλέλεσθαι: to discuss with one another (among themselves) what is encountered (cf. 'dialectic'). 'Discourse' and *being*!

3   Reading 515 c 5 according to Schleiermacher [instead of the Oxford edition εἴη, εἰ φύσει τοιάδε – Ed.]. Cf. *Platons Werke*, trans. Friedrich Schleiermacher, Berlin: Reimer, 3rd edition 1855–1862, Division III, Volume I (1862), p. 232 and note on p. 368.

4   Cf. p. 22.

5   ὀρθός (rectus – right): straight, without diverting, without detour; not by way of the shadows, the thing itself.

6   *Odyssey* XI, 489 f.

7   See Supplement 3.

8   *Metaphysics* Z, Ch. 1; see Supplement 5.

9   Parmenides Fr. 3: τὸ γὰρ αὐτὸ νοεῖν ἔστιν τε καὶ εἶναι. (In Kirk, Raven and Schofield, op. cit., p. 246, which gives the alternative translations 'Thought and being are the same' and 'For the same thing is there to be thought of and to be'.) [Trans.] .

10   Immanuel Kant, *Kritik der Urtheilskraft*, ed. Karl Vorländer, 4th edition, Meiner 1924, p. 117.

11 Light (brightness) is 1. what is first (primarily) sighted, 2. what is primarily transparent for sight as such.

12 'Das Lied von der Glocke', line 192.

13 Cf. Kant, *Critique of Pure Reason*, B XI [Ed.] .

14 Cf. the saying of Protagoras (in Plato, *Theaetetus* 152 a) [Ed.] .

15 See above p. 2.

16 See Supplement 6.

17 See above p. 35.

18 490 b 3: ὅ ἐστιν [not as in the Oxford edition ὃ ἔστιν – Ed.].

The Idea of the Good and Unhiddenness

§ 12. The Idea of the Good as the Highest Idea: Empowerment of Being and Unhiddenness

During our interpretation of the third stage this question was intentionally held back and reserved for the concluding consideration of the allegory.[1] This task must now be carried through. We can now ask what the interpretation of the highest idea, and the relation of ἀλήθεια to the idea of the good, show about the essence of truth itself.

How did we encounter anything like *ideas*? It was by asking how Plato wants us to understand the region outside and above the cave. He informs us about this in the passage where he himself gives an interpretation of the cave allegory (517 a-c). Stated without allegory, the ascent from the cave to the light of the sun is ἡ εἰς τὸν νοητὸν τόπον τῆς ψυχῆς ἄνοδος, 'the way upwards, measured out by the soul in its knowing, for reaching the place where one encounters what is accessible to νοῦς'. Plato speaks of a τόπος νοητός. νοῦς is the faculty of non-sensory seeing and perceiving, of understanding things *as what* they *are,* their essence (what-being), the *being* of things. τὰ νοητά, the perceivable in νοεῖν, the perceived in non-sensory seeing, the look, the given-as . . . (e.g. book, table), are, as we know, the ἰδέαι. τὸ νοητόν is here equivalent τὸ γνωστόν. And now Plato says (517b 8–c 1):

> ἐν τῷ γνωστῷ τελευταία ἡ τοῦ ἀγαθοῦ ἰδέα καὶ μόγις ὁρᾶσθαι.
>
> 'In the region of that which is genuinely and truly knowable, what is ultimately seen is the idea of the good, but it can be seen only with great difficulty, under great exertion.'

The ascent into the light thus comes to an end. The τέλος (end), that which is ultimately seen, is not grasped just as a finishing and going-no-further of something, but as the all-encompassing, forming, determining *limit.* It is only here that liberation is brought to complete fruition as a becoming-free *for*, a self-binding *to,* being. In the meantime we have learnt to understand more clearly the interrelation between liberation and unhiddenness.

We thus come to the question of the nature of this ultimately perceivable idea, ἰδέα τοῦ ἀλαθοῦ. What does the clarification of its essence tell us about the essence of ἀλήθεια? I mentioned that Plato already treats the idea of the good in the final section of Book VI (506–511), that is, *before* the presentation of the cave allegory at the beginning of Book VII. This section, and the passage at the end of the cave allegory (517 a-c), are Plato's two principal (in truth his only) communications of what he understands by the idea of the good, thus of the highest point of his philosophy.

We already heard that this idea is μόγις ὁρᾶσθαι, that it can be viewed only with difficulty. It is therefore *even more* difficult to *say* anything about it. Accordingly, in the two passages, Plato speaks of the ἰδέα τοῦ ἀγαθοῦ only indirectly and symbolically, insisting always on the correspondences of the symbolism, on the need to follow these through rigorously and exhaustively. We already know what symbolizes the Idea of the good: it is the sun.

After everything we have said it is worth considering whether, if we immediately demand a propositional explanation of the highest idea, we are proceeding in a truly Platonic manner. If we ask in this way we already deviate from the path of authentic questioning. But inquiry into the idea of the good generally proceeds along this false track. One straightaway wants to know what the good is, just like one wants to know the shortest route to the market place. The idea of the good cannot be interrogated in this uncomprehending way at all. It is thus no wonder if through this way of questioning we do not receive an answer, i.e. if our claim upon the intelligibility of this idea of the good, as something to be measured in terms of our ruling self-evidences, is from the very beginning decisively repulsed. Here we recognize – how often – that questioning also has its rank-order.

This does not mean, however, that the idea of the good is a 'mystery', i.e. something one arrives at only through hidden techniques and practices, perhaps through some kind of enigmatic faculty of intuition, a sixth sense or something of the kind. The sobriety of Platonic questioning speaks against this. Instead, it is Plato's basic conviction, which he expresses once again in his old age, in the so-called *Seventh Letter* (342 e–344), that the highest idea can be brought into view only through the method of stepwise philosophical questioning of beings (asking down into the essential depth of man). The viewing succeeds, if at all, only in the comportment of questioning and learning. Even so, what is viewed remains, as Plato says (341 c 5): ῥητὸν γὰρ οὐδαμῶς ἐστιν ὡς ἄλλα μαθήματα, 'it is not sayable like other things we can learn'. Nevertheless, we can understand the unsayable only on the basis of what has already been said in a proper way, namely in and from the work of philosophizing. Only he who knows how to correctly say the sayable can bring himself before the unsayable; this is not possible for just any old confused head who knows, and fails to know, all kinds of things, for whom both knowing and failing to know are equally important and unimportant, and who may accidentally stumble upon a so-called puzzle. Only in the rigour of questioning do we come into the vicinity of the unsayable.

What method shall we adopt to understand the direction in which this idea of the good should be sought? For at the moment we cannot wish for more than this. Two methods suggest themselves. First we could carry through a comprehensive and formal interpretation of the main section at the end of Book VI. However, this procedure would take us too far from the purpose of these lectures, and, despite the close connection between the end of Book VI and the cave allegory, we would be completely diverted from the path of our earlier discussion. Only the second method is appropriate, that is, we attempt to remain within the sequence of events presented in the cave allegory, and to follow through to its final conclusion the ascent begun in the third stage. This means proceeding from the ideas to the ultimately seeable idea, to what is located out beyond the ideas as something ultimate and highest. In this way we shall clarify what is said in Book VI concerning the ἰδέα τοῦ ἀλαθοῦ.

The step from the ideas to the ultimately seeable idea presupposes an adequate understanding of the essence of idea as such. We must already understand what 'idea' means if we are to grasp the ultimate idea in its finality. Only in this way can we understand what is meant by τελευταία ἰδέα. We also say 'highest idea', and quite rightly, because it is the ultimate step in an *ascent*. It is the highest not only in the sense of being the last reached, but also in its rank. Of course everything depends on understanding why distinctions of rank are essential here. The highest idea is *idea in the highest degree*: τελευταία means that wherein the essence of idea is *fulfilled*, i.e. that from which it is *originally* determined.

We recall that in clarifying the *idea* as such we already encountered superlative determinations: the idea is something highest, namely the most beingful being and the most unhidden being. The ideas are the most beingful beings because they make being comprehensible, 'in whose light', as we still say today, a particular being is a *being* and is *what* it is. The ideas are also the most unhidden, i.e. the primordially unhidden (in which unhiddenness *arises)* in so far as they are what first let beings show themselves. But if there is a highest idea, which can become visible *over* all ideas, then it must exist *out beyond* being (which is already most beingful) and primordial unhiddenness (unhiddenness as such). Yet the good, as that which exists out beyond the ideas, is also called *idea*. What can this mean? It can mean only that the highest idea holds sway most primordially and authentically by *allowing both the unhiddenness of beings to arise*, and the *being of beings to be understood*[2] (neither of these without the other). The highest idea, although itself barely visible, is what makes possible *both* being and unhiddenness, i.e. it is what *empowers* being *and* unhiddenness as what they are. The highest idea, therefore, is this empowering, the empowering for *being* which as such *gives* itself simultaneously with the empowerment of *unhiddenness* as *occurrence*. In this way it is an intimation of αἰτία (of 'power', 'mastery').

Note that what we say about the highest idea is unfolded purely from what was previously clarified concerning the essence of the idea. We must once again underline the necessity of freeing ourselves at the very outset from any kind of sentimental conception of this idea of the good, but also from all perspectives, conceptions, and definitions belonging to Christian morality and its secularized corruptions (or any kind of ethic), where the good is conceived as the opposite of the bad and the bad conceived as the sinful. It is not at all a matter of ethics or morality, no more than it is a matter of a logical or epistemological principle. Such distinctions are of interest to scholars of philosophy (who also existed in antiquity) but are not the concern of philosophy.

§ 13. Seeing as ὁρᾶν and νοεῖν. Seeing and the Seeable in the Yoke of the Light

We must now see if what has been said can be verified from Plato's own presentation. With this intention we turn to the final section of Book VI of the *Republic*. In regard to the 'state' (as we somewhat inappropriately translate πόλις) and its inner possibility Plato maintains as his first principle that the authentic guardians of human association in the unity of the πόλις must be those who philosophize. He does not mean that philosophy professors are to become chancellors of the state, but that philosophers are to become φύλακες, guardians. Control and organization of the state is to be undertaken by philosophers, who set standards and rules in accordance with their widest and deepest freely inquiring knowledge, thus determining the general course which society should follow. As philosophers they must be in a position to know clearly and rigorously what man is, and how things stand with respect to his being and ability-to-be. 'Knowing' does not mean having heard things, or having and repeating opinions, but to have appropriated knowledge in the proper way, and to ever again appropriate it. This is the knowledge which itself has leapt ahead and continually takes the same path back and forth. Plato sees this knowledge as passing through quite definite stages, beginning from the most external meanings of words and reports of what everyday experience sees or hears. Beginning from what people commonly (and within certain limits rightly) say and opine about things, knowledge advances to the genuine understanding that seeks beings from the idea (from the perceiving of ideas). In order to clarify this highest knowledge in its essence, Plato in Book VI already distinguishes two basic types of knowledge, αἴσθησις and νοῦς, i.e. seeing (ὁρᾶν) in the usual sense (sensory perception), and νοεῖν, comprehending perceiving (non-sensory seeing). To these two types of seeing there correspond two regions of the visible: ὁρώμενα, what is accessible to the eyes, the senses, and νοούμενα, what is graspable in pure understanding. Already at this point Plato brings the essential determinations of non-sensory seeing into line with the characteristics of sensory seeing. He characterizes comprehending perceiving, i.e. ultimately the perceiving of ideas, by putting this in exact correspondence with seeing in the usual sense.

For something visible in the usual sense to be seen what is necessary is firstly δύναμις, τοῦ ὁρᾶν, the capacity to see with the eyes, and secondly δύναμις τοῦ ὁρᾶσθαι, the faculty and enablement for being seen. For it is in no way self-evident that a being, a thing itself, should be *visible*. These two elements, however, the ability to see and the visible itself, cannot occur in simple juxtaposition; there must be something which *enables* seeing on the one hand, and being-seen on the other hand. What enables must be *one and the same*, must be the ground of *both,* or, as Plato expresses it, the ability to see and the ability to be seen must both be *harnessed together under one yoke* (ζυλόν). This yoke, which makes possible the reciprocal connectedness of each to the other, is φῶς, brightness, light. Only what lies in the light of the sun is visible; on the other hand, only the eye whose looking is illuminated by light (the illuminated view) *sees* the visible. The looking eye, however, is not the sun. Instead, it is and must be, as Plato says, *like the sun,* ἡλιοειδής. Neither the looking nor the looking eye (nor what is itself seen with the eyes) themselves give light and brightness, but the looking and the eye is ἡλιοειδέστατον, the most sunlike of all tools of perceiving.

Now it must be borne in mind that, for the Greeks, the sense of sight is the *exemplary* sense for perceiving beings. The ancients considered that things are given most completely in seeing, namely in their immediate presence [*Gegenwart*], indeed in such a way that the present being has the character which, for the Greeks, belongs to every being: πέρας,[3] i.e. it is firmly *circumscribed* by its look, its *form*. The ὄψις is the πολυτελεστάτη αἴσθησις. The most sunlike faculty is what owes most to *light,* which is claimed by light, which therefore illuminates in its own essence, making- free and giving-free.

It is for this reason that the sense of seeing provides the guideline for the meaning of knowledge, i.e. knowledge does not correspond to smelling and hearing but to *seeing.* Precisely this latter kind of perceiving is suitable to serve as the guiding phenomenon in the depiction of *authentic* perceiving with its corresponding *higher* seeing. Everything depends on carrying over this clarification of the relationship between seeing and the visible (the yoke) into the region of genuine knowledge, into the understanding of *being.* We are already acquainted with this as the comprehending perceiving of the ideas. Here also there must be a *yoke* between higher seeing (νοιεῖν) and what is visible in it (νοούμενον), a yoke which gives the δύναμις to the perceiving as also to the perceivable. And what must pertain to the perceived, in order that it should be perceivable? The ἀλήθεια!

Plato says (508 e 1 ff.) that a being is only accessible as such when it stands in ἀλήθεια In a way that is self-evident for a Greek, he quite unambiguously understands ἀλήθεια not as a property and determination of seeing, of knowledge, nor as a characteristic of knowledge in the sense of a human faculty, but as a determination of what is known, of the things themselves, of the beings.

Τοῦτο τοίνυν τὸ τὴν ἀλήθειαν παρέχον τοῖς γιγνωσκομένοις καὶ τῷ γιγνώσκοντι τὴν δύναμιν ἀποδιδὸν τὴν τοῦ ἀλαθοῦ ἰδέαν φάθι εἶναι.

'This, therefore, which grants unhiddenness to the knowable beings and which lends to the knower the power of knowing, this, I say, is the idea of the good [the good as the highest idea].'

Here ἐπιστήμη (λνῶσις) and ἀλήθεια are clearly distinguished, but at the same time it is explained how this highest idea is atria, ground and *condition* for the knowing of the 'subject' (if we may speak in this way), and for unhiddenness on the side of the 'object'. The way it harnesses the knowing and the knowable beings under *one* yoke can be properly comprehended only if one correctly expresses the correspondence to ordinary seeing in the domain of sensory perception, seeing with the eyes. We heard that the yoke which harnesses together the eye and the visible object is the light, for this illuminates the object and 'lights up' the eye itself, i.e. makes it free to receive. *Seeing* is both the faculty to see *and* the visible as such *in the yoke* of the light – it is not itself the light-source, but is sun *like,* has the *character* of the source and in this way *corresponds* to it. So also here: just as sensory seeing is not the yoke, the light, the light-source itself, just as little in the field of non-sensory seeing is the faculty of knowledge, thus the understanding of being, or on the other side the manifestness of being, the highest and genuine source of the possibility of knowledge. Instead, just as seeing is not the sun itself, but rather sunlike, determined in its possibility through the sun, so are perceiving, and the unhiddenness of beings in their being, in *one* yoke, but are not themselves what conditions them as yoked; they are not themselves the good, but only ἀγαθοειδῆ (509 a 3), i.e. what *owes* its look and inner essence to the good.

To be sure, the understanding of being, and unhiddenness, allow beings to become accessible. They enable something. *This* enablement, however, is itself empowered by a higher one. So Plato says (509 a 4): ἔτι μειζόνως τιμντέον τὴν τοῦ ἀλαθοῦ ἕξιν. 'What the good can do is to be valued still more highly' than the faculty of the ideas itself. It is thus clearly stated that the ideas are what they are, namely the most beingful beings, and the most unhidden in the indicated sense of letting-through, only by virtue of an empowerment which exceeds them both (the most beingful and the most unhidden) in their unity.

This empowering is the highest idea. An idea, as we know, is something perceivable; it *is* not just on its own account, but is itself the being that it is in a per-ceiving [*Er-blicken*], in a forming pre-figuring. In its essence an idea is bonded to perceiving and *is* nothing *outside* this perceiving.

Notice the constant difficulty we have in understanding the idea of the good, namely that we never experience anything tangible and of substantive content, but we always interrogate and gain access to it only as something decisive in the enablement of being and truth. The ἀγαθόν has the character of ἕξις, of that which *makes possible,* i.e. of that which bears in itself the first and final *power.* Only in respect of this enablement of the very existence of being [*daß überhaupt Sein ist*] and occurrence of truth, can we ask about what Plato intends with the idea of the good.

By way of summary, also for the purpose of clarification, we can obtain help from a diagram, which only says anything if we think through the indicated connections in living understanding. We know that Plato, like the Greeks in general, understands genuine knowledge as seeing, θεωρεῖν (put together from θέα, look, and ὁρᾶν). Authentic knowledge of beings in their being is symbolized through sensory seeing, the seeing of the eyes.

To seeing there belongs something seen. In order that these two sides, and their inner connection as contraposition, should be *possible*, what is necessary – to remain at the level of sensory symbolism – is light. This light itself, again in sensory imagery, has its source in the sun, ἥλιος. As we shall see, Plato says that the sun, as the source of light, is not only the enabling condition of this connection, this becoming-seen of a being, but that it is also the condition of this being's (nature in the broadest sense) *existence,* of its origination, growth, nourishment and the like.

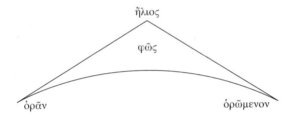

In Plato's correspondence: the νοεῖν and the known being as the νοούμενον. The ideas correspond to the symbol of light, brightness. The overall correspondence of the symbolism is that, just as light requires another source, so do the ideas themselves presuppose another idea standing over them, the good.

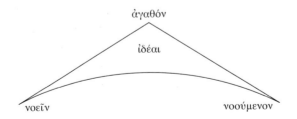

So much for the correspondence.[4]

§ 14. The Good: Empowerment of That upon Which All Depends

We have paused at Plato's statement that the power of the good is to be valued even more highly than the ideas. He wants to say: when we ask about the *essence* of being and unhiddenness, our questioning goes *out beyond* these, so that we encounter something with the character of *empowerment* and nothing else. Empowerment is the *limit* of philosophy (i.e. of metaphysics). Plato calls that which empowers ἀγαθόν. We translate: the good. The proper and original meaning of ἀγαθόν refers to what is good (suitable) for something, what can be put to use. 'Good!' means: it is done! it is decided! It does not have any kind of *moral* meaning: ethics has corrupted the fundamental meaning of this word. What the Greeks understand by 'good' is what we mean when we say that we buy a pair of good skis, i.e. boards which are sound and durable. The good is the sound, the enduring, as distinct from the harmless meaning suitable for aunties: a good man, i.e. respectable, but without insight and power.

After characterizing the idea of the good, Plato again presses forward (509 a 9-b 10):

ἀλλ' ὧδε μᾶλλον τὴν εἰκόνα αὐτοῦ ἔτι ἐπισκόπει.

Πῶς;

Τὸν ἥλιον τοῖς ὁρωμένοις οὐ μόνον οἶμαι τὴν τοῦ ὁρᾶσθαι δύναμιν παρέχειν φήσεις, ἀλλὰ καὶ τὴν γένεσιν καὶ αὔξην καὶ τροφήν, οὐ γένεσιν αὐτὸν ὄντα.

Πῶς γάρ;

Καὶ ταῖς γιγνωσκομένοις τοίνυν μὴ μόνον τὸ γιγνώσκεσθαι φάναι ὑπὸ τοῦ ἀγαθοῦ παρεῖναι, ἀλλὰ καὶ τὸ εἶναί τε καὶ τὴν οὐσίαν ὑπ' ἐκείνου αὐτοῖς προσεῖναι, οὐκ οὐσίας ὄντος τοῦ ἀγαθοῦ, ἀλλ' ἔτι ἐπέκεινα τῆς οὐσίας πρεσβείᾳ καὶ δυνάμει ὑπερέχοντος.

'Let us once again bring the analogy into view [further explore the essence of the sun, in which the idea of the good is depicted].'

'How?' [asks Glaucon]

'The sun, I believe you will agree, grants to the *visible* things not only their capacity to *be seen*, but also their origination, growth,

nourishment, even though the sun itself is not something that
becomes.'

'How could it be?'

'It may therefore *also* be said that the good not only grounds the
knowability of the knowable things, but also that their *being,* and
their being *what* they are, is granted by the good, even though the
good itself is not a being [*ein Sein*], but rather something over and
beyond being [ἐπέκεινα τῆς οὐσίας], exceeding this in dignity and
power.'

Thus Plato now emphasizes that things are indebted to the sun not
only for their visibility, but also for the fact that they *are*. What is living is
indebted to the sun for its growth, for its γένεσις, i.e. its origination and
dissolution, its coming into being and disappearance from being. To be
sure, in such a way that the sun is *not* itself anything that becomes, but,
as lying out beyond all becoming, remains always the same.

Now to the *interpretation* of this symbolism in respect of the
corresponding domain of *knowledge*. What is known are beings in
general. Now just as, in the sensory realm, beings possess not only
visibility but being, so there belongs to the νοούμενον not only ἀλήθεια
but also οὐσια. And just as, in the above sensory imagery, the sun
cannot *be* becoming [nicht Werden *sein* kann], but rather *grants*
becoming, so τὸ ἀγαθόν cannot be a being [*nicht ein Sein sein kann*],
therefore also cannot be unhiddenness, but is *beyond* (ἐπέκεινα), out
beyond both being and unhiddenness.

It is clear, therefore, that the good is δύναμις, thus still has the
character of idea (of enablement, empowerment), indeed has this in
the highest degree; being and unhiddenness are under its empowering
power, ὑπ; ἐκείνου. But in this empowering the good surpasses both,
namely in so far as beings are *seen,* i.e. known, and also in so far as
they are *beings*. This surpassing, however, is not simply an indifferent
lying over and above, a being-situated somewhere or other for itself as
it were, but is a surpassing in the sense of the idea, i.e. in the sense
of being-as-idea [*Idee-seins*]. But in so far as being-as-idea means
empowerment for being, the making manifest of beings, this surpassing
of the idea of the good means that this idea surpasses being as such
and truth. This empowerment which surpasses pertains precisely to the
possibility of the *ideas*, to the enablement of that which the ideas *are:*

namely that itself which makes beings accessible in their *unhiddenness* and thus accessible *as* beings, i.e. in their *being*.

The good, the ἀγαθόν, is therefore the enablement of being as such and of unhiddenness as such. Or better, what Plato calls the good is that which empowers being and unhiddenness to their own essence, i.e. what is prior to everything else, that upon which everything else *depends*. The ἀγαθόν can only be understood in this sense. *Empowerment* of being; not an existing 'good' (a 'value'), but what is *prior to* and *for* all being and every truth. It is not the *word* ἀλαθόν or our translation of it (which can easily be misleading) which is decisive, but what is named by this word. And what is this? It is just what we are interrogating in our questioning concerning being and unhiddenness, what such questioning is all about and that to which all such questioning returns. We are inquiring here into what *grants* being and unhiddenness.

Precisely this same characterization of the highest idea is given by Plato in a passage at the end of the cave allegory (517 c 3 f.):

ἔν τε νοητῷ αὐτὴ κυρία ἀλήθειαν καὶ νοῦν παρασχομένη[5]

'In the region of comprehending perceiving it [the idea of the good] is master, in that it grants unhiddenness and νοῦς, i.e. disclosedness in the understanding of being.'

Again we see that the good is the empowerment of being and unhiddenness to their ownmost unitary essence.

This is all that Plato says concerning the highest idea. But it is enough, indeed more than enough, for whoever understands. To understand the little that Plato does say is nothing less than to really *ask* the question concerning the essence of being and truth, to grasp and lay hold of the *task* inherent in such questioning, thus to follow this questioning to wherever it may lead, to *stand by* this questioning instead of avoiding it through cheap solutions. We must grasp the unfolded essence of being (presence) and the unfolded essence of truth (manifestness) from their ownmost unitary subjugation (yoking), i.e. from the essence of that which rules them (in their essential *unity*) in its prevailing; to begin with we must grasp *that* this is a self-asserting [*ein Sich-durchsetzen*], an enduring withstanding [*durchstehendes Standhalten*].

We misunderstand Plato's idea of the good if we try to obtain a better idea of it by busily searching through his other dialogues for passages where he uses the word ἀγαθόν, or if we believe that later in Plato's career, because he no longer uses the word, he must have given up this idea. He would have had to give up the idea of philosophy! On the contrary, wherever being and truth are interrogated, so is the good. Thus, although the word does not occur in the *Seventh Letter* (a work of Plato's old age), nothing else but this is intended. For here he says (342 ab) that the genuinely knowable, i.e. what is to the highest degree question-able, is τό ἀληθῶς ὄν, that which constitutes being and unhiddenness as such. Here Plato emphasizes (cf. 344 b), with remarkable severity and firmness, that this cannot be thought out and conceived at one stroke, but that only in proceeding through what is proximally question-able, through definite individual levels of the sciences, does the questioner, and only the questioner (not some random dreamer), come to what is primary and ultimate. Everything proximally question-able is τὸ ποῖον, but the primary and ultimate is τὸ τί (343 b).

And just where the later Plato went farthest in his interrogation of being and truth, in the *Sophist* dialogue, the essence of being is found in δύναμις, i.e. in empowerment and nothing else (247 d–e). It was left to Plato's contemporary interpreters to 'prove' (in the way they do prove) that Plato was not serious about this idea of the δύναμις character of being.

The good is the empowerment, the δύναμις, the enablement of being and unhiddenness in their essence. In other words, what is at stake in the *interrogation* of being and unhiddenness is empowerment *to* this essence. *What* this empowerment is and *how* it occurs has not been answered to the present day; indeed the question is no longer even asked in the original Platonic sense. In the meantime it has almost become a triviality that the *omne ens* is a *bonum*. For whoever asks in a philosophical manner, Plato says more than enough. For someone who wants only to establish what the good is in its common usage he says far too little, even nothing at all. If one takes it merely in this latter way, nothing can be done with it. This clarification of the idea of the good *says* anything only for a philosophical questioning.

But if 'the good', i.e. what is at stake in the interrogation of being and truth, is itself still an 'idea', then what we have already said about ideas in general applies to the *highest* idea in the *highest* degree. The idea is the sighted, the sight-*able*; it refers essentially to *seeing*. It does not hover around on its own, but is seeable and perceivable only *in* that viewing which as such perceives the visible, which as such forms and pre-forms the idea itself. The highest perceivable thing requires the deepest perceiving. The highest as well as the deepest: neither without the other. The idea, and especially the highest idea, is neither something objectively present nor something subjectively construed. It is precisely that which empowers all objectivity and subjectivity to what they are, by establishing a yoke between subject and object, a yoke under which they can first become subject and object. For a subject *is* such only when it relates itself to an object. This *yoke* is the decisive thing and is accordingly the *first* determination of what is yoked. The inadequate, indeed quite erroneous, conception of what stands in the yoke prevents the comprehension of the yoke and the definition of the yoked (commonly: 'object' – 'subject'; actually: manifestness, understanding of being).

§ 15. The Question Concerning the Essence of Truth as the Question Concerning the History of Man's Essence and His παιδεία

If, therefore, the perceiving of the idea constitutes the ground upon which man as a being comports himself to beings, then to the highest idea there must correspond a perceiving that occurs most deeply in the essence of man. The questioning which penetrates through to the *highest* idea is thus simultaneously a questioning down into the deepest perceiving possible for man as an existing being, a questioning of the history of man's essence that aims at understanding what empowers being and unhiddenness. We have followed this question of the history of man's essence in our interpretation of the cave allegory, and we have seen that it is a quite definite occurrence with quite definite stages and transitions.

What Plato says in the *Seventh Letter* (344 b 3) has precisely the same meaning. Only when this whole path of liberation has been traversed in all its stages, with full commitment to inquiry and investigation, does there occur the flash and illumination of understanding:

ἐξέλαμψε φρόνησις περὶ ἕκαστον καὶ νοῦς συντείνων ὅτι μάλοτ᾽ εἰς δύναμιν ἀνθρωπίνην (344 b 7/8).

'Only then is the perceiving of essence unfolded, the perceiving that stretches as far as possible, namely as far as the innermost capacity of man reaches.'

What the cave allegory is all about, therefore, is the liberation and awakening of the innermost power of the essence of man. Accordingly, at a later point, where he interprets the depicted events in his own practical sense, Plato says (521 c 5 ff.):

Τοῦτο δή, ὡς ἔοικεν, οὐκ ὀστράκου ἂν εἴη περιστροφή, ἀλλὰ ψυχῆς περιαγωγή, ἐκ νυκτερινῆς τινος ἡμέρας εἰς ἀληθινήν, τοῦ ὄντος οὖσαν ἐπάνοδον, ἣν δή φιηοσοφίαν ἀλνθῆ φήσομεν εἶναι.

'This therefore [the whole liberation from the cave to the light] is not, as it appears, merely a whirling of the slate in the hand [a children's game amongst the Greeks], but is a turning around of the essence of man, a leading of this out from a kind of darkened day towards the authentically unhidden. It is this ascent to beings that we say is philosophizing in the genuine sense.'

What therefore does the clarification of the idea of the good now tell us about the essential determination of truth? Four things:

1 that truth itself is not ultimate, but stands under an empowerment;
2 and not just by itself, but together under the same yoke with being;
3 that in so far as man is the questioner, who inquires about what is prior to and for all being, what empowers truth to its essence itself occurs in the historical-spiritual Dasein of man;
4 not in man as such, but only in so far as he continually transforms himself in his history and returns to the ground of his essence.

Truth as ἀλήθεια is therefore nothing that man can possess or fail to possess in certain propositions or formulas learned and repeated, and which ultimately correspond with things. Instead, it is something that empowers his ownmost essence to what it is, in so far as he comports himself to beings as such, and in so far as man, in the midst of beings, himself a being, exists.

For this reason it is said in the *Phaedrus* (249 b 5):

οὐ γὰρ ἥ γε [ψυχὴ] μήποτε ἰδοῦσα τὴν ἀλήθειαν εἰς τόδε ἥξει τὸ ὄχημα.

For the soul could not take on this form [namely that of man, his fate, i.e. it could not make up the essence of man], if it did not already have in itself the fulfilled vision of unhiddenness.'

If the soul did not already understand what being means, man could not exist as the being that comports itself to beings and to itself.

All these accumulated determinations only indicate ever more clearly and unambiguously what the whole interpretation of the cave allegory is meant to impress upon us: that the question of the essence of truth as unhiddenness is the question of the history of human essence.

Only now can we understand the statement we originally passed over at the beginning of Book VII, the statement that introduces the whole allegory (514 a 1 f.):

Μετὰ ταῦτα δή . . . ἀπείκασον τοιούτῳ πάθει τὴν ἡμετέραν φύσιν παιδείας τε πέρι καὶ ἀπαιδευσίας.

'Picture to yourself [namely the following image as given in the cave allegory] our human nature in respect of its possible positionedness [*Gehaltenheit*] on the one hand, or lack of bearings [*Haltungslosigkeit*] on the other hand.'[6]

Παιδεία is not education [*Bildung*], but ἡ ἡμετέρα φύσις: that which prevails as our ownmost being, both in respect of that to which it empowers itself, and also of what, in its powerlessness, it loses, of that into which it degenerates. It is not a matter just of παιδεία, but παιδείας, τε πέρι καὶ ἀπαιδευσίης, of the one as well as the other, i.e. of their confrontation or setting-apart, of what is *between* both and out of which they both arise, so that they may then assert themselves against each other. παιδεία is the *positionedness* [*Gehaltenheit*] of man, arising from the 'stance' [*Haltung*] of the withstanding that carries through [*sich durchsetzenden Standhaltens*], wherein man, in the midst of beings, freely chooses the footing [*Halt*] for his own essence, i.e. that whereto and wherein he empowers himself in his essence. This innermost empowerment of our own essence to the essence of man, this free choice of footing by an entity given over to itself, is, as occurrence, nothing else but philosophizing, as the questioning that presses through to being and unhiddenness, i.e. to what itself empowers unhiddenness.

So the cave allegory is already *introduced* by the clear statement that it treats of ἡμετέπα φύσις (φύσις: arising and standing in the open), of the essence of man. But at the same time we now know that this questioning concerning the essence of man *precedes* all pedagogy, psychology, anthropology, as well as every humanism. This questioning grows from, and is in no way different to, the questioning of the essence of truth, with which question there is coupled, under a yoke, the question of the essence of being. In so far as both questions are posed, questioning goes out beyond them in asking what empowers both being and truth in their essence, as that which *carries* the essence of human existence. The essence of truth as ἀλήθεια is *deconcealment*, in which occurs the history of man's essence. So understanding the whole interpretation is a matter of grasping again and again this one thing in its fundamental meaning: that the question of the essence of truth is the question of the history of man's essence, and vice versa.

We do *not* understand philosophy as

1   a cultural phenomenon, a realm of man's creativity and of the works which issue from it;

2   a kind of unfolding of individual personalities as spiritual creators;

3   a region of learning and teaching within a system of scientific values, a science;

4   a worldview, completion, rounding off and model of thought; also *not* as

5   philosophy of existence;

but as a *questioning* which in a fundamental way changes Dasein, man, and the understanding of being.

And what has become of all this? Much that is great and that has been effective in later history, but also just as much that is miserable and now becoming widespread. But nothing has happened that would amount to a primordial re-origination, nothing that would once again set us in motion within this occurrence. And we today! 'Plato's doctrine of ideas' has its essence ripped out and made accessible for the superficiality of today's Dasein: ideas as values and παιδεία as culture and education, i.e. what is most pernicious from the nineteenth century, but nothing from 'antiquity'!

Notes

1 See above pp. 34–5.

2 Plato places ἰδέα *over* ἀλήθεια, because envisability [*Sichtsamkeit*] becomes essential for ἰδεῖν (ψυχή) and not deconcealment as the essencing of beyng [*als Wesung des Seyns*].

3 τὸ πέρας = boundary, end, goal.

4 See Supplement 7.

5 παρέχειν: to give – to bind.

6 Paul Shorey (Loeb) translates: 'compare our nature in respect of education and its lack'; Desmond Lee (Penguin) translates: 'picture the enlightenment or ignorance of our human condition'; Francis Cornford (Oxford U. P.) translates: 'the degrees in which our nature may be enlightened or unenlightened'. [Trans.]

3

The Question Concerning the Essence of Untruth

§ 16. The Waning of the Fundamental Experience of ἀλήθεια. The Philosophical Obligation to Re-awaken It: the Abiding Origin of Our Existence

The interpretation of the cave allegory has thus been brought to a conclusion. For what reason did we undertake it?

1   In order to show that if we say ἀλήθεια instead of truth we are not, owing to some kind of stubbornness, introducing a new translation or a different linguistic meaning, which, moreover, has a mere etymological antiquarian character and is otherwise without force. Instead, we are seeking to better understand how this basic word arises from a *fundamental experience*, an experience which tells us something about the fundamental stance of man in his philosophical comportment to beings.

2   In order to more clearly grasp the *essence* of ἀλήθεια as unhiddenness. To be sure, we have not gone back to the ultimate fundamental experience, but we have consciously sought,

3 to make a testimony to ἀλήθεια come alive for us, a testimony
which could grow in the *domain* of this fundamental experience,
so that we can *arrive* in this same domain.

Have we succeeded in this? There is no straightforward objective
answer to this question. The result appears to consist merely in our
now being somewhat better instructed concerning the connections
between word-meanings. In each case it has become clear that the
unhiddenness of beings in its various modifications refers to the essence
of man and his liberation to himself, indeed *is* nothing else than precisely
the occurrence- character of this liberation, and that truth is thereby not
an arbitrary property of man but the ground of his existence; further, that
Plato regards the enactment of this transformation of unhiddenness
as the fundamental requirement for παιδεία in its antagonism to
ἀπαιδευσία.

To be sure, the question arises as to whether this clarification of the
essence of ἀλήθεια as unhiddenness can still become actual for us
today, in such a way that the whole content of this essence of truth (as
we have comprehended it) could also determine our existence, which
means at the same time determining our questioning. Before looking
at this problem more closely, we must evaluate what we have obtained
from the allegory for the questions developed in the first lecture, the
questions which made us realize that the word 'true' is *ambiguous*. We
saw that the word is used of things (true gold) and of sentences (true
propositions), whereby the prevailing view is that 'true' and 'truth' apply
in the first place and originally to propositions. For what reason, and
by what right, we were unable to clarify. Does the clarified essence of
ἀλήθεια make it comprehensible why 'true' and 'truth' are today used
quite unproblematically in this peculiar double sense?

We now see:

1 What is primordially true, i.e. unhidden, is not the proposition
about a being, but the being itself – a thing, a fact. A being is true,
understood in the Greek way, when it shows itself as what it is:
true gold. By contrast, bogus gold shows itself as something it is
not: it covers up, it conceals its what-being, it conceals itself as
the being it actually is. Therefore true is primarily a characteristic
of the beings themselves.

2 The proposition is true in so far as it *conforms to* something already true, i.e. to a being that is unhidden in its being. Truth in this sense of *correctness* presupposes unhiddenness.

The two meanings of 'true' (true thing and true proposition), which are commonplace and which have long ago become self-evident and worn out, spring from ἀλήθεια in different ways. The *ambiguity* of the German word could originate and continue only because 'true' primordially means 'unhidden'. Thus, in the double meaning of our contemporary everyday understanding of truth (true), the fundamental meaning of ἀλήθεια is *still* effective, albeit faded and hidden.

But does that not prove how *little* has come down to us of the fundamental experience which corresponds to ἀλήθεια? In purely theoretical reflection we can see and understand how ἀλήθεια belongs to the φύσις of man, and from this we can 'scientifically' explain contemporary linguistic practice; that is all. What we strove for – a return into *history* [*Geschichte*], such that this becomes *our* occurrence [*Gescheheri*], such that our own history is renewed – is not thereby achieved. Our understanding remains at the level of a merely historical familiarity, perhaps something different to previous interpretations, perhaps only using different concepts and words, perhaps 'new' in the sense that we take an interest in it, that we can thereby instruct others, that we can know better and can feel superior to those who uncomprehendingly translate ἀλήθεια as 'truth'. But this is not very much, nor is it worth the effort. We must once again admit that, even if we recognize it ever so clearly as belonging to the essence of man, *we* are *no longer touched* by this ἀλήθεια of Plato. It is not an occurrence which touches us intimately.

If we do not deceive ourselves, this is indeed the situation. What accounts for this absence of genuine historical touching? Does the cause, perhaps, reside in ourselves? For a long time our own history has run along a path that does not reach far enough down into the essence of man, and in a region within which we can no longer be touched by the occurrence expressed by the word ἀλήθεια.

Yet, that this occurrence of ἀλήθεια could not maintain its effectiveness, that it no longer touches our Dasein and genuinely stirs us: is that ultimately due only to us and our own groundlessness, or has this got *just as much* to do with that occurrence itself? Does Plato himself already detach ἀλήθεια from its fundamental originating experience? Is he at least on the way toward doing this? Such is in fact the situation. What already happens in Plato is the waning of the fundamental experience, i.e. of a specific fundamental *stance* [Grund*stellung*] of man towards beings, and the weakening of the word ἀλήθεια in its basic meaning. This is only the beginning of that history through which Western man lost his ground as an existing being, in order to end up in contemporary groundlessness.

It is due to *us* as well as to Plato that ἀλήθεια remains relevant merely to the past, without becoming *history* for us. Yet, one might very well ask, should and must ἀλήθεια at all costs become this? Can we not simply rely upon ourselves and define the essence of truth from our own standpoint? Can we not take account of history by choosing from the past just what we want, in such a way that one person appeals to Aristotle, another begins with Plato, a third perhaps relies on Plotinus, still others on Kant or on another series of philosophers?

Do we have a *choice* here? We? Who are we then? Despite all progress and transformations we are only the beneficiaries of the beginning of Western philosophy, beneficiaries of that which goes to the essence of our Dasein, i.e. its total existence, which consists precisely in the fact that we *comport* ourselves to those beings which we are not as well as to *that* being which we are, and that we must always already seek a *stance* for this comportment.[1] So long as we *are* in this way, we remain bonded and obligated to that beginning whether we know it or not, whether we know much or little about it, whether we work it out laboriously by way of learned reflection, or whether we can feel it immediately and continually in everyday life, e.g. in the trivial event of a journey through the city by electric tram. We can only travel by tram (to formulate it in an extreme way) because our Dasein stands in the history of the beginning of Western philosophy, i.e. of the question concerning the meaning of beings, of the possibility of the development of the theoretical question concerning particular beings, of the science of nature, of 'physics'. That we travel in such a way means nothing else but that the beginning of Western philosophy, albeit without our recognizing it, is immediately *effective*. To be sure, whether something like this, namely that we travel or even must travel by electric tram, signifies a *success* of man, or is rather the opposite, cannot be decided without further ado.

For us, so long as we still understand what 'us' and 'we' mean, there is no choice in the question of whether ἀλήθεια to remain merely something from the past or rather become history. There is no choice, assuming that we have not already dispensed with grasping the awakening of the essence of man as a philosophical fundamental task. There is no choice for us, assuming that we have not already become caught up in the misrecognition of human essence, believing perhaps that the fate of man will be decided through the regulation of the international economy. We have no choice, assuming that we do not believe our history first begins where the presuppositions of the contemporary external world situation and its contemporary external misery begin.

It is we as much as Plato who are responsible for the fact that ἀλήθεια remains merely something from the past, without becoming history. To the extent that we remain resolved to maintain ourselves in existence, ἀλήθεια *must* become history for us. This means: to the extent that we remain resolved to hold ourselves in the manifestness of beings as such and *to be* in this resolve; to grasp that beings and beings are not necessarily the same, that not all beings whatsoever, just because they are situated in the world, have the right and dignity to everything; that *all beings* and each and every *arbitrary* being do not *belong* to every arbitrary being; to understand that every being has its law, its origin, its rank; and that without firm ground, origin, and rank, being is less than nothing; that then not even nothingness can any longer be grasped, and the existence of man becomes crushed in the lawlessness of groundless levelling. If we still want to understand beings, and if we are resolved to exist out of this understanding, ἀλήθεια must occur. That it did *once* occur is the abiding origin of our existence, so long as this itself, not that of the individual but *our* history, lasts. In order that ἀλήθεια might still *remain* an occurrence, even as the most external and remote possibility, our only recourse is that we should *ask* after it. This is the only way in which we can really bind ἀλήθεια to our own Dasein.

§ 17. The Neglect of the Question Concerning the Essence of Hiddenness. Transformation of the Question Concerning the Essence of Truth into the Question Concerning the Essence of Untruth

But *how* can ἀλήθεια again become history for us?[2] Only by the question concerning the essence of truth again becoming an actual and essential *question*, only in so far as we *get serious* with this question. This means first of all that in this questioning we do not leap over anything worthy of questioning. In this way we must once again experience the actuality of actual questioning, renouncing the hunger for results.

The first thing we must ask in relation to our own procedure is: why do we maintain that in Plato and Aristotle, thus more or less at the time (broadly considered) of the origin of the word ἀλήθεια, the fundamental experience of which it speaks was already waning? We must now demonstrate what we dared to assert, which must not remain a mere historical observation. Are there clear indications of the fundamental meaning of ἀλήθεια becoming ineffective? And are we able, from that which conditions the *waning* of the fundamental experience, to discover what is needful for *preserving* this same experience, even for *reappropriating* it in a more primordial way?

There is indeed a clear indication here: it is that Plato conceives ἀλήθεια as something pertaining to *beings*, such that beings *themselves* are said to be unhidden. Plato *equates* the unhidden with what is (beings), in such a way that the question of unhiddenness *as such* does not come to life. This is proved by the fact that he does not inquire into the *hiddenness* which must run up against *unhiddenness*. More accurately, in interrogating the essence of truth, Plato does co-interrogate the essence of un-truth, but only in a quite particular sense. If the essence of truth is unhiddenness, then the way in which hiddenness is interrogated contains the standard for the ground, origin, and genuineness of the question concerning unhiddenness.

The word ἀλήθεια most often stands simply for beings themselves, or more precisely, for the *most beingful* beings. Why does ἀλήθεια so to speak *disclose* beings and their being? What and how *'is'* being then? As *presence*! Why does unhiddenness disclose being as understood in just *this* way?

What is unhidden, i.e. that *to which* un-hiddenness *pertains*, are the genuine beings; but it is not these as such that are intended. This is shown by the previously quoted[3] words of Aristotle, φιλοσοφεῖν περὶ τῆς ἀληθείας, concerning ἀλήθεια as the object of philosophy, whereby he means beings themselves, in their unhiddenness naturally, but not unhiddenness as such, not the *essence* of truth. There are countless examples of this usage in Plato. Here ἀλήθεια already stands for that *to which* it pertains, but not for what it *is* in itself. Unhiddenness rules, and the attempt is made to attain it, but it is not as such further placed in question.

Yet does not the cave allegory prove the contrary? We attempted to show in detail that through all its stages there occurs a transition from one unhidden to another, and that unhiddenness constitutes the fundamental occurrence of the story. How can we now repudiate our own interpretation?

We shall certainly not do this. But what does our interpretation of the cave allegory really establish? We must look more closely at what we have actually obtained. It is just this, that Plato does not specifically place ἀλήθεια in question, but always treats only of what is involved in the unhiddenness of beings as such. It is *we* who, subsequently in our interpretation, have gathered together all these considerations about light, freedom, idea, beings, in order from the unity of these to assess what can be learned about the essential determination of unhiddenness itself. When we say that ἀλήθεια is deconcealment, this is an *interpretation* which analyses the ground of unhiddenness itself.

For Plato, therefore, unhiddenness is a theme, and at the same time not a theme. Because this is the situation with regard to *un*-hiddenness, an explicit clarification of the *hiddenness* of beings does not eventuate. But just this neglect of the question of hiddenness as such is the *decisive* indication of the already beginning ineffectiveness of *un*hiddenness in the strict sense. We must therefore maintain, as the guiding proposition for what follows, that the way in which one inquires into and discusses *hiddenness* is the index for the degree of primordiality of the question concerning unhiddenness as such. For the unhiddenness of beings is precisely *wrested* from hiddenness, i.e. it is obtained in *struggle* against the latter. The way in which the struggle *against* the hiddenness of beings, which means *for un*hiddenness, is engaged and followed through, shows *how* the opponent in this struggle is understood, i.e. how man himself estimates his own power, and lack of power, to truth.

But *what* is it that stands over against truth as unhiddenness and is opposed to it? Well, just the 'untruth'! So we are faced with the task of asking about how Plato and the Greeks of his time conceive of *untruth.* How does this struggle against untruth occur? Properly understood, this too is not a question about a past concept of untruth, namely Plato's concept, but asks if and how the hiddenness of beings, which opposes unhiddenness, makes itself effective. It asks if and how hiddenness is experienced precisely as what must be robbed and torn away, such that ἀλήθεια may occur, i.e. such that hiddenness may give way to unhiddenness. Since, for the Greeks, truth originally has a privative, negative character (what is no longer hidden), we must, in order to grasp the primordial essence of ἀλήθεια, place this 'negation' in question. But the necessary first step for this is the question concerning *that which* opposes truth, concerning the *essence* of untruth. To be sure, whether we thereby grasp the totality and essence of that against which ἀλήθεια seeks to assert itself, is an unavoidable, but subsequent, question.

Once again, the ancient word for truth is privative; it expresses a removal from, a ripping away, a going against . . ., therefore an *attack.* Where is the enemy situated? What kind of struggle is it? Only if we really grasp these two things do we have any intimation of the essence of ἀλήθεια, i.e. of the origin of that which constitutes the innermost ground of the possibility of our *existing* Dasein.[4] If truth is an attack, then the enemy must be un-truth. But if truth means un-hiddenness, then the enemy of truth must be hiddenness. Then it is *not only* falsity and incorrectness which is the enemy of truth. If this is the situation, then un-truth is itself *ambiguous*, and it is precisely this ambiguity which ultimately conceals within itself the whole dangerousness of truth's enemy, thus the endangerment of every essential determination of truth. In order that we should see clearly here, we expressly state that we understand 'un-truth' ['*Un-wahrheit*] in the sense of *not-truth* [*Nicht-Wahrheit*], which need not necessarily mean falsity, but can and must mean much else besides. Not-truth is not-un-hiddenness. The not un-hidden is

1 what is *not yet* unhidden,

2 what is *no longer* unhidden.

So we already see that untruth as not-unhiddenness is ambiguous in a quite *essential* sense; perhaps it has many meanings in a sense we still do not fathom and that becomes a *question* for us.

If the awakening and forming of the word ἀλήθεια is not a mere accident (the origination of a sound-formation) and not an external matter, if it actually refers to an attack, then, in order to understand this, we must place ourselves before and against the enemy. The active insight into the essence of truth as unhiddenness can only be effective if we inquire into the un-truth.

Through the double concept of untruth, our task of asking about the essence of *truth* has *changed.* Untruth is not an opposite that occurs alongside (next to truth), and that must *also* and subsequently be taken into account, but the *one* question concerning the essence of truth is *in itself* the question concerning the essence of *un*-truth, for this latter belongs to the *essence* of truth.

This is the *decisive* result of the interpretation of the cave allegory and of the whole previous reflection: the insight that the question concerning the essence of truth as unhiddenness must be transformed into the question concerning *untruth.* In other words, a decisive *answer* to the question of essence is already contained therein, an answer which only sharpens and broadens the questioning. However, we *lose* this insight again as soon as we make it into an opinion or piece of gossip, e.g. by going around saying that the question of the essence of truth is the question of the essence of untruth. In that case it would be better to stay with the old opinion that truth is correspondence between judgement and object.

At the same time, however, we likewise know from the cave allegory that the question of the essence of truth is the question of the essence of man. Thus the question of the essence of un-truth, as the fundamental question of the essence of truth, will also become a question specifically oriented to the essence of man.

Yet the question of un-truth in the service of the question of the essence of truth: is this not a *detour*, and perhaps a long-winded one? Why do we take this detour if it is precisely the essence of *truth* that we wish to know? We shall no longer take this reservation seriously. The question concerning untruth is *not* a detour, but is the only possible path, the *direct* path, to the essence of truth. But perhaps this path to the question of the essence of un-truth is very arduous, perhaps even the traces of this path can be found only with great difficulty. This is indeed certain. The proof lies in the fact that this path has hardly been trodden and is today totally unknown. Even the short, narrow, and steep stretch that was earlier trodden and opened up, is today long overgrown with the weeds of mere opinions, and covered over by doctrines and ideas which have become self-evident. The questioning, or better, the non-questioning concerning the essence of untruth, stands under the self-evident dogma that untruth is easy to understand if only one knows what *truth* is; then one just has to think of its denial. And one knows what truth is, namely a property of a proposition (judgement). However, if we are shaken out of the miserable triviality of such talk, we shall not presume to rectify everything at one stroke, but with care and patience we shall learn to grasp that one thing above all is necessary: to *rediscover* that stretch of the path of the question concerning the essence of untruth which was trodden *once before*. We have no thoughts of making this short, narrow, and steep stretch into a broad and comfortable highway suitable for everybody. All our efforts are directed to merely rediscovering this stretch of road and actually *going* along it. It is that stretch of the road of the question concerning untruth which, for the first and last time in the history of philosophy, Plato actually *trod:* in his dialogue the *Theaetetus*, which also bears the title 'The Dialogue on Knowledge'.

However, to actually travel on this road, and to actually once again ask the question of the essence of untruth, we must mark out our own way still more rigorously and definitely by reference to the traces which Plato's philosophical work left buried in the history of the spirit. Our interpretation of the cave allegory proceeded by artificially isolating this small section from the larger context of the dialogue. For the following exposition of the question of untruth it is not permissible to limit ourselves to isolated portions (doctrines) of Plato, e.g. by collecting, in the usual way with the help of a lexicon, passages where Plato talks about untruth. This procedure is not only unfruitful, but pretends to a thoroughness where none exists; it is only an opportunity to avoid the text and the challenge of its *question.*

We develop and awaken the question of untruth upon the path of a quite specifically oriented interpretation of the Platonic dialogue. We shall proceed as we did with the interpretation of the cave allegory. It is not primarily a matter of instruction in the general procedure of interpreting a philosophical text (this only incidentally), but of awakening the (pre-determined) question of the essence of untruth as the properly understood *fundamental question* of the essence of truth. For the immediate purpose of these lectures it is therefore not necessary for you to have an autonomous command of the Greek text. In fact you should also be able to co-enact the questioning itself *without* the text. It will be beneficial if you have a Greek text or translation beside you. A translation is enough, preferably Schleiermacher's (easily obtainable from Reclam[5]), which still has not been substantively improved upon and remains the most beautiful. To be sure, the original text is basic for one's own work on the dialogue, and that means simultaneously one's *own* translation. For a *translation* is only the end result of an *interpretation* which has been actually carried through: the text is *set over into* an autonomous questioning understanding. While I do not advocate working with mere translations, I must also warn against thinking that command of the Greek language by itself guarantees an understanding of Plato or Aristotle. That would be just as foolish as thinking that because we understand German we already understand Kant or Hegel, which is certainly not the case.

The task and goal of the interpretation must be to bring the *questioning* of this dialogue to you in the actual proximity of your ownmost Dasein, so that finally you no longer have a foreign text and an accidental Reclam edition in front of you, but have *in yourselves* a question that has become awake and inwardly awakened. If you still find it unconditionally necessary to read current philosophical literature, this is a sure sign that you have not grasped anything of what we have been dealing with thus far.

§ 18. Justification of the 'Detour'. Preliminary Clarification of Fundamental Concepts: ψεῦδος, λήθη and ἀ-λήθεια

We ask therefore, quite specifically, about the essence of *untruth*. But a renewed reflection on this intention must nevertheless make us wary. It is as clear as day that our endeavour lacks all prospects. Even if, in asking about the essence of truth, it is not a detour to inquire first into the essence of untruth, we are nonetheless able to grasp the essence of untruth only if we have already adequately determined the essence of *truth*! For truth is precisely what is *denied* in un-truth. There is an old doctrine of logic according to which negation *presupposes* something *capable* of being negated, thus something already affirmable, affirmed, thus affirmation. To want to *begin* with negation, whether this is a detour or not, therefore infringes against the most elementary law of logic.

To be sure, we could reply to this query by saying that the foregoing considerations have treated truth at sufficient length, so that something capable of negation is pre-given, which, when actually negated, is untruth. This is correct. But are we really paying attention to the matter at hand? If we argue in this way, are we not again clinging to the mere words 'truth' and 'untruth', as if we had not discovered that truth means unhiddenness? Truth itself is already substantively a negation. In unhiddenness, 'no' is said to hiddenness. Then everything is the wrong way around: truth is denial (negative), un-truth is affirmation (positive).

But has not *untruth* always counted as the negative, not only in the sense of what *is* denied, but of what *should* be denied, of the invalid and unworthy, of what should be *avoided* in the interest of truth, of what must be overcome and opposed? Certainly! But from where is the intrusiveness and stubbornness of un-truth supposed to come, if untruth is merely something negative, if it does not possess its own positive *power*? Is there in the end *more* to un-truth than the mere 'not-being-present' of truth? Is this 'more' perhaps just what is most essential to it? Must we not therefore attempt to bring out this *positivity* of un-truth, i.e. attempt to conceive of un-truth *otherwise* than as mere negation of truth? Thus the doubts, which once again threatened to keep us from the indicated short steep stretch of road, disappear, and for two reasons:

1 We have seen that truth *qua* unhiddenness is already a *negation* and should not, as the positive, be set over against un-truth as the negative.

2 Even if un-truth *qua* falsity is something negative, its essence cannot consist in *mere* negation, but must exercise its own power.

We remain, therefore, on the path we have chosen, and we *inquire* into untruth. We do not rely on having *defined* truth, and we do not believe that the essence of untruth can be conjured up by mere negation (i.e. without inquiring into it at all).

Although disposing of the indicated methodological reservation has not advanced our substantive understanding of the essence of truth and untruth, it has brought out an important point: truth and untruth (unhiddenness and hiddenness) are not simply opposites, i.e. opposing denials such that by adding the 'not' and the 'no' the other is already grasped. Instead, the 'not' and the character of the 'no' clearly *belong* to the essence of *both,* i.e. to truth as *un*-hiddenness, but also, in another way, to *un*-truth *qua* falsity, as something invalid (something that stands *against* truth). In the end it is precisely this 'not' which lends to truth, and in a different sense also to untruth, their characteristic *power* and power*less,* but which also makes it so difficult to grasp the *essence* of both and the essence of their *connection,* so that already in *the asking* and at the outset we mostly go astray. Briefly put: un-hiddenness *and* hiddenness are bound up with what is null and invalid, not on the basis of a formal external differentiation of the two, but *in themselves.* In the question of the essence of truth the question of the 'not' and negation must play a special role.

We shall recapitulate Plato's path toward clarifying the essence of untruth by simply *travelling along* it. As with the interpretation of the cave allegory, we begin with certain preparatory considerations. In the former case we inquired first into the *word* for truth, ἀλήθεια, and its meaning. Likewise, we now inquire into the linguistic expression used by Plato and the Greeks to name the opposite of ἀλήθεια (truth). The Greek word for un-truth in this sense, which subsequently attains the status of a technical term, is τὸ ψεῦδος. We can gain some clarity about this term by comparing it with the word for truth.

At a purely linguistic level, we notice two things about this counterword:

1 that this word has a quite different *stem,*

2 that this word has a different *form,* i.e. no *alpha privatum* (the un- in un-truth), therefore it does not have a *negative* character at all.

With us, on the other hand:

1 'truth' and 'untruth' have the same stem (it is different, however, with 'true' and 'false'!),

2 un-truth is already in its linguistic construction the negation of truth.

Therefore, remembering our previous considerations, we shall conclude that the meaning of ψεῦδος arose from a quite different fundamental experience to ἀλήθεια; in any case not the experience of hiddenness, of concealing (covering up) and uncovering, for otherwise something of this latter experience would have come to linguistic expression (λαθ-). ψεῦδος as word-form comes from a different stem, as distant as can be from λήθη (λάθω), and does not, like un-truth, have a negative character. If we translate ψεῦδος (correspondingly the adjective ψεῦδος, ψευδές) simply with untruth, falsity, incorrectness, the genuine meaning of the Greek word must escape us.

Therefore, we shall further conclude, it cannot be finally settled whether we are justified in referring the essence of untruth to the fundamental experience of *hiddenness,* or whether, on the contrary, the meaning of ἀλήθεια is determined by the meaning of ψεῦδος rather than by the fundamental experience of ἀλήθεια (especially if we remember that truth arises precisely in the struggle *against* untruth, ψεῦδος). Perhaps the word ἀλήθεια is indeed an accidental formation and its meaning must be understood from ψεῦδος. We have evidence that this may be so from the Greek of Plato himself, namely from his characterization of the true as the not-untrue, ἀ-ψευδές.

Truth as what opposes untruth is then grasped as not-ψεῦδος, ('ἀ-ψεῦδος'): cf. ἀψευδέω, to say the truth; ἀψευδής, true; and, as the genuine counter-concept to ψεῦδος, ἀ-τρεκές[6] (= not turned around, not distorted, not deformed) in Pindar. Cf. Democritus Fragment 9: ἡμεῖς δὲ τῶι μὲν ἐόντι οὐδὲν ἀτρεκὲς συνίεμεν μεταπῖπτον δὲ κατά τε σώματος διαθήκην καὶ τῶν ἐπεισιόντων καὶ τῶν ἀντιστηριζόντων[7] (cf. the other fragments, further Herodotus: ἀτρέκεια). Here, therefore, the peculiar state of affairs arises whereby the meaning and essential conception of truth is guided by ψεῦδος and its meaning.

Yet what do ψεῦδος, the cognate form ψενδής, -ές and the corresponding derivation ψεύδειν, ψεύδεσθαι, all mean? It is convenient that in our language we use a foreign word to clarify the meaning of ψεῦδος: 'pseudonym', from ψενδές (false, untrue) and ὄνομα (name), an untrue name, a false naming. But does 'pseudonym' actually mean this? Clearly not. A false naming would occur if I answered the question 'what is that thing called?' (it is chalk) by saying 'a sponge'. That would be an incorrect designation. On the other hand, when e.g. Kierkegaard publishes one of *his* works under the name 'Johannes Climacus', this naming is not simply a false name (in the sense of not corresponding to the real author); instead, Kierkegaard publishes his own work, as we say, 'under' a different name. Under, i.e. *under the protection* of this name. It is not that the name fails to correspond, that it is incorrect, but that it *hides* the real author, that it covers up and conceals, which is decisive for the pseudonym (the cover name). A pseudonym, therefore, is not a false name *(qua* incorrect) but a concealing name. (The name itself is even very 'correct', but in a hidden sense.) On the title-page of the book the reader is faced with a name behind which a different, indeed a well-known, author is hiding. In this facing-towards of the name lies the attempt at distorting the actual state of affairs, in such a way that this state of affairs does not come into view, yet appears to do so – for the book, as is customary, has a title and an author. In this distortion the real state of affairs is turned around such that it indeed presents itself, but in so doing precisely hides itself. The fundamental meaning of ψεῦδος is to thus *twist* a thing, a relation, a saying or a showing: in short, *distortion.* We can easily see that hiding and concealing thereby play a role and belong essentially to the meaning. But it is not hiding in the sense of simply removing something and making it inaccessible. Instead, it is hiding precisely *through* showing and letting be seen. The real state of affairs shows itself from one side, so that *one* side is turned towards us, but the view of it is *skewed* and the object somehow appears twisted. Yet this twisting or distortion remains hidden as such, for the object is indeed turned towards us (a book with title and name of author).

We hold fast to this: τὸψεῦδος, is distortion, or again *that which* is distorted, thus the mendacious. It is clear that some kind of concealment belongs to ψεῦδος, but we already notice that concealment and concealment is not necessarily the same. Here we come across modifications of hiddenness that are interrelated and refer to quite central phenomena. Only *one* meaning of ψεῦδος is mentioned here (having consideration for what we shall later encounter in the *Theaetetus:* the μὴ ὄν). Distorting (τὸ ψεῦδος) means twisting the facts in such a way that they face us only from *one* side, thereby disguising and covering up *something else* behind them. It may even be that what is concealed is not something else hidden behind the side that faces us, but just the fact that there is *nothing* behind it. Then the *impression* arises of something behind it, so that it looks like something without actually being what it shows itself as. ψεῦδος is therefore deception, a pretence to something where there is nothing, and so is in itself idle and worthless. From this we can understand the verb ψεύδειν: to turn idle, to make worthless, to make into a non-entity, into something bogus, into something behind which there is nothing, thus into something which itself is not. At the same time we can understand the meaning of ψεύδεσθαι: to act deceptively, especially in speaking, saying and declaring, to speak in such a way that what is meant gets covered up and concealed. Already in Plato, and then in a terminologically fixed manner in Aristotle, ψεύδεσθαι functions as the counter-concept to ἀληθεύειν (to bring something unhidden clearly before oneself and to have it before one). Characteristically, Aristotle refers the *two* moments of hiding and letting-be-unhidden to the λόγος, understood as *propositional determination*. Aristotle was the first to speak in this way.

We saw previously that the primordial meaning of each word is different. A crucial question for understanding the problem of truth is whether the fundamental meaning of ἀλήθεια is strong and vital enough to change ψεύδεσθαι in *its* sense (this possibility exists), or whether, on the contrary, the fundamental meaning of ψεύδεσθαι and ψεῦδος gains the upper hand over ἀληθεύειν (cf. ἀψενδεῖν, saying the truth) and thus determines the essence of truth.

It will emerge that ψεύδεσθαι comes to have control,[8] and indeed:

1 because seen from λόλος (why?);

2 because in this way it itself becomes 'in-correctness';

3 because ἀλήθες for its part becomes ἀψευδές, not-incorrectness, i.e. correctness;

4 this predominance over ἀλήθεια is made easier,

  a. because ἀλήθεια is not grasped with sufficient primordiality,

  b. because ἀλήθεια is made equivalent to παρουσία, the opposite of λήθη,[9]

  c. because the λόος, comes to predominate, truth is thereby levelled out to seeing, showing itself, appearing (δοκεῖν δόξα).

We begin by reaffirming that ψεῦδος (distortion) arises as the counter-concept to ἀλήθεια, that ἀληθεύειν as deconcealing is oriented to ψεύδεσθαι and comes to mean the same as ἀ-ψεύδειν, thus modifying itself to become the counter-concept to distortion (not-distorting). By this remarkable juxtaposition ἀληθεύειν loses its fundamental meaning and is uprooted from the fundamental experience of unhiddenness. Thus ἀλήθεια comes to oppose the kind of concealing which is a hiding and disguising, i.e. which is not hiddenness and concealment simply as such, but specifically distortion (while distortion may itself *contain* the moment of hiddenness, the latter does not come forth). This covering up (distortion) is thus first in a *defensive stance* with respect to uncovering (making unhidden); in this way 'uncovering' obtains the meaning of not distorting, not concealing, hitting the mark, which is something different to the previous meaning of simply wrenching what is hidden from out of hiddenness. However, the defensive meaning of 'conceal' can immediately change over into *offence;* i.e. not hidden from . . ., but, actively, to erect a façade, thus to mis-lead and *lead* into error.

The situation, therefore, is that the terms of the opposition truth/ untruth are linguistically quite independent from each other: ἀλήθεια – ψεῦδος. The apparently irrelevant fact that the word for untruth has a different stem to the word for truth acquires great significance for the history of the concept of truth. We cannot help asking whether the

Greeks did not also have a counter-concept to ἀλήθεια. If in Greek the counter-*concept* to ἀ-λήθεια were *linguistically* grasped in a way that corresponds to our practice (simply as unhiddenness), then the counter-word would have to be formed from the same stem, such that the un-, the *alpha privatum*, would simply fall away: 'λήθεια'. Is there anything of the sort in Greek? Indeed! They had λήθη, λάθω, λήθομαι, λανθάνω, λανθάνομαι. All these words revolve around the fundamental meaning of being hidden and remaining hidden, but with a curious crucial modification and weakening, which, in order to fully grasp the real meaning of ἀλήθεια, we must keep clearly before us: for the most part, λήαη is understood as *forgetting*.

From our many-sided clarification of ἀλήθεια we have already discovered something which must be repeatedly emphasized vis-à-vis later conceptions of truth, especially the contemporary conception: ἀλήθεια does not pertain primarily to the knowing comportment, i.e. to declaring and judging, but to things [*Sachen*], to beings [*Seienden*]. It is the same with λήθη: this does not refer to forgetting as some kind of subjective condition or experience, but means the hiddenness of beings. What is essential for the proper conception of λήθη is insight into the fundamental meaning of ἀλήθεια: unhiddenness applies to the beings themselves. Thus also λήθη is the slipping away and withdrawal of beings as an objective occurrence. This withdrawal is precisely the reason that knowers can no longer direct themselves to beings, ἀλήθεια is the consequence of λήθη, not vice-versa.

To clarify the meaning of the word λήθη (from which originates 'Lethe', still used to refer to the river of forgetting) I choose a well-known passage from the historical work of Thucydides (II, 49 *finis)*. In Chapter 47 Thucydides begins his account of the second year of the Peloponnesian War, in which the Lacedaemonians' second invasion of Attica succeeded and when the plague first broke out in Athens. Chapter 49 gives a detailed description of the course and consequences of this disease, and says towards the end: 'After surviving the disease many lost their limbs; some lost their eyes', τούς δέ καί λήθη ἐλάμβανε παραντίίκα ἀναστάντας τῶν πάντων ὁμοίως καί ἡγνόησαν σφάς τε αὐτούς καί τούς ἐπιτηδείους. 'Others were overcome, right after an initial recovery, by the remaining – hidden [*Verborgenbleiben*] of all beings, so that they did not know either themselves or their friends.' λήθη τῶν πάντων ὁμοίως: 'the remaining- hidden of all beings befell them'.

Λήθη, in the genuine Greek sense, is not a 'lived experience' (the Greeks, thank God, knew no such thing), but is a fateful occurrence that overtakes human beings, an occurrence, however, that pertains to all beings: they fall into hiddenness, they withdraw, they are simply absent.

We know, however, or to put it more carefully, we should now reflect in a more penetrating way upon this fact, that the Greeks understood the being of beings as presence. The most serious and therefore most dangerous thing that can happen to beings is their becoming absent: the emergence of *absence*, the being-gone, the gone-ness of beings. A λήθη of beings occurs: hiddenness, not in the sense of a preserving hiding away, but simply as being-gone. What occurs is a removal, a becoming-absent of beings from man. It is as if man is dragged into this happening. This gone-ness of beings is the ground and condition of the possibility that these people now no longer know anything even of themselves as being [*als seienden*] or of their closest friends. This ἄγνοια, this no longer knowing, i.e. no longer being able to direct oneself towards, is the consequence of λήθη, exactly corresponding to the way ὀρθότης (directing oneself to beings) presupposes the ἀλήθεια of beings (unhiddenness). It is typical of the Greek language to say λήθη (being hidden in the sense of being-gone) of the *beings* to which man should be able to comport himself. The Greeks say that beings are gone, so that one knows nothing more of them. We say, by contrast, that someone who no longer knows anything is 'somewhere else', 'not all there'. It is therefore quite wrong to translate λήθη as forgetting in the ordinary sense of a subjective psychological event. (I still leave open the question of whether one can at all comprehend forgetting by conceiving it as a psychological event or occurrence in consciousness.) What is important for us is that λήθη means an objective occurrence which affects man in his existence, which comes over him and seizes him, i.e. which intervenes in the manifestness of beings. This objectively occurring gone-ness of beings is the *condition* of the possibility of someone no longer knowing anything, of someone being 'completely gone'. ἐλάμβανε is frequent in Greek; λαμβάνει φόβος, ἄλγος, ὕπνος fear seizes him, sleep seizes him, and so forth, all as objective (if we may use this misleading expression here) 'powers'.

The Greek λήθη (and λανθάνομαι) only gets the meaning of forgetting via the indirect manner of a specific derivation, whereby, however, the objective sense is still present. What is decisive for this derivation is precisely its origin in the fundamental meaning of remaining-hidden. λανθάνω means that I am or remain hidden, to myself or to others. This fundamental meaning of the word leads to a linguistic usage quite characteristic of Greek, namely combination with a participle as we know this from Homer *(Odyssey* VIII, 93, a verse which we still remember from school): ἐνθ' ἄλλονς μέν πάντας ἑλάνθανε δάκρυα λείβων. 'He remained hidden to all the others as someone shedding tears'; *we* say, by contrast, that he shed tears without anyone else noticing it. For the Greeks, remaining-hidden stands in the foreground (it is expressed in the *verbum finitum*), always as an existing state of affairs, as the character of the beings (also of a particular human being). But we turn the state of affairs around into something subjective, and express it by saying that the others did not notice his weeping.

In this way the wisdom of language provides us with an important testimony to the fact that the remaining-hidden and being-unhidden of things and human beings (to themselves as to others) was experienced by the Greeks as an occurrence of the beings themselves, and also belonged to the fundamental experiences which determined the existence of ancient man. λανθάνω ἥκων: I remain hidden as someone who comes; we say: I come without anyone noticing. Thus the meaning of λανθάνομαι as letting something be hidden to *me*, i.e. I let it withdraw, slide away from me and be gone, I allow forgetting (being-gone) to come over something, *I* do not turn towards it, *I* let it rest, *I* forget it. Only by way of this modification do λανθάνομαι and λήθη come to have the meaning of forgetting in the sense of a subjective state of affairs (but precisely in the meaning of being-gone).

We said that λήθν has the fundamental meaning of hiddenness, but with a notable modification. We now see the character of this modification: it is a weakening. What comes forth from the essence of hiddenness is not the veiledness, nor even the mysterious preservation and safekeeping, but much more the removal, the simple putting-away, withdrawing, getting-out-of-view. Hiddenness, λήθν, has withered away to a simple not-being-present, being-gone, absence. In this way we see not only the character of the modification of λήθν, but also its implications. For precisely this same withering away also comes to expression in the counter-concept, ἀλήθεια. As the counter-phenomenon to being-gone, ἀλήθεια has the meaning of not-being-gone, i.e. being present. The true is what is not-gone, i.e. what is *present*. But what is present is, for the Greeks, beings. Thus beings as the actual are the true as the not-gone. In this way we can comprehend why, for the Greeks, ἀλήθεια can mean both presence and *being* (assuming that we bear in mind that the Greeks understand being as presence). It is not at all self-evident that actuality and truth should be equated, but this springs from the quite specific meaning of being and truth in Greek. For the Greek meanings of truth and being meet up in the moment of the not-gone as the not-hidden, and in the not-gone as the present. Not-gone, therefore not hidden, therefore true; not-gone, therefore present, therefore existing. It is for this reason that the Greeks mean the same thing by ὄντως ὄν and ἀληθῶς ὄν. (*We also* say: 'really and truly is', but without giving it a thought.)

This relation, or even identity, between being and truth, is not at all self-evident in itself, but is made necessary by the ancient concepts of being and truth. The essential thing is that each reinforces the other in the progressive withering away of, and the progressive uprooting from, their fundamental experience. The meaning of being as presence is the reason that ἀλήθεια (unhiddenness) withers away to mere being-present (not- gone). But this means that the ancient understanding of being, at its very origin, prevents the incipient fundamental experience of the *hiddenness* of beings from unfolding into its ownmost depth. The Greek understanding of being (being = presence) brings it about that ἀλήθεια immediately forfeits the power of its fundamental meaning. The weakening to mere not- goneness, presence, is completed. However, this weakening of the meaning of the fundamental experience of 'hiddenness/unhiddenness' helps the meaning of ψεῦδος, which has a quite different origin, to gain the upper hand over ἀλήθεια, such that the meaning of hiddenness contained therein is again suppressed. ἀλήθεια, truth, is understood from ψεύδεσθαι as the *un*distorted, as correct orientation, as correctness. On the other hand, the weakened meaning of ἀλήθεια now rebounds on the concept of *being*. Truth is understood as being-correct in the sense of correct assertion (correctness or validity); thus being is also understood as the being of assertion (ὄν = ὄν λεγόμενον): what is correctly asserted, and *only* this, *is*. Being is thus oriented to the assertion. A tangible testimony to this is the fact that, ever since Aristotle, the characteristics of being have been called 'categories': determinations that belong to the proposition. In this way the concept of being loses its primordial innermost meaning, i.e. presence; this *temporal* moment is completely shaken off.

What I have briefly sketched here results in the two fundamental experiences of εἶναι and ἀλήθεια, a particular kind of time on the one hand, and hiddenness/unhiddenness on the other hand, these most stirring fundamental experiences of ancient existence, shrivelling up, disintegrating, and leaving behind a faded everyday self-evidence. The philosophy that follows, rootless as it is, makes it a first principle that the concept of being is the clearest and simplest of all concepts, without need of, and inaccessible to, any interrogation. To be sure, the whole world has recently been gossiping about the problem of being, and one acts as if the question of being is lying out there on the street. We can leave all this to its own poverty and blindness.

§ 19. Summary: Unhiddenness and Being; the Question Concerning the Essence of Untruth

The question concerning the essence of truth first defined itself as the question concerning the essence of unhiddenness. What belongs to this was brought out by an interpretation of the cave allegory. A basic characteristic of unhiddenness consists in its being something which occurs with beings themselves. Nevertheless, this occurrence belongs in a particular way to the history of man as an existing being. Unhiddenness does not persist somewhere by and in itself, or as a property of things. Being occurs as the history of man, as the history of a people. We called this occurrence of the unhiddenness of beings 'deconcealment'.

Deconcealing is in itself a confrontation with and struggle against concealing. Hiddenness is always and necessarily present at the occurrence of unhiddenness, it asserts itself unavoidably in the unhiddenness and helps the latter to itself. To really ask after the essence of unhiddenness therefore means being serious about the question of the essence of hiddenness. But in relationship to truth this is not-unhiddenness, not-truth, i.e. un-truth in the broad sense. The question of the essence of truth therefore changes into the question of untruth.

Untruth in the broad sense now emerges as thoroughly ambiguous. The not-unhidden, the not-true, is on the one hand the concealed in the sense of the not-deconcealed, and on the other hand it is the hidden as the *no- longer* deconcealed. Both the not-yet and no-longer deconcealed are in turn ambiguous: either the still never deconcealed, still never made manifest, although deconcealable [*Entbergbare*]; or on the other hand the hidden as the no longer deconcealed, which was, however, previously manifest, and which can again completely sink back into hiddenness. Or again, something concealed but which is still in a certain way deconcealed and shows itself, i.e. the distorted. This will suffice as a schematic formal indication of the various modes of un-truth.

Of these various modifications of untruth it is only the last mentioned that is typically recognized: untruth in the sense of distortion, as we ordinarily use this word. That and *how* this mode of untruth *alone* came into view, and to a certain extent was made into a problem, is no trivial matter, but is the ground of an innermost distress [*Not*] which the existence of man has had to bear ever since. This is what essentially determines the course and direction of the history of the Western spirit and its peoples.[10]

The question of untruth in the quite specific meaning of falsity was first developed, and for subsequent times substantially decided, by Plato, in his dialogue the *Theaetetus*.

The explanation of the words ψεῦδος and λήθη has again led us, from the opposite side as it were, to a connection we encountered in the first lecture, the connection between unhiddenness (truth) and beings (being). We can foresee that the question of the essence of untruth is very intimately tied up with the question of being, indeed of un-being [*Un-Sein*].

To once more summarize, in five points, our view of the question concerning the essence of truth:

1 The question of the essence of truth in the sense of the unhiddenness of beings is a question concerning the history of man's essence as an existing being.

2 The existence of man is grounded in the fact that, as understanding being and as himself a being, he stands in the midst of beings.

3 The question of the essence of truth as the question of the history of man's essence is itself a question concerning being as such, whose comprehension makes existence possible.

4 The question of the essence of truth as un-hiddenness is itself the question concerning hiddenness, therefore concerning untruth in the broadest sense.

5 This modified question of the essence of un-truth brings a more primordial direction to the question concerning the history of man's essence.

We shall now attempt to set this new question of the essence of truth, i.e. as the question concerning the essence of untruth, into motion.

Notes

1 See above pp. 83 f.

2 In parentheses, probably not delivered [Ed.]: Only by us *awakening* such an occurrence – without imagining that we can reverse history overnight; without the childish idea that the proof of success or failure of this task (which is not of today) is perhaps the removal of unemployment and the like. At bottom, whoever thinks in this way imagines that the essence and spirit of man is something one gets at the pharmacist.

3 See above p. 9.

4 See above pp. 82 ff.

5 *Platons Theaitetos oder Vom Wissen,* translated by Friedrich Schleiermacher, edited by Dr Curt Woyte, Leipzig: Philipp Reclam 1916 (unchanged edition 1922). Cf. today: *Platon Sämtliche Werke,* from the translation of Friedrich Schleiermacher, edited by Walter F. Otto et al., 6 vols, Reinbeck: Rowohlt 1957–1959; Vol. 4 (1958), pp. 103–81.

6 Switching of stems τρεκ and τρεπ.

7 Democritus Fr. 9, in Kirk, Raven and Schofield, op. cit., pp. 411–12, where the translation is given as: 'We in actuality grasp nothing for certain, but what shifts in accordance with the condition of the body and of the things which enter it and press upon it'. [Trans.]

8 See below pp. 193 ff.

9 See *Theaetetus* 144 b 3: οἱ . . . λήθης γέμοντες.

10 See Supplement 8.

PART TWO

An Interpretation of Plato's *Theaetetus* with Respect to the Question of the Essence of Untruth

1

Preliminary Considerations

We set the whole following endeavour under a principle enunciated by Plato in the course of the dialogue (187 e 2): κρεῖττον γάρ που σμικρὸν εὖ ἢ πολὺ μὴ ἱκανῶς περᾶναι. 'More is accomplished by a proper treatment of little than by an inadequate treatment of much.'

§ 20. The Question Concerning the Essence of ἐπιστήμη: Man's Attack on the Self-evidences of His Self-understanding

The necessary method of interpretation leads us to the centre of our *question*. We do not therefore go schematically through the dialogue[1] from beginning to end; we completely abandon the attitude of the mere reader. In somewhat impertinent fashion we cut into, as *co-questioning* auditors, the already progressing conversation, without knowing the beginning or end, yet at a point where we immediately feel something of the whole.[2]

We encounter Socrates, the mathematician Theodorus, and the young Theaetetus, all in conversation, at just the moment when Socrates says to Theaetetus (184 b 4 ff.):[3]

Ἔτι τοίνυν, ὦ Θεαίτητε, τοσόνδε περὶ τῶν εἰρημένων ἐπίσκεψαι.
αἴσθησιν γὰρ δὴ ἐπιστήμην ἀπεκρίνω. ἦ γάρ

Ναί.

'With regard to what we have been talking about, Theaetetus, consider this further point. You answered that perception is knowledge, did you not?'

'Yes.'

Socrates at this point refers back to what was previously discussed. During this earlier discussion Theaetetus claimed that the essence of knowledge consists in *perception.* From this we conclude that the leading question of the conversation is: it τί ἐστιν ἐπιστήμη; what *is* 'knowledge'? Socrates put this question forward quite clearly at the beginning of the dialogue (146 c3), challenging Theaetetus as follows:

ἀλλ’ εὖ καὶ γενναίως εἰπέ·τί σοι δοκεῖ εἶναι ἐπιστήμη;

'So tell me frankly: what does that seem to you to be, "knowledge"?'

In the course of the conversation (151 e) Theaetetus arrives at his answer: the essence of knowledge is αἴσθησις, 'perception' [*Wahrneh-mung*], as we shall provisionally translate it. The correctness or otherwise of Theaetetus' answer is then considered. At the moment we begin to listen in, this question takes a new and positive turn.

As auditors – genuine auditors, i.e. co-questioners – we allow ourselves to be drawn into the question 'what is knowledge?' A peculiar and at bottom eccentric question. What 'knowledge' is might be of interest to scholars, but even scholars will not direct their primary interest to such a question, nor will they take it very seriously. On the contrary, they will apply themselves to *particular* knowledge in particular *domains,* in order to gain an overall view and command of these domains. But what knowledge is *as such* is a quite *empty* question. Now the philosophers (especially those representing contemporary philosophy) will admit that it does appear this way, but will nonetheless insist that precisely this is the authentically *philosophical* question! For what is the difference between this science of *philosophy* and the other sciences? The sciences have divided up all beings among themselves. They have divided up the individual domains of the knowable for the purpose of their research. No specific domain is left over for philosophy. Yet one thing does remain for it to do: to inquire into knowledge as such, into the possibility of knowledge in general, and this means, for them, to inquire into the possibility of *science* as such. What knowledge is as such is the province of theory of science, whose most general task is sought in *theory of knowledge*. Accordingly, the question posed by Plato in the *Theaetetus* must be the fundamental question of the theory of knowledge, and so it comes about, particularly in the modern period, that the *Theaetetus* is commonly characterized as Plato's main epistemological dialogue. One sings the praises of Plato and the Greeks because they were already sufficiently advanced as to pose epistemological questions, because in fundamental respects they had already reached a stage that was not subsequently attained until the nineteenth century. Yet although this is the common and generally accepted conception of the *Theaetetus'* leading question, it remains erroneous, groundless, superficial and unphilosophical.

The question 'what is knowledge?' gets conceived as the question 'what is *science*?' because knowledge in the proper sense is equated with scientific knowledge. This is a false interpretation of the leading question and thus of the whole dialogue. We shall confirm this in the course of our interpretation, but it is not the *aim* of our exposition to show it.

Doubts have been expressed – happily so – about whether we are still moving along the path of our leading question. We are inquiring into the *essence of truth*! It would indeed be a serious matter if we had become diverted from our path. On the other hand, possession of factual knowledge is of no great consequence. Whether you 'know' this or that (e.g. where Megara is, when Schleiermacher was born, who Friedrich Schlegel was) does not count for much. What is essential is that you are ready and willing to pose *questions.*

Not only is the question posed by Plato not an epistemological question, it is not a question concerned exclusively with theoretical knowledge or with the kind of knowledge that is the business of the learned. The question τί ἐστιν ἐπιστήμη asks after the essence of that with which we are acquainted under the word ἐπιστήμη.[4] Confronted by this question, we raise the preliminary problem of what ἐπιστήμη meant for the *Greeks prior to* this Platonic question. Only by first answering this preliminary question can we determine what is being interrogated in this dialogue.[5]

Tί ἐστιν ἐπιστήμη: if Plato asks in this way, then he already *understands* what ἐπιστήμη means, in so far as ἐπιστήμη *says* something for every Greek. What ἐπιστήμη so self-evidently says is not discussed in the dialogue but is presupposed. However, we ourselves must first become clear about the *ordinary* meaning of ἐπιστήμη *prior* to all philosophical discussion, thus as the *point of departure* for the philosophical dialogue.

Ἐπίσταμαι means: I direct myself to something, come closer to it, occupy myself with it, in a way that is fitting and measures up to it. This placing of myself toward something is at the same time a coming to *stand,* a standing *over* the thing and in this way to *under*-stand it (= σοφία); e.g. understanding the *production* of something in craftwork, the production of shoes for example, understanding the care and *preservation* of something in agriculture or animal husbandry, understanding the management and *implementation* of something, e.g. the practice of war, the art of war. ἐπιστήμη originally means all this: the *commanding knowing-one's-way- around* [*beherrschende Sich-auskennen*] in something, familiarity in dealing with something.

We draw out two points from this basic meaning of ἐπιστήμη:

1. This commanding knowing-one's-way-around in something extends across all possible human activities and all possible domains, in accordance with their respective modes of dealing.

2. On the negative side it emerges that ἐπίστασθαι and ἐπιστήμη do not originally have the meaning of scientific-theoretical instruction. To be sure, scientific knowledge is *also* called ἐπιστήμη (e.g. γεωμετρία in *Theaetetus* 146 c/d). It is nevertheless clear that what we call 'science', i.e. the methods and institutions and results of theoretical research, is just *one* kind of knowing-one's-way around in something.

The leading question of the dialogue, τί ἐστιν ἐπιστήμη, is therefore completely misinterpreted, and evacuated of its primordiality and significance, if one renders it as 'what is the essence of theoretical-scientific knowledge?', or even as 'how is science as such possible?' This is a question of the old Marburg school, but it is not Plato's question. Plato inquires into this multifaceted knowing-one's-way-around as it pertains to the *whole* range of human comportments, whether in shoemaking, warfare, geometry, or anything else. Plato asks about what this actually *is*.

If one wants to translate the Greek ἐπιστήμη by the German 'Wissen' [knowledge], then one must also take this German word in its corresponding primordial meaning and hold fast to this. As a matter of fact our language recognizes a meaning of 'know' which corresponds precisely to the original meaning of ἐπιστήμη: we say that someone knows [*weiß*] how to behave, knows how to succeed, knows how to make himself liked. It is this 'he knows, he understands how' that we must assume if we wish to use the word 'knowledge' in the sense of the Greek ἐπιστήμη. Plato is inquiring into what *this* kind of knowledge is, and not into science as such. Only if we make it clear to ourselves that it is this kind of knowledge which is interrogated, the kind of knowledge which prevails *prior* to and *alongside* all science, can we understand why a *question* is at all possible and necessary: precisely because ἐπιστήμη in its many *modifications* prevails over the whole Dasein of man, yet, as is already indicated by the use of the same *word* for such disparate things as shoemaking and geometry, all this knowing somehow appears to be the same. Only when we understand the question in the full scope of its origin can we comprehend why, later on, the answers moved in a quite specific direction, with the result that the concept of ἐπιστήμη was *narrowed down,* so that in Aristotle it becomes, in part, synonymous with what we call science.

While we thus have a clearer view of *what* is put in question, we still do not comprehend this question sufficiently well to be able to really participate in the questioning. What is still lacking is a clear specification of *how* ἐπιστήμη is interrogated. To be sure, this appears to be obvious from the very *form* of the question: τί ἐστιν, what is this and this? A question of this kind does not initially present any difficulties. What is more simple, more transparent, more commonplace, than this (as we call it) question of what? For example, we ask about what this thing here is, and we answer: a book, i.e. we give the *name* of the thing. But with this latter what- question we did not actually want to discover the name of the thing, what the thing is called; rather, we wanted to know what it *is*. Still, giving the name, e.g. 'book', is an initially satisfactory answer, because this is a so- called type-name, i.e. its meaning indicates what things like this are *in general*. But we can immediately pose the same question: we can ask what 'book' is. Then we are asking about what is necessary for something to be a book *as such,* irrespective of its content, size, format, paper, print, binding, decoration. Good, so the first answer was *itself* placed in question. But where is it stated what a 'book as such' is? What are we looking *to* when we ask in this way? From where are we supposed to obtain this information? Now this appears to be easy: we take particular books and compare them! Particular books? But how do we know that they are *books,* if we are indeed asking what a book is? In this way, with the apparently harmless and simple question 'what is that?', we immediately fall into great confusion. When we place something under the what-question, we must already know the 'what' in order to identify examples, yet it is the 'what' that we are initially asking about.

But this is not the only difficulty. In the case of what-questions concerning present things it may be relatively easy to assemble examples. But what is the situation in the case of the question 'what is knowledge (ἐπιστήμη)?' Knowledge does not exist in the same way as books and stones. How, given the various modes of knowledge, are we to decide in general and in advance whether a particular instance of knowledge is genuine? Is anything of the sort present like a thing? Or does such a thing *exist* only if one knows beforehand what belongs to it? Are we not asking precisely about what must always and primarily pertain to knowledge for it to be 'genuine'? If we ask *in this way,* the what-question takes on a quite specific meaning. We do not want to discover various peculiarities of ἐπιστήμη, properties of a knowing which happens to occur somewhere or other, but we are interested in what is *at stake* in knowing-one's-way- around in something. We are inquiring into what is *decisive* for it. Our questioning attempts to take a *measure*: it asks after the measure and law of the possibility of knowing-one's-way-around. Questioning is preparation for, and enabling of, a law-giving. The question 'what actually is that – knowledge?' means: what actually is at stake therein, i.e. how does it come about that, in knowing, man stands under a *claim*?

If we fully reflect upon the fact that what is in question is a human activity, and indeed not a trivial one but a fundamental activity of man that rules over and makes possible his whole Dasein, then the leading question of the *Theaetetus*, 'what is knowledge?', turns into the question of how man is to understand himself in his fundamental activity of knowing-his-way-around in things, of the conditions which must pertain if he is to be a knower. In this question 'what is ἐπιστήμη?' man asks after himself. He places himself in question. Such questioning brings man himself before new possibilities. The apparently innocuous what-question is revealed as an attack by man on his own self, on his proximal persistence in the usual and common, on his forgetting of first principles. It is an attack by man on what he proximally believes himself to know, and at the same time it is a determining intervention in what he himself can be, in what he wants to be or wants not to be.[6]

§ 21. Fundamental Content of the Greek Concept of Knowledge: Fusion of Know-how and Seeing Having-Present of That Which Is Present

We are not concerned with making unambiguous a hitherto perhaps ambiguous word (ἐπιστήμη) such that we arrive at a *definition*. The 'concept' that is sought for this, as for every philosophical word, is not a type- concept for present things, but an attacking *intervention* in the essential possibility of human existence. With this question, set in train by Plato, man acquires and secures a new stance and self-transparency, which then continues over centuries. How man subsequently *takes* himself *as* a knower: this means what subsequently counts for him as knowable or not knowable. This is not self-evident, nor is it simply given to man like a nose or ears, nor does it come to man in his sleep, nor is it the same at all times. Reflection upon *what* this question places in question and upon *how* this questioning proceeds, immediately shows us that in a primordial sense it is a question concerning *man*. But along the path of this question there also moves, and already has moved, the question concerning the essence of *truth*. If participating in the leading question of the *Theaetetus* is supposed to bring us to the question concerning untruth, we can suspect that also with this question, and perhaps really only with this question, will we be driven along the same path of the history of man's essence.

That we treat the *Theaetetus* (the question of knowledge) as foundational for the question of truth seems justified: truth is a 'property' of 'knowledge' (so it appears). But we still do not see how by following the question 'what is ἐπιστήμη?' we are supposed to arrive at the question of *untruth.* We do not even see how the question of knowledge connects with the question of *truth*, especially if we reflect that although we indeed encounter truth (ἀλήθεια) in connection with *knowledge*, in the cave allegory knowledge is precisely not conceived as ἐπιστήμη (knowing-one's- way-around-in-something, having a command of something) but rather as *seeing* (ὁρᾶν, ἰδεῖν). Knowledge as 'seeing' and as 'knowing-one's-way- around' are, in the first instance, two fundamentally different things. Yet in the Greek concept of knowledge in the broadest sense they are *unified.* The peculiar fusion of these two fundamental meanings of knowing- one's-way-around and of seeing, constitutes the basic content of the Greek concept of knowledge. For this reason we must undertake a brief reflection wherein to some extent we anticipate the following content of the dialogue. This reflection is necessary if we wish to understand the next step of the dialogue in the sense of our problem. The inner preparation for understanding this dialogue (and Plato's other works) involves, together with the clarification of the *what* and *how* of the questioning, the elucidation of how ἰδεῖν and ἐπίστασθαι, seeing and knowing-one's-way- around, are united in the Greek understanding of the essence of knowledge in the broadest sense. We give this elucidation only in its main features and with the intention of thereby once again making visible our question concerning the essence of truth *qua* unhiddenness.

It is clear that the fundamentally different comportments of 'seeing' and 'commanding' can together (unitarily) make up the essence of knowledge only if they agree with each other in some essential way. What is this unitary principle? We can only grasp it by understanding both ἰδεῖν and ἐπίστασθαι in a *more primordial* fashion. For this purpose we must pay attention to what is *at stake* in both.

First *seeing.* Why is precisely seeing with our eyes, thus, as we say, a specific activity of our *senses*, that comportment in terms of which the Greeks so to speak *sensorily* depict knowledge?[7] One might think: because seeing is a kind of apprehending which allows particularly sharp and exact differences to be discerned, thus making a diverse domain accessible in its diversity. But this is not the reason. Rather, seeing corresponds most closely to what ordinarily and pre-conceptually counts as knowledge because it is somehow an apprehension of *beings*. However, as must always be emphasized, the Greeks understand beings as *that which is present.* The way beings are apprehended and determined must accord with what is to be apprehended. The apprehending and knowing of what is present as such, of beings in their presence, must be a *having-present* [*Gegenwärtig-haben*]. And seeing, holding in view, is in point of fact the predominant, most conspicuous, most immediate, at the same time the most impressionable and far-reaching mode of the having-present of something. Owing to its distinctive character of *making-present* [*Präsent-machens*], sensory seeing comes to be the definitive example of knowledge as the apprehending of beings. The essence of seeing is making-present and holding-present, keeping something *in* presence, so that it is *manifest,* so that it is *there* in its unhiddenness.

It is precisely this basic feature of holding-present which enables ἐπίστασθαι and ἐπιστήμη to co-determine the essence of knowledge, albeit in a different and in a certain sense more important direction. ἐπίστασθαι means to know-one's-way-around in something, to understand how something is produced, run, preserved, protected or destroyed; to understand the being of a being; to understand how things stand with a being, even if it is *not yet,* or is *no more,* or if in particular cases it is not immediately to hand. Knowing-one's-way-around involves a farther apprehended and farther reaching readiness for, and disposing over, that which constitutes the being of a being, what belongs to its presence and persistence. Thus knowing-one's-way-around in something is a more extensive and simultaneously more penetrating (because geared to being) having-present of something. That ἐπίστασθαι co-determines the essence of knowledge, that it becomes *definitive* for the unfolding of the Greek concept of the essence of knowledge, means that the *content* of the essence of knowledge (i.e., according to what was earlier presented, of the actual *occurrence* of knowledge itself), its conception as 'seeing' and perceiving, undergoes an inner enrichment and broader grounding.

Knowledge is the having-present of what is present as such, having disposal over it in its presence, even when, indeed precisely when, it is absent, when it is *not* at one's disposal. Beings show themselves in their *meaning* for such disposal over; they are as such manifest, unhidden.

Thus knowledge (knowing-one's-way-around) becomes *disposal* over the unhiddenness of beings, i.e. the having and possessing of truth. Seeing means having disposal over something in its presence and persistence; to have disposal over beings *as* they show themselves and must show themselves, therefore over *how* they are manifest and unhidden. Knowing-one's-way-around is disposal over the unhiddenness of beings. Knowledge and knowing-one's-way-around is to maintain oneself within the unhiddenness of comprehended beings, to possess their truth.

This explanation of the essence of ἐπιστήμη provides some insight into the connection between knowing-one's-way-around (ἐπιστήμη) and truth (ἀλήθεια). Both mean possession of truth in the sense of the unhiddenness of beings.

From these connections we can now also understand the trajectory which the dialogue takes at the moment when we as auditors approach the speakers.

Notes

1 See Supplement 9.
2 See Supplement 10.
3 See Supplement 11.
4 See Supplement 12.
5 See Supplement 13.
6 The aggressive intervention depends on the action of *essence* in the beings, on primordiality, on in-tention [*Vor-satz*]: *how* the beings are to be beings; and this again borne along and secured by the place where man first finds himself and takes hold of himself, anti-cipates himself [*sich vor-greift*]: in the beginning of Western philosophy (Heraclitus, Parmenides).
7 Cf. *Phaedrus* 247 e 3 ff.: ὄψις as εἰπεῖν of θέα of οὐσία at the ὑπερουράνιος τόπος.

2

Beginning of the Discussion of Theaetetus' First Answer: ἐπιστήμη Is αἴσθησις. Critical Demarcation of the Essence of Perception

§ 22. Αἴσθησις as φαντασία. The Self-showing in Its Presencing

The leading question of the dialogue is: τί ἐστιν ἐπιστήμη; knowledge now being understood as knowing-one's-way-around in something. The first answer given is: ἐπιστήμη is αἴσθησις. We translate: knowledge is 'perception' [*Wahrnehmung*]. This translation is literally (lexically) correct. It is doubtful, however, whether it expresses the proper content of the specifically Greek problem contained in this answer.

How then is this thesis (knowledge is perception) arrived at? Let us consider this question on the basis of what we discovered from our earlier reflections on ἀλήθεια! If knowledge is in some sense possession of truth, and if the essence of knowledge consists in perception, then perception must carry, within itself, something like truth. Moreover, so that the attempt to answer the question of the essence of knowledge might strike out in the direction of the indicated answer, in order, therefore, that *perception*, as happens in the dialogue, can so naturally be brought forward as the bearer of *truth*, this must happen somehow at the instigation of perception (αἴσθησις) itself. Something must be contained in perception which immediately suggests that *it* (perception) should be taken as what shows the characteristic of possessing truth, and which thus allows it to be 'knowledge' of the *first* order. Now truth, ἀλήθεια, means the unhiddenness of beings, thus the fact that beings are manifest, that they show themselves. For the Greeks, wherever it happens that beings show themselves, ἀλήθεια is there. However, τὸ αἰσθάνεσθαι, becoming perceived, concerns nothing else but ὅ φαίνεται, that *which* shows itself, so we have the equation: αἰσθάνεσθαι = φαίνεται, becoming perceived = self-showing. Without further ado, Plato describes that which shows itself as φαντασία. This equivalence of αἰσθάνεσθαι and ὅ φαίνεται (φαντασία) is to be found in the dialogue at 152 c 1.

We must beware of translating this Greek word φαντασία by our word 'fantasy' [*Phantasie*], understanding this as imagination, and, in turn, understanding imagination as a psychological event or experience. We cannot get close to the meaning of the Greek word φαντασία in this way. Rather, what the word here refers to is:

1 Not any kind of subjective psychological activity or the faculty thereto, e.g. 'power of imagination', but something objective [*Gegenständliches*].

2 From what was just said one might suspect that φαντασία, while not meaning imagination in the sense of a mental comportment, nonetheless refers to the object of imagination, i.e. what imagination is directed at, the imagined, what is only mentally construed, the un-real as distinct from the real, as when we say that someone is talking pure 'fantasy'. But this is also not the meaning of φαντασία. Instead, φαντασία in the Greek sense is simply the self-showing in its self-showing, in its self-presenting, in its *presence*, exactly like οὐσία: what is present (τὰ χρήματα) in its presence.[1]

A φαντασία is e.g. the moon itself that appears in the sky, that presents itself and is present; this is something that shows itself. Schleiermacher translates φαντασία quite correctly as 'appearance' [*Erscheinung*]; only one must not misunderstand this in the sense of 'illusion' [*Schein*]. The selfshowing is the genuinely Kantian concept of 'appearance'. This book is an appearance, i.e. it is something that shows itself from itself. This is the meaning of φαντασία.

At 152 c 1 Plato makes a further crucial statement: φαντασία ἄρα καὶ αἴσθησις ταὐτόν, which roughly translated means 'appearance and perception are the same'. αἴσθησις is equivalent to self-showing beings as such (cf. Parmenides: τὸ γὰρ αὐτὸ νοεῖν ἐστίν τε καὶ εἶναι²). What does this *belonging together* consist in? αἰσθάνεσθαι means to have immediately before oneself, e.g. in 'seeing'. What shows itself belongs to perceiving. Thus αἴσθησις also stands for φαντασία, for the perceived as such. If we follow the usual practice and translate αἴσθησις as 'perception', also understanding this in the usual way as a psychological process, then the Platonic statement would have to say that e.g. the self-showing moon, and the psychological process of perceiving the moon, are the same, which is an obvious absurdity. On the other hand, if we hold strictly to what φαντασία means, i.e. the self-showing thing itself, we must ask why αἴσθησις and φαντασία are equated. What must αἴσθησις mean in this case? φαντασία is nothing else but what is perceived as such in its perceivedness, i.e. what shows itself in its self-showing. This leads us to the crucial insight that αἴσθησις means the perceivedness of something. To be sure, perceivedness always involves *being* perceived and thus the *occurrence* of a perception. So αἴσθησις has the characteristic double meaning that is also to be found in our word 'perception', and that plays a special role with Kant: 'the perceived' in its *perceivedness*, and the 'per-*ception'* [Wahr*nehmen*] in which perceivedness occurs.

The thesis is therefore: knowledge, knowing-one's-way-around in something as the possession of truth, i.e. of unhiddenness, is *perceivedness*. As we have explained it, Theaetetus' statement asserts the identity of αἰσθάνεσθαι and φαντασία perception and presence. But if we translate this statement along the lines of contemporary psychology it will be declared absurd. Understanding αἴσθησις psychologically as perceptual event misses the essential content of the Greek word. In this case the present problem cannot be comprehended, especially if one also employs a concept of truth and knowledge equally unfaithful to the Greek notion. On the other hand, if we grasp αἴσθησις as the perceivedness of something, it becomes clear that αἴσθησις involves self-showing, facing, presence, i.e. the manifestness of something, a kind of unhiddenness. What αἴσθησις signifies is the immediate unhiddenness of colours, coloured things, sounds and the like. Here, accordingly, is truth; here, accordingly, is knowledge.

It should be noted that Theaetetus does not advance his thesis identifying knowledge and αἴσθησις because perception is presented in the doctrines of psychology as the *lowest* cognitive faculty and because one should obviously begin at the lowest level. That would be to think in modern terms. Theaetetus also does not refer to αἴσθησις because he is a 'sensualist' and thus a representative of a poor theory of the psychical etc., but because as a Greek he understands αἴσθησις: because perceivedness appears the most immediate mode of the unhiddenness of something, thus the most tangible 'truth'. We can see, therefore, how a clear-thinking mind can come quite spontaneously to this answer, which looks so outrageous to a sophisticated 'philosopher'. For the Greeks, nothing is more self-evident than to interpret possession of ἀλήθεια (i.e. knowledge) first of all as αἴσθησις.

However, the question arises as to how things stand with this now quite comprehensible thesis that ἐπιστήμη is αἴσθησις. Does αἴσθησις as perceivedness fulfil the demand we make of the essence of knowledge? Do we require of knowledge nothing *else* besides the perceivedness of something? How do things stand with this perceivedness itself? Through this self-showing, something becomes manifest, unhidden. Is perceivedness really the unhiddenness of *beings*?

This question can only be decided by inquiring into the essence of αἴσθησις, especially into whether it itself is or can be the possession of unhiddenness, i.e. into its ἀλήθεια-character. What does this mean?

We have heard that ἀλήθεια means the unhiddenness of beings. Thus, wherever possession of *truth* is found, possession of unhidden *beings* must also be present, i.e. the possessor must have a *relationship* to beings as such. The question of whether the perceivedness of something is unhiddenness leads to the question of whether αἴσθησις as such, in perceptual comportment as perceiving, contains a possible relationship to *beings*. The inquiry we now begin is occupied with the question of whether perceptual comportment as such can bring itself into a *relationship* to beings as beings, such that the unhiddenness of beings is *given* in the perceivedness occurring in such comportment.

§ 23. The Senses: Only Passage-way, Not Themselves What Perceives in Human Perception

In order to decide this question, it is necessary to investigate what this perceiving bringing-itself-into-relationship *consists in*, who or what is actually *capable* of such a relationship to the perceivable and perceived, and *bears* this relationship. Thus Socrates begins the critical demarcation of the essence of αἴσθησις with the words (184 b 8):

Εἰ οὖν τίς σε ὧδ' ἐρωτώη· τῷ τὰ λευκὰ καὶ μέλανα ὁρᾷ ἄνθρωπος καὶ τῷ τὰ ὀξέα καὶ βαρέα ἀκούει; εἴποις ἄν, οἶμαι, ὄμμασί τε καὶ ὠσίν.

[Theaetetus] Ἔγωγε.

'If then anyone should ask you, Theaetetus, how one sees white and black things, and how one hears high and low tones, you would say, I suppose, with one's eyes and ears?'

'Yes.'

In agreement with Theaetetus, Socrates gives clear decisive expression to an obvious and everyday observation. It should be noted that the kind of perceiving here in question is not perception in general, i.e. perception by *any kind* of being, e.g. by animals, but the perception by *man* as human *comportment* (that from ψυχή and λόγος to the ὄν). This accords with the leading question of what knowledge is, namely that over which we human beings are empowered. We '*see*'; '*how*' do we see? *Who* sees? What is it *that sees* when we see? Who are 'we'? It is clear that in human perception, thus in seeing, hearing etc., the eyes and ears etc. come into play. It is they 'with which' (ᾧ) we perceive; literally, that which is thereby at work, that which so to speak 'performs' the perception. Wherever perception and perceivedness are found, nose, tongue, eyes and ears are at work. What comes into play with perception, what 'therefore' undertakes and carries out the perceiving, is 'therefore' in all logic that which takes up a *relationship* with the perceived and perceivable, i.e. with smells, colours, sounds etc. Accordingly, what is now inquired into is that which as such takes up the relationship in perceiving comportment. Can this be the body? How do we perceive warm and cold, light and sweet things? Certainly through the body! However, it is agreed that each faculty only makes accessible what is given to *it*, and nothing else.

For example, with perception as 'seeing' the eye is at work. But can we say that *therefore* the eye is what carries out the perception? Can we, without further ado, equate being-at-work in a perception with carrying out the perception? If we express *both* by the word ᾧ and say that perception occurs 'through' the eyes, this 'through' is ambiguous. Therefore a more rigorous and exact use of words is required. To be sure, Plato also emphasizes that it would be pedantic and small-minded to fixate on individual words and always to insist on definitions. 'Seeing *through* the eyes' and 'seeing *with* the eyes': this is initially an irrelevant distinction. But here we are concerned to clarify something essential: what constitutes (or better, *takes up*) the 'relationship' in perceiving 'comportment'. It was said that this (in the case of seeing) is the eyes. What therefore are 'the eyes'? Socrates asks *Theaetetus* (184 c 5):

σκόπει γάρ· ἀπόκρισις ποτέρα ὀρθοτέρα, ᾧ ὁρῶμεν τοῦτο εἶναι ὀφθαλμούς, ἢ δι' οὗ ὁρῶμεν, καὶ ᾧ ἀκούομεν ὦτα, ἢ δι' οὗ ἀκούομεν;

'Just consider! Which of the two answers better fits the facts: the eyes are that, ᾧ ὁρῶμεν ἤ, δι' οὗ *that which* carries out the seeing, or, that *through which* the seeing occurs?'

The corresponding question for hearing and the ears. ('ᾧ' is ambiguous; 'through' does not give the meaning. Therefore we say for ᾧ 'what': *what* does the perceiving, as distinct from 'through which'.)

The essential determination of eye, nose, ear, tongue, thus depends on whether these themselves carry out the perception and are at work as it were, or whether they are such that perception occurs in *passing through* them. Theaetetus admits that the second characterization is more accurate.

Why should this be so? Theaetetus himself does not give the reason, but passes the problem over to Socrates. The proof provided is in its external form indirect, for the matter leads Plato to a fundamental reflection. To understand this, to draw out everything from it pertaining to the leading problem, we must, here as elsewhere, put aside the problematics and advances of contemporary disciplines like psychology (especially psychology). Instead, we shall call upon the unprejudiced pre-scientific everyday self-understanding of man on the one hand, and upon a clear and expansive philosophical mode of questioning on the other. Both are still missing in what is familiar to us as 'psychology'.

The thesis, also conceded by Theaetetus, runs as follows: the eye (ear and so forth) is such that we perceive in *passing through* it (δι' οὖ); it is not *that which* performs the perception. The proof is indirect, i.e. the *contrary* of the asserted thesis is assumed, and the consequences of this assumption are then followed through and checked against the facts. Assuming, therefore, that it *is* the eye, ᾧ, i.e. that the eye is *not* that *through which* we see but is *that which* performs the seeing, then we must make the corresponding assumption in regard to the nose, tongue, hand etc. Thus the ear would be what performs the hearing. The eye would come into a relationship with colour, the ear into a relationship with sound, the nose into a relationship with smell, the tongue into a relationship with taste, the hand into a relationship with touch. What does all this amount to? Let us make the situation quite clear! Eyes, ears, nose, tongue, hand, are all situated at various points on the human body such that each is concerned with *its own* respective perceptual object. Accordingly, the colours seen by the eyes, the sounds heard by the ears, the smells etc. are *distributed* over the corresponding points of the body. The individual perceptual objects (colours, sounds etc.) and perceptions would then occur at different points of the body. *What* then do we truly 'perceive'? What do we take immediately into 'view', into *presence*? The crucial passage runs as follows (184 d 1 ff.):

Δεινὸν γάρ που, ὦ παῖ, εἰ πολλαί τινες ἐν ἡμῖν ὥσπερ ἐν δουρείοις ἵπποις αἰσθήσεις ἐγκάθηνται, ἀλλὰ μὴ εἰς μίαν τινὰ ἰδέαν, εἴτε ψυχὴν εἴτε ὅτι δεῖ καλεῖν, πάντα ταῦτα συντείνει, ᾗ διὰ τούτων οἷον ὀργάνων αἰσθανόμεθα ὅσα αἰσθητά.

'It would be strange, my boy, if so many perceptual objects [such as show themselves, φαντασίαι and αἰσθήσεις] should be dispersed at different places within us, like the warriors in the belly of a wooden horse, and that they should not all converge and meet [assembled and braced] in something like an idea, i.e. in some single sighted nature, the 'soul', or whatever it is to be called.'

This situation would be δεινόν, strange and disturbing. Why so? What is supposedly perceived by the eyes, ears, and so forth, would not be perceivable by the human being at all; he would have to betake himself sometimes to this place, sometimes to that place of the body, indeed he would have to be at several places at once. That would be possible only if he, the human being, could thereby stay *the same* as he who sees, hears etc. But the assumption is that the *eye* is what sees, that the *ear* is what hears. Perceiving is dispersed over different parts of the body, and the presence of these parts in the same body, even if we assume nerves, does nothing to remove this dispersion; on the contrary, the body upholds this dispersion. Here seeing occurs, there hearing, there tasting; but *who* is it that sees and hears? On the assumption that the eye performs the perception (correspondingly with the other senses), the situation becomes very odd: *nobody* would be able to see *and* hear *and* smell. It would not be possible for someone to simultaneously hear and see something, to have both perceptions at once. The whole essence of man would be, in respect of perception and perceivability, broken up and fractured. The essence of man would be quite impossible. It is therefore evident that the assumption cannot be maintained.

§ 24. The Soul as the Relationship That Unifies the Perceivable and Holds It Open

But bringing this situation to mind, this situation which we too today, despite all progress in the natural sciences, cannot reflect upon often and rigorously enough, does not merely have this negative result. At the same time it points to something positive, namely to what clearly must *be* in order that perception can be *as* we know it and live in it as human beings. This directs our attention to what is decisive for enabling perception to take place. In so far as some*one* does in fact exist, i.e. in so far as the *unity* of the human being is a fact, the question arises as to how this unity is possible.

The strangeness of the depicted situation is explained, and then disappears, if 'everything converges' in a *unity*. According to Plato's reflection, there must be 'something like a *single* sighted nature' *in* which all these, colour, sound, smell, taste, 'converge', i.e. something like a singular *envisability* [*eine einzige Sichtsamkeit*]. This latter would then be the centre, ἧ . . ., from which (by means of which), through our eyes and ears (as 'tools' so to speak), we have the perceptual object *immediately* before us. What one calls this singular envisability is at bottom irrelevant. One *can* call it 'soul' [*Seele*]. But if so, if we have already used this word 'soul', ψυχή, and continue to use it, we must understand it precisely in the sense of μία τις ἰδέα, and in no other way.

What does Plato mean with this statement? This is what we wish to clarify, so far as is possible at the present point. In the following we shall come to a more concrete and denser characterization. The impossibility of this uncanny state of affairs implies that there must be something like an ἰδέα. We have long ago ceased to find anything surprising and questionable about Plato's use of this word ἰδέα; for Plato is indeed the 'inventor' of the 'theory of ideas'. This terminology, to whose origination and later domination Aristotle contributed, was probably the most disastrous thing that could have happened to the Platonic philosophy. For in this way it was rigidified into a formula, thus made moribund and philosophically powerless. When we encounter this word in Plato, particularly in the passage now under discussion, it is not permissible to interpret it according to the usual understanding of ideas and theory of ideas. Instead, we must constantly be aware that with the word ἰδέα Plato means something which relates to his innermost philosophical questioning, something which opens up and guides this questioning, and something which for the entirety of Plato's career *remains* a question. Instead of 'explaining' ἰδέα in terms of the dry school conception of a so-called Platonic theory of ideas, we must grasp the possibility and necessity of this word, at any rate its surprising occurrence in our passage, and we must grasp this from the given constellation of problems. Only in this way can we give to the word ἰδέα a meaning grounded in the matter itself, instead of everything *running firmly towards* the ἰδέα and thus over ἀλήθεια and οὐσία, such that finally the decision is made for *metaphysics*.

First we should recall the earlier treated *general* word-meaning: ἰδέα is what is sighted, specifically in its being-sighted. Where ἰδέα, there sight and visibility (envisability, the formation of vision). 'Sight' is ambiguous: *that which sees*, sight as the power of seeing; and self-showing, sight as view. Both are 'sight', i.e. offering a view or presence. Seeing is the seeing of a view or look, having a view of . . . What binds the two together, as their ground, is *the envisable* [*das Sichtsame*].

However, *this* kind of 'seeing' and 'sight' must be understood in a transposed meaning rather than as sensory seeing with one's eyes. It is this sight which in perception first *makes out* something like a look, something present in such and such a way. What is retained in this transposed meaning is seeing as the immediate perception of something in its 'look', i.e. in its self-presentation, in that which it *is*; perception of what-being itself in its immediate presence. Where ἰδέα, therefore *perceivability* in this sense.

And now back to the context of our questioning. We are concerned with what is perceived by the individual sense-organs. More precisely, the assumption was made that every organ is occupied, from its own place on the body, merely with *its own* perceptual object. This assumption led to the collapse of human essence. Human beings do *exist*; but how? How do things stand in regard to what is perceived by the individual sense organs? Do the eyes and ears determine this for themselves? No, on the contrary: in genuinely unprejudiced, self-absorbed perception, the eyes and ears are not noticed by us at all. Let us pay close attention to this all too everyday state of affairs! We do not see colour in our eyes, and we do not hear sounds in our ears, but rather – where then? Perhaps in the brain? Or perhaps somewhere in a soul which haunts the body like a goblin and runs from one sense-organ to another? We perceive colour, sound etc. nowhere 'inside', neither in the body nor in the soul, but 'outside'. But what does that mean? At any rate this: we see colour *on* the book cover, we hear the sound *of* the door that someone slams, we smell, *in* the corridor or *in* the lecture room, the aroma coming from the cafeteria. Book, door, lecture room, on or in which we perceive the object of perception (colour, sound, smell): these themselves all belong to the circle of present things that surrounds us, and of which we can say it is one and the same space. But this space too, e.g. the whole spatiality of this building, is given to us only as *one*, in so far as it discloses itself to us in *one* region of the perceivable. The unity and self-identity of the region from which the perceivable so to speak springs out, is itself, even if the perceivable is *in* space, no longer anything spatial.

Where, therefore, and to where, do these perceivable objects (colour on the book, sound of the door) *converge*? εἰς μίαν τινὰ ἰδέαν, answers Plato, in a certain *singular* sighted nature; μία τις, Plato says cautiously, for it is not yet fully determined but at this stage is supposed only to announce itself. It is not yet settled what this singularity *is*. To begin with we are only to look, and make clear to ourselves that, prior to all theory, every perceived thing whatsoever encountered by us converges in *one* region of the perceivable surroundings; what is perceived must maintain itself over a broad field, yet concentrate itself into the singularity which is ἰδέα.

This singularity does not first originate from, through, and with, individual perceptions and their perceptual objects, e.g. colour and sound, but this one region of perceivability is such, εἰς ὅ . . . – it is 'something, toward which . . .', which is therefore *already there*. It *waits*, as it were, upon what converges in it, upon what at this time and at that time, indeed constantly, we encounter in perception.

Therefore, without any experimental psychology, physiology and the like, we discover the fact that a unitary region of perceivability stands ready and open beforehand for the perceptual object and its plurality. This fact is not of any lesser importance because it can and must be demonstrated without any scientific instruments and experiments, however indispensable these may remain in their field. This *single* pre-given region of possible perceivability, says Plato, one could, if one wishes, call 'soul'. So, what *is* the soul? It is just this singular environing region of perceivability, more precisely, it is this sighted nature in its being-sighted. The 'soul' is what holds up this *one* region of perceivability, as one with this region itself. This self-maintaining region which surrounds us belongs to ourselves, and is thereby a constant sameness, as Plato says quite emphatically: αὐτό τι ἡμῶν αὐτῶν,[3] something in itself that is in or by ourselves.

A concept of soul is obtained which lays the foundation for the reflections that follow. This concept is nothing artificial but arises from the unprecedented sureness with which the Greeks see those self-evident states of affairs which make up the genuinely questionable.

This is not the only way in which Plato clarifies the 'soul'. A quite different method (albeit one which ultimately agrees with what has just been indicated) is employed in the *Laws* (Book X, 891 ff.), where the phenomenon of κίνησις (movement), more precisely self-movement, provides the guiding thread for the essential determination of the soul. Here we pursue the essence of the soul only in the sense of the clarified μία τις ἰδέα. We can now say it is that which, ᾧ or ᾗ . . ., i.e. *what* can perceive, what in perception takes up the perceiving *relationship* to the perceptual object. More exactly, in so far as the soul is the singularity that holds up and maintains, for our own self, the region of a unified perceivability, it has always already and *as such*, in its very essence, taken up the relationship to the perceivable. Indeed it is *here* nothing else but precisely this relationship to the perceivable that holds up the region of possible perceivability, the region-opening and holding-open relationship to the perceivable.

Only such a relationship to what is perceivable in general, has the capacity to employ, in its perceiving, anything like sense-organs. For the soul, conceived in this way, is in itself *relational*, it reaches out to . . ., and as such it is already a possible intermediate, between which eye, ear etc. can now be interpolated. Only on the basis of such a possible interpolation does the soul become something we may characterize as δι' οὗ, as the passage-way *through which* something is perceived. A passage-way has no meaning at all if a stretch or span did not previously exist within which it is as it were inserted. We do not perceive colour and sound because we see and hear, but the reverse is the case: only because our self is relational in its essence, i.e. maintains a region of perceivability as such and *comports* itself to this, can the same self have different kinds of perceptions (e.g. seeing or hearing) within one and the same region. What kind of necessity attaches to our possession of sense-organs is an unavoidable question for philosophy, but is beyond the scope of our present inquiry.

'Soul', therefore, must be first of all the relational [*das Verhältnishafte*], i.e. that which in itself takes up a relationship to something, such that this, ᾗ . . . (*that which* takes up a relationship), and then the δι' οὗ . . . (*in passage through which* perception occurs), first become possible. Therefore Plato says (184 d 4), grasping this state of affairs more precisely:

[ψυχή] ἧ διὰ τούτων οἷον ὀργάνων αἰσθανόμεθα ὅσα αἰσθητά, the soul is that 'which allows us to perceive all the objects of perception through the senses as instruments'. It is therefore the relationality of the self which makes it possible for the corporeal to be structured organically. Only in this way can a corporeal structure be a *body*. Something can be a body in the proper sense only in so far as it is rooted in a soul, i.e. a soul does not in any way get 'breathed into' a body.

How then is a decision arrived at concerning the first statement of Theaetetus? In what way does the dialogue thus achieve its goal?

1. The argument proceeds by demonstrating that αἴσθησις as sensory sensation is necessarily grounded in *something else* which first makes it possible for things to show themselves and be perceived. Theaetetus – as we also do today – takes 'perception' in the broadest possible sense. αἴσθησις now becomes restricted to sensory sensations ('we see a tree' = 'we see it with our eyes') and is thereby underdetermined, because in truth it has a richer essential constitution. The *word* αἴσθησις is rejected, but it is nevertheless preserved in the sense of per-ceive [*ver-nehmen*], to have before oneself, διὰ-νοεῖν. Only now, therefore, do we see what The-aetetus actually intends. At 184 d 4 it is also stated that the 'soul' is 'what does the perceiving'. Theaetetus does *not* stand for any kind of 'sensualism', as if he wanted to say that 'knowledge is sensation' in the sense of having sensations (affections) and 'experiences'.

2. The argument proceeds by inquiring into that *with which* or *through which* (τῷ) we perceive. The eyes and ears: *what are* they? This question leads us to the ground of the relationship between αἴσθησις and φαντασία, thus to the ground of the ταὐτόν, of the belonging together in *one*, of the singularity and its unity, unification, gathering, presence, unhiddenness, deconcealment. It then emerges that the 'relationship' does not consist of and in the instruments of the body. Instead, the relationship (συντείνειν) is ἰδέα, seeing of the sighted, having sight (νοεῖν) of the visible (look, presence): *envisability*. The relationship is the soul itself. It is not firstly soul on its own account, and then, in addition, a relationship to the things.

3. To what degree the soul is now uncovered, and the aim of the dialogue fulfilled, requires no further discussion. 'Soul' serves to name the relationship to being (presence of the look) and thus to unhiddenness. The body and its physical constitution is admitted into this relationship, a relationship within which the historical human being *is*.

§ 25. Colour and Sound: Both Perceived at Once in διανοεῖν

This reflection, by developing a fundamental concept of 'soul', demonstrates what was merely asserted by Theaetetus, namely that the eyes and ears do not take up the relationship to the perceivable, and that it is therefore impossible, πάντα ταῦτα[4] εἰς τὸ σῶμα ἀναφέρειν, for everything perceivable to relate back to the body as that which unifies them. On the other hand, to the perception of sound, colour and the like, there belongs something like bodily interpolation. Sight (ὄψις), hearing (ἀκοή): every such αἴσθησις has a definite bodily character.

Furthermore, despite the unity of everything perceived, indeed *on the basis* of this, there occurs a *dispersion*. Through the various passage-ways (sight, hearing), each perception (αἴσθησις) is held fast to a definite track that admits only a specific kind of perceptual object: sight colour, hearing sound. No αἴσθησις provides what another does, none can replace any other, none can reach over into the domain of any other. Each isolated in itself, and in *this* sense undeniably dispersed, the individual modes of perception give *their own* perceivables and nothing further. But the eyes and ears are just passage-ways; they are not the perceiving itself that takes up the relationship to the perceivable.

Yet we see a colour and hear a sound *at the same time.* We say 'at the same time', meaning not only that the 'acts' (as one says) of seeing and hearing occur at the same point of time, but that sound *and* colour are perceived *together* with each other, that one is given along with the other. What do this 'and' and this 'both together' mean? Do we *hear* the togetherness of sound and colour? But we cannot hear a colour at all, nor can we *co*-hear *it* along with a sound. On the other hand, we cannot *see* a sound, neither can we *co*-see a sound *with* a colour. Through which organ of sense do we perceive the 'with' (the one *with* the other) and the 'both'? Therefore Socrates asks (185 a 4 ff.):

Εἴ τι ἄρα περὶ ἀμφοτέρων διανοῇ οὐκ ἂν διά γε τοῦ ἑτέρου ὀργάνου, οὐδ' αὖ διὰ τοῦ ἑτέρου περὶ ἀμφοτέρων αἰσθάνοι' ἄν.

[Theaetetus] Οὐ γὰρ οὖν.

'When therefore you are in the vicinity of both and perceive both [colour and sound] at once, you cannot perceive them both together through either the one or the other sense organ.'

'Not at all.'

This, to be sure, only registers something negative. In perceiving sound and colour, we also perceive something else: the 'and'. Yet the eyes and ears are *not* involved in perceiving the 'and'. (Or has anyone ever seen or smelled or heard the 'and'?) We must therefore inquire into *which* sense-organ comes into play here. For this, however, some preliminary work must still be completed, in particular we must clearly show *what* it is we perceive when we perceive *both* colour *and* sound at once.

Plato expresses the matter in the following way: περὶ ἀμφοτέρων τι διανοεῖν. This is Plato's description of the situation in which colour and sound are given in one and the same perception, i.e. in one and the same region of perceivability, and *at one and the same time*. It is common practice, also followed by Schleiermacher, to translate διανοεῖν as 'thinking' [*Denken*]. However, this is not only un-Greek, but testifies to a lack of comprehension of the question at issue. In the course of what follows we shall come to understand how through such a lexically correct and apparently harmless 'translation' the whole problem is blunted and has its ground pulled out from under it. But quite apart from this, διανοεῖν does not at all mean 'thinking'. Rather: νοεῖν means 'perceive', and διά means 'through': to perceive in going through, through between the one and the other, to perceive each on its own account *and* their interrelations.[5] We must hear an ambiguity, and so understand this 'perceiving' in the specific fruitful ambiguity that the word possesses in our language too, and not by chance; on the one hand perceiving in the sense of *accepting*: I have taken it, I have heard it, it has come to my ears, but also perceiving as in hearing witnesses at a trial: I have examined him, I have questioned him, meaning to *fore-take* something [*etwas vor-nehmen*], to fore-take and take in with regard to something. In διανοεῖν there resides this *fore-taking* assimilating accepting of something which thereby *shows* itself. We shall presently discover quite convincing evidence for this interpretation of διανοεῖν. To translate διανοεῖν with 'thinking' is simply thoughtless, for what one means by this word is not further *reflected*, and one completely overlooks the fact that Plato, precisely in unfolding the question of ἐπιστήμη, is concerned above all to delineate the essence of διανοεῖν in the indicated sense. To be sure, these efforts of Plato later gave rise, through misrecognition of what he was doing, i.e. through corruption of his ideas, to the concept of 'thinking' and 'ratio', which then led Western philosophy on the road towards the total decadence of today.

Let us recall how the matter stands with our question. When we perceive something in respect of colour *and* sound, this cannot be perceived either through sight or through hearing. Which organ, therefore, is at work? This can only be ascertained if we have previously established what it actually is that we perceive in such a situation. The inquiry into this question extends from 185 a through to 186 c 6. The decision about whether αἴσθησις is or is not the essence of knowledge depends on the result of this inquiry.

It is no exaggeration to say that the possibility of Western philosophy through to Kant rests upon this short section of our dialogue, as too does the transformation made by Kant himself. To be sure, what was later built up, and arranged in disciplines, by reference to this short section of the *Theaetetus*, counts as 'progress', but progress is inessential to philosophy. It is always the beginning that remains decisive. The authenticity and power of philosophical understanding can only be estimated by whether and how we measure up to the origin, by whether, if we ourselves are to begin over again, we *are able* to make anything of this origin. The prerequisite for this is that we leave aside everything which was *later* thought up, read in, and merely learnt, and that we feel, out of the most vital actuality, the origin of an elementary questioning. If philosophy is not to remain just a useless and groundless shifting around of concepts – a business in which the undisciplined agility of the literati and the dry 'accuracy' of the schoolmaster always hold the upper hand – it must be constantly returning to this origin.

Notes

1 See above p. 38.
2 See n. 9, p. 38 above. [Trans.].
3 Freely cited according to 184 d 7 f.: εἴ τινι ἡμῶν αὐτῶν τῷ αὐτῷ. [Ed.].
4 184 e 2; Oxford edition: τὰ τοιαῦτα.
5 See Supplement 14.

3

Stepwise Unfolding of Perceiving in All Its Connections

Our question and task are once more established. What organ is in play when we perceive something in respect of *both* colour *and* sound? To answer this question we must first show *what* is perceived in this situation and *how* this perceiving itself must be.

The inquiry (185 a 8–186 c 6) proceeds in *four* clearly distinguishable steps (A–D).

A. Step One: Perceiving of Beings as Such

§ 26. A Strange 'Excess' in the Perceived over and above the Sensory Given: 'Being' and Other Characters as the Necessary but Unnoticed Co-perceived

The first step continues until 185 b 6. Let us imagine ourselves in a quite ordinary situation, where we 'hover', so to speak, within an immediate perceiving simultaneously of colour and sound. Lying in the meadow we see the blue of the sky, while simultaneously we hear the singing of the lark. Colour and sound reveal themselves to us. We perceive both. *What* do we then perceive in respect of *both?* What *can* we perceive here?

We shall let *Socrates* ask this (185 a 8):

Περὶ δὴ φωνῆς καὶ περὶ χρόας πρῶτον μὲν αὐτὸ τοῦτο περὶ ἀμφοτέρων ἦ διανοῇ, ὅτι ἀμφοτέρω ἐστόν;

[Theaetetus] Ἔγωγε.

'In regard to sound *and* colour: don't you first of all perceive, taking them in, that they both *are?*'

'Yes.'

We perceive *both* colour and sound, both the blue of the sky and the song of the lark, first and foremost as *existing,* πρῶτον μέν, 'in the first place', can be said only if *something else* is also perceivable, indeed something over which this 'in the first place' has priority. Thus Socrates says:

Οὐκοῦν καὶ ὅτι ἑκάτερον ἑκατέρου μὲν ἕτερον, ἑαυτῷ δὲ ταὐτόν;

[Theaetetus] Τί μήν;

'Not also (besides that they are perceived as beings) this, that each is different from the other and the same as itself?'

'What else?'

We perceive, therefore, the *existing* objects of perception: colour *and* sound. Colour is one being, sound is another; or to put it the other way around, the one exists as something different in relation to the other. As beings, both colour and sound are different to each other *and* the same as themselves. Different with respect to each other, the same with respect to themselves, the one *and* the other existing: just this is meant when we say that we perceive *both as beings.*

Socrates continues:

Καὶ ὅτι ἀμφοτέρω δύο, ἑκάτερον δὲ ἕν;

[Theaetetus] Καὶ τοῦτο.

'Therefore both together, the one *and* the other, are *two*, and each on its own account is *one*?'

'Yes, that also.'

Only because the one being *and* the other being are perceived is it possible to *count* them. The one and the other are not already as such two; we must first add 'and' as a 'plus'. Every plus is an and, but not every and is a plus. A plurality is still not something countable as such, it is not yet a so-and-so-many. Both must first be given *as beings,* one and the other, and then we *can* take them as two, although we need not do so.

Socrates continues:

Οὐκοῦν καὶ εἴτε ἀνομοίω εἴτε ὁμοίω ἀλλήλοιν, δυνατὸς εἶ ἐπιστέψασθαι;

[Theaetetus] Ἴσως.

'Are you not also able to tell whether they are *like or unlike* each other?'

'Presumably.'

So in looking at both (in the broadest sense of 'look') we can ascertain their difference or non-difference (in this case, that they are different).

The first step towards Plato's goal has thus been taken: he has indicated what we *can* perceive when we simultaneously perceive colour and sound. The emphasis on δυνατός in Socrates' last question is significant, for Plato wants to draw attention to the circumstance that, while we do not *necessarily* have to expressly apprehend what is additionally given in our co-perception of colour and sound, we always need to be able to do this. What is thus indicated is nothing trivial and arbitrary, but refers to an interrelation, *above all* to the fact that both colour and sound must be perceived *as existing* before we can perceive their difference and sameness, equivalence and non-equivalence, countability etc. By the same token, when they show themselves to us as *different*, we perceive them, whether we are aware of this or not, as an existing one and another.

We perceive all this (being, being one, different, both, the same, two, one, identity and non-identity) *in addition* to the colour and sound. So we have an irremovable *excess* (as we provisionally call it) of perceivables within the region of perception, and it is incumbent on us to again soberly re-enact the proof that Plato provides for this. We do not know what this excess (existing, being different and the same) is. However much the nature of this 'more' may trouble us, and however helpless we may be in this regard, the important thing for the moment is just to *see that* there is an excess.

There is one more point to be made. Right at the beginning of the discussion (185 a 4), Socrates asks: εἴ τι ἄρα περὶ ἀμφοτέρων διανοῇ', 'how is it then we perceive something, when we take in both of these together?' He grasps the perceiving of *both* as διὰ. . ., as an assimilating perceiving [*durchnehmendes Vernehmen*] (translating διανοεῖν in this way and not as 'thinking'); and this assimilating perceiving is able to perceive the demonstrated excess, or as Plato now says instead (185 b 5): ἐπισκέψασθαι. The latter expression stands immediately for διανοεῖν and certainly does not mean 'thinking'. It means, rather, to look at a thing, thereby perceiving something about it. Schleiermacher translates the word as 'to inquire into' [*erforschen*], but this is quite erroneous.[1] The immediate perceiving of colour and sound together is not inquiry of any kind. This is the first clear evidence that Siavoeiv does not mean 'thinking', but must be understood in the sense of a specific kind of perceiving and accepting.[2]

But even if this and other evidence (which we shall presently come to) were lacking, we should have already grasped, from the whole constellation of problems, that Plato highlights precisely the following: that in the perception of something heard and seen we perceive *more* than sound and colour, that this 'more' pertains to the *existence* of colour and sound and is perceived so self-evidently and *immediately* that at first we do not pay the least attention to it. That the blue sky 'blues', that it is in blueness, that the lark which sings is in singing: all this remains so obvious that we do not give it any further notice. We *delight* in the natural blue-existing sky and in the singing-existing bird. At the moment, however, we are not concerned with delighting in them, but with seeing what we take in *over and above* the colour and sound, also and precisely when in such delight we pay no regard to this, and even less inquire into it. Precisely when we are lying in the meadow and thinking of *nothing* else do we perceive this 'excess', i.e. these several beings, the one and the other, and each itself the same.

B. Step Two: Inquiry into What Perceives the Excess in the Perceived

§ 27. The Sense-Organs: No Passage-way to the Common in Everything Perceived

The *second step* of the inquiry (185 b 7–186 a) now follows. Socrates poses the crucial question:

Ταῦτα δὴ πάντα διὰ τίνος περὶ αὐτοῖν διανοῇ; οὔτε γὰρ δι᾽ ἀκοῆς οὔτε δι᾽ ὄψεως οἷόν τε τὸ κοινὸν λαμβάνειν περὶ αὐτῶν.

'Now in what way do you perceive all this [the indicated excess] attaching to them [colour and sound]? For it is impossible, either through hearing or sight, to discover, or take in, what they have in common.'

Again there is a new word for διανοεῖν: λαμβάνειν, to take. But what is the organ through which we take the excess to ourselves? This question is and must be posed, because it was previously shown that everything perceivable is perceived through an *organ*. It is now said that this excess is τὸ κοινόν, i.e. what colour and sound have in *common*. Plato says (185 b 8 f.): τὸ κοινὸν περὶ αὐτῶν, and not (as at 185 b 7) αὐτοῖν; i.e. the excess is common not only to colour and sound, but to colour, taste, sound, smell and touch. When salty things, smooth things, rough things etc. are perceived, they are perceived *as existing*; each is the same as itself and different to the others. This common character applies to *everything* we perceive, to everything perceptible in its diversity.

Colour, sound, taste etc. are all existing, each identical with itself and different from one another. Do we *hear* this being-different, do we see it with our eyes? Do we hear or see their existing? Of course we do not. So in any case one thing is undeniable, namely that we cannot immediately discover the appropriate organ, and yet, just as in other cases of perception, we must be able to indicate one. Assuming one could inquire into whether colour and sound are salty, it would immediately be clear which organ would decide this: the salty is perceived through the tongue. But are we clear about the organ through which we perceive 'being' or 'being non-identical'? Here we are at a loss; we are unable to discover an organ through which existing, being-different etc. are perceivable. The only thing we can no longer deny is *that* these latter are perceivable, that we *are able* to perceive 'being', 'difference', 'sameness' etc. After all the foregoing considerations it is also clear that we perceive these *through* something; it is just that we do not know what this is, and we are not, without further ado, able to discover it. So the same question arises, this time more pointedly (185 c 4–8):

Καλῶς λέγεις. ἡ δὲ δὴ διὰ τίνος δύναμις τό τ' ἐπὶ πᾶσι κοινὸν καὶ τὸ ἐπὶ τούτοις δηλοῖ σοι, ᾧ τὸ 'ἔστιν' ἐπονομάζεις καὶ τὸ 'οὐκ ἔστι' καὶ ἃ νυνδὴ ἠρωτῶμεν περὶ αὐτῶν; τούτοις πᾶσι ποῖα ἀποδώσεις ὄργανα δι' ὧν αἰσθάνεται ἡμῶν τὸ αἰσθανόμενον ἕκαστα;

This passage does not tell us anything new, yet for what follows, and for the whole, it is crucial to understand its *methodological* intention. Schleiermacher translates:

'Very good. By what means is the faculty exerted which reveals to you what is common to all these things, and which allows you to ascribe being or non- being to them, and those other attributes of which we were speaking?'

Since the received way of rendering this text shows that the inner unfolding of the problem has not been understood, we are forced to alter it; or better, we do not need to change the text, but only to remove a misleading way of writing. The sentence, presented in the form of a question, begins with Καλῶς λέγεις. ἡ δὲ δὴ διὰ τίνος δύναμις . . . and ends with περὶ αὐτῶν; If we leave the accents off δια τινος (nor did the Greeks write these) then we can just as easily, indeed we must, read it as διά τινος, where the sentence no longer is, or no longer *needs* to be, a question.[3] The question first begins with τούτοις πᾶσι ποῖα . . . The sentence ἡ δὲ δὴ διά τινος. . . now becomes a more pointed summary of what the inquiry has thus far unfolded, and has the following meaning:

'Thus the faculty that somehow provides a passage-way, reveals to you what is *common* to your perceptions of colour, sound, and everything else, and which you call "is" and "is not".'

What has occurred through our writing διά τινος? What is the significance of our transposition of the question into a simple declaration? In the context of the whole train of thought it has the methodological meaning that Socrates once again establishes the *existence* of an excess of perception, thus of a *faculty* which provides a passage-way (that we do not recognize) to this and makes it perceivable. This is the undeniable state of affairs. With regard to what was previously seen, Socrates can once again, with full clarity, put the vital question:

τούτοις πᾶσι ποῖα ἀποδώσεις ὄργανα δι᾿ ὧν αἰσθάνεται ἡμῶν τὸ αἰσθανόμενον ἕκαστα;

[δηλοῦν now stands for διανοεῖν] 'With what sense-organs do you perceive this common element [this δηλουμένοις, over and above colour and sound]?'

It is indubitably the case that something must provide a passage-way (διά τινος); i.e. it is not doubted that ἡ δύναμις is διά τινος. What remains in question is just the nature of this passage-way. Only by so asking do we arrive at the inner sense and movement of the thought. Otherwise the entire section would become superfluous and fail to correspond with the whole; it would not belong in the text at all. What is so extraordinary about every Platonic text is that each 'and', 'but', and 'perhaps' is set in a quite definite unambiguous position, i.e. these words are not just idle.

What then is the answer? To begin with there is none. Instead, Theaetetus himself attempts, by giving his own account of the matter, to establish what, in all perceptions of colour, sound, smell etc., is additionally perceivable. We see that the young Theaetetus does not simply defer to Socrates' superiority but wishes to enact the proof for himself in an originary way. This leads him to grasp the peculiar excess in what is perceivable in the perceptible (ταῦτα πάντα, 185 b 7) more directly and precisely. He gives linguistic expression to this through nominalization (185 c 9 ff.):

Οὐσίαν λέγεις καὶ τὸ μὴ εἶναι, καὶ ὁμοιότητα καὶ ἀνομοιότητα, καὶ τὸ ταὐτόν τε καὶ τὸ ἕτερον, ἔτι δὲ ἕν τε καὶ τὸν ἄλλον ἀριθμὸν περὶ αὐτῶν.

'Being and non-being, identity and non-identity, sameness, countability.'

This nominalized grasping of the excess is not without significance. Theaetetus adds, on his own account:

δῆλον δὲ ὅτι καὶ ἄρτιόν τε καὶ περιττὸν ἐρωτᾷς, καὶ τἆλλα ὅσα τούτοις ἕπεται,

'In some cases we also perceive odd and even and the like',

thereby making the fundamental point that to this excess there belongs everything ὅσα τούτοις ἕπεται, 'which follows from what has already been shown'. This does not refer to what occurs in later, differently directed perceptions, but means all determinations that can be *built up* from being and non-being, sameness and difference, identity and non-identity etc., all the concrete characters which in their content essentially involve and presuppose being, i.e. every being such-and-such – as that which determines beings as the beings they are. In this way Theaetetus shows not only that he grasps the full scope of this excess of perception, but that he is himself able to pose Socrates' question in all its sharpness (185 d 3 f.):

διὰ τίνος ποτὲ τῶν τοῦ σώματος τῇ ψυχῇ αἰσθανόμεθα,

'through which bodily organs does the soul perceive the perceptions [of the indicated excess]'.

This is important because it now becomes clear that the soul also needs a δι' οὗ. At first the question was: ᾧ or δι' οὗ? We now see that in the new version of the question both are taken together, ᾧ (ᾗ) and δι' οὗ, but without them any longer being confused with one another. The soul is that which, ᾧ . . ., that which carries out the perceiving, that which perceives; the question remains, δι' οὗ . . ., through what, in what way, does it perceive the totality of the perceivable.

Socrates confirms to Theaetetus that he is 'doing well' in his elucidation of the question:

'Υπέρευ, ὦ Θεαίτητε, ἀκολουθεῖς, καὶ ἔστιν ἃ ἐρωτῶ αὐτὰ ταῦτα (185 d 5 f.).

'Bravo, Theaetetus! You follow me exactly; that is just what I meant by my question.'

If one surveys the foregoing discussion (and what follows), one might wonder at the laborious and repetitious way in which the problem is unfolded. One is tempted to pass over the inner course of the dialogue seeking eagerly for results. But in this case one would miss what is essential, one would never achieve the proper philosophical stance which alone allows the decisive content to be appropriated. In all genuine works of philosophy the decisive content does not stand there in so many words, but is what brings into motion the *totality* of a living interpretation. So I shall refer, under four points, to what must be kept in mind concerning this whole question.

1 For the first time in the history of philosophy, the excess in perception (over and above what is given in sense) is systematically demonstrated and treated as a fundamental problem.

2 This excess and its presence within the sphere of perception is initially so strange that everything depends on being sufficiently unprejudiced to simply accept and register it, even if there is no obvious way of grasping it more precisely or explaining its possibility.

3 On the contrary, the investigation must (therefore the seemingly constant repetitions) ever again confirm this excess, in order then to properly inquire into its origin.

4 Plato has intentionally brought the discussion and development of the question to a head, so that we are struck by the surprising turn which its solution involves.

Only if we pay attention to all this we can obtain some insight into the inner sureness of the dialogue, and into the unprecedented conscientiousness and sobriety of its individual steps. We begin to have

some intimation of the model of actual working philosophizing that is
presented to us.

§ 28. The Soul as What Views the Κοινά in διανοεῖν

By resolute immersion in the entire content of the question Theaetetus
becomes capable of giving the decisive answer himself, albeit rather
cautiously. It appears to him that (185 d 8 ff.):

πλήν γ' ὅτι μοι δοκεῖ τὴν ἀρχὴν οὐδ' εἶναι τοιοῦτον οὐδὲν τούτοις
ὄργανον ἴδιον ὥσπερ ἐκείνοις, ἀλλ' αὐτὴ δι' αὐτῆς ἡ ψυχὴ τὰ
κοινά μοι φαίνεται περὶ πάντων ἐπισκοπεῖν.

'There is no special organ for this [for this excess] as there are for the
others [colour, sound, smell], but the soul itself views, through itself,
what all things have in common.'

So we see that the κοινά (being – non-being, sameness – difference)
are precisely what allow us to grasp more concretely this region of inner
perceivability. In their total constellation, it is precisely these Koiva which
co-constitute the region of perceivability.[4] That wherein they agree
is a singularity, indeed a singularity in which they *come together*, ἕν,
εἰς; ὃ συντείνει (184 d 4), such as belongs (as we already know) to
the soul, and to which only the soul, according to its essence, has a
relationship.

There is no *specific* organ, certainly no corporeal, bodily organ, for
perceiving being, non-being, sameness, difference and so forth, as in
the perceiving of colours, sounds etc. Instead, the soul itself, δι' αὐτῆς,
in perceiving the first mentioned characters (being), does so through
and by itself, in this way grasping the common.

How has this answer been arrived at? On the one hand negatively, by
the circumstance that no bodily organ can be discovered for perceiving
e.g. difference. On the other hand *positively*, because what is to be
perceived (being, difference etc.) is itself such that it can be perceived
only through the soul. Why this should be so is not immediately clear.
Indeed, is it not all too easy and naive to call upon the soul in this way?

When the body cannot manage it, we appeal to the soul for assistance! But this is not the situation. We should reflect upon *how*, and *how alone*, the so-called 'soul' was brought into the present context of questions. As μία τις ἰδέα εἰς ἢν πάντα ταῦτα συντείνει as 'something like a singular sighted nature, into everything perceptible is brought together'. We interpreted this to mean that the soul holds up the *singular* region of perceivability into which everything perceivable converges and is held in unity and sameness.

But is it this which is now spoken of? Let us see! Perception of the excess is treated in the context of being, non-being, being-different, difference. These have already received the character of κοινά. In what way are they common? E.g. being: we perceive colour and sound as existing. We perceive *their* being, i.e. in perceiving being we perceive something that is common to both. This singularity, being, which they have in common does not contain anything of colour and sound, neither anything of smell. Being-different is likewise a κοινόν. To be sure, difference separates one from the other (colour from sound)! It is therefore definitely not something they have in common! So it appears. Colour and sound are different only in so far as they can be distinguished. They can be distinguished from each other only in so far as they are held up together and compared. They come together in comparison, albeit only to emerge as different; this means that *each* is different, that difference pertains to both, that they *agree* in being-different: a singularity, and indeed such that 'both are extended therein', and must be so extended, in order that they can be different. So we see that this κοινά this totality belonging to the excess, shows us what is perceived in this *one* region of perceivability, *into which* colour, sound etc. show themselves in their diversity. Therefore the κοινά have precisely the character referred to earlier, namely that it is the soul which relates to them: a singularity, an extending of one to the other.

The connection between the excess of perception and the soul itself is thus understood in a properly *positive* sense; we understand why it must be the soul, and this alone, which perceives τὰ κοινά. Plato says: αὐτὴ δι' αὐτῆς ἡ ψυχή, the soul perceives everything of this kind through itself. But what can διά mean here, where no *bodily* organ, indeed no kind of organ *whatever*, can be meant? Perhaps a 'soul-organ' and 'forces'? Not at all! But does the soul itself 'possess' a possible passage-way? It does not have this, but rather is this itself, thus holding up the region of a unitary perceivability. Holding up this region, the soul passes through this. *Intrinsically* and as such it *extends over* to the other which can be given to it, and it maintains itself only in such extension. As that which intrinsically perceives, the soul is itself a being-extended-to, a passage-way, an extending over to. It is the soul which, in its own relating of itself to something giveable, makes possible comportment towards . . ., i.e. through its precursory perceiving it constructs its own extension, within which a passage-way can as it were draw itself in.

The verbal form of Theaetetus' answer also provides us with further verification of the meaning we attribute to διανοεῖν. It was introduced as a comportment wherein we perceive something in respect of *both* colour *and* sound. We have already seen (185 b 5) that ἐπισκέψασθαι[5] too means this, i.e. to see something in looking at something; now (185 e 2) ἐπισκοπεῖν, to direct the perceiving apprehending look towards something. In the perceiving of being, non-being, being-different etc. the soul is itself *seeing, immediately* perceiving. Indeed, in what follows Plato uses the expression ἐπισκοπεῖν in a still more comprehensive sense, which is completely appropriate to his formulation of the question.

After the young Theaetetus has brought forth the decisive answer to the question, Socrates says (185 e 3 ff.):

Καλὸς γὰρ εἶ ὦ Θεαίτητε, καὶ οὐχ, ὡς ἔλεγε Θεόδωρος, αἰσχρός.

'Why, you are beautiful, Theaetetus, and not, as Theodorus said, ugly.'

In his first description of the young Theaetetus, Theodorus had said that the former was snub-nosed and goggle-eyed, albeit not in such a pronounced way as Socrates. Why then does Socrates now call him 'beautiful'? The reason is immediately given:

ὁ γὰρ καλῶς λέγων καλός τε καὶ ἀγαθός,

which means literally 'for whoever speaks beautifully is beautiful as well as good'.

In estimating the beauty of a person, everything depends on his λέγειν.[6] That he 'speaks beautifully' does not mean that he uses brilliant words in the manner of an orator. λέγειν means to gather, to present and reveal something as gathered, and in this way to show it to others. Whoever *shows* something as beautifully gathered is himself beautiful and capable. Only someone who is *inwardly* gathered and connected is capable of such a thing, i.e. someone who possesses that illuminative power of essence which alone makes him fit (ἀγαθός) for human existence.

Incidentally, the καλὸς καὶ ἀγαθός is also what the Greeks understand by the 'classical'. It is quite unnecessary to call upon the assistance of art historians to tell us what the classical is. It is a question of the existence of man. Since the Greeks did not at all 'enjoy' works of art as we do, καλός is a determination which does not primarily relate to works of art, but concerns the Dasein of man. To this Dasein there also belongs the *uncanniness* of which Sophocles speaks in the *Antigone* (line 332 f.): 'There are many uncanny things, but nothing is more so than man himself'. Such is Greek classicism. This remark, at such a decisive point in the dialogue, indicates a positive step towards the understanding of the whole problem.

The καλῶς λέγειν is the genuine beauty of human existence, precisely because man in his essence is ζῷον λόγον ἔχον, the 'living being possessed of speech', i.e. to whose innermost essence there belongs speech. In so far as man speaks out about the beings to which he comports, and thus also about himself, he deconceals beings and makes them manifest, thereby letting *truth* occur. Theaetetus is 'beautiful' in the Greek sense, and is called so by Socrates (Plato), because, immersing himself in the vital question and following its connections through, he confined his utterances to what he was truly able to make his own.[7]

This answer of Theaetetus also spares Socrates from a long and tedious discussion (185 e 7 f.):

τοῦτο γὰρ ἦν ὃ καὶ αὐτῷ μοι ἐδόκει, ἐβουλόμην δὲ καὶ σοὶ δόξαι.

'This, my dear Theaetetus, was also my opinion, and was what I wanted to show you.'

Socrates now sums up the unitary clarification achieved by Theaetetus (185 e 6 f.):

φαίνεταί σοι τὰ μὲν αὐτὴ δι' αὐτῆς ἡ ψυχὴ ἐπισκοπεῖν, τὰ δὲ διὰ τῶν τοῦ σώματος δυνάμεων.

Here we again encounter ἐπισκοπεῖν. But notice that it is used for the perceiving of colour, sound etc., as well as (in the same sense) for the perceiving of being, non-being, being-different etc.

'In perceiving something the soul apprehends two things: τὰ μέν, the one in itself and through itself; τὰ δέ, the other by means of the bodily faculties.'

In other words, and in regard to the guiding question, it is denied that in perceptual comportment to the perceived the taking up of a relationship to the latter is twofold. Clearly, a duo is now combined and simultaneously separated. Both are present in perception: one, the indicated excess, being, non-being etc. is perceived by the soul itself; the other is likewise perceived by the soul, but by means of bodily faculties.

The second step of the inquiry has thus been completed; the answer has been given as to how the soul perceives being, non-being and the like.

C. Step Three: The Soul's Relation to Being as Striving for Being

In the *third step*, which extends from 186 a 2 to b 10, the soul's relationship to being is more precisely characterized.

§ 29. The Priority of Striving for Being in the Soul as Relationship to the Perceived

Let us once again bring the whole into view. The perceiving comportment to the perceived involves a *relationship* of the perceiver to the perceivable. The clarification of the essence of perception (perceivedness) must establish what this relationship consists in. For this it was first necessary to investigate the content of the perceived. Besides colour, sound, smell etc. there was something more – the being of these, otherness, sameness and so forth – and corresponding to this 'double' content something twofold in the *relationship* to the perceived, a relationship that is taken up first of all through the soul itself and that simultaneously occurs through the bodily organs.

However, something is still missing in the foregoing discussion of this perceptual relationship. We saw merely that the content of the perceived contains an excess, and that this must be related in its perceivability and perceivedness to the soul itself. But nothing has so far been said concerning the *character* of the soul's relationship to being, non-being etc. This is now clarified in the third step.

Why is this necessary? Since no organ comes into play here, it is puzzling how the soul *through itself* has a relationship to being. If it is capable of clarification, the nature of this 'through itself' will at the same time characterize the *essence* of the soul more clearly; to be sure, 'soul' in the indicated sense. But the third step also contains the complementary counter-inquiry to the first step: there the excess as such, here the nature of its relationship to the soul. The discussion of the question of αἴσθησις leads to the goal, for ψυχή becomes visible in such a way that it is now possible to determine its essence, thus to confer on the word a fulfilled and grounded meaning and legitimate its name.

However, the soul is not any kind of thing, to which a relationship can now be attached; instead, it is itself the relationship to . . . To be such a relationship is to be soul. Therefore the inquiry into the more precise nature of the soul's relationship to being, non-being etc. will have to ask about how the soul *relates*, as relationship, *to* the indicated excess. After the foregoing discussion, this excess is now what is *more familiar* to us; what now occurs is a retrospective inquiry concerning the *relationship* which belongs to this excess, namely that of the soul. In exhibiting the excess the first thing encountered was εἶναι (185 a 9: ἐστόν), being. This is what we perceive πρῶτον, before everything else; it is what we apprehend first, and not by chance but necessarily so.

The third step sets out from here, and asks (186 a 2 f.):

Ποτέρων οὖν τίθης τὴν οὐσίαν; τοῦτο γὰρ μάλιστα ἐπὶ πάντων παρέπεται.

'So then, to which of the two [the moments of the relationship of perceiving to the perceived] do you assign being? For this, more than anything else, already belongs to all things.'

In this concise characterization of being (which we shall encounter again later) every word is important. We already know that everything belonging to the excess is κοινόν, common to all the individual modes of sensory perception. The discussion is again introduced (as with the first step) by showing that being comes first, for all the other determinations such as sameness, difference, otherness etc. are already in themselves *being*-the-same, *being*-different, *being*-other. Among these κοινά, being has priority as always already assumed and present. Whatever we perceive by seeing, hearing, smelling, tasting, shows itself to also have, somehow and above all, the character of a being [*Seienden*], in some sense of being [*Sein*], Being is what is least not-there, i.e. it is what can never be gotten rid of so to speak, when we perceive something through the senses, and indeed ἐπὶ πάντων: the comprehensive function of being with regard to all regions of the perceivable. Whatever we imagine, perceive, think, posit, already has the character of a being.

This curious, comprehensive intrusiveness of being, over and into all regions of the given and perceivable, distinguishes it precisely as what belongs to the perceivable 'first of all' (πρῶτον), as there, παρά, i.e. present, as what 'presences' ['anwest'] whenever beings show themselves (not just when we apprehend them!). This, apparently, teaches us nothing about what being is as such, but only about how it behaves so to speak.

The question must now be answered as to whether being is perceived through a bodily organ or through an organ-free comportment, immediately by the soul itself. Theaetetus answers:

Ἐγὼ μὲν ὧν αὐτὴ ἡ ψυχὴ καθ' αὐτὴν ἐπορέγεται.

'In my view, οὐσία belongs to what the soul, through and by itself, strives for.'

Schleiermacher translates ἐπορέγεται in the wrong way, and misses the problem, when he says: it belongs to what the soul conceives [*erfaβt*][8] through itself; the Greek word is not λαμβάνει, but ἐπορέγεται. ἐπορέγεσθαι means to strive after something, and indeed the middle voice: what is striven for is not just striven for by the soul, but is so for it itself and *only* for it. For this reason there appears not αὐτὴ δι᾽ αὐτῆς, but καθ᾽ αὐτήν; to be sure, κατά means as much as διά, but it also conveys that, in striving, what is striven for is related back to the striving soul itself.[9]

We thus have a fundamental characteristic of the soul's relationship to being. Being is that towards which the soul strives, not just from time to time and to any purpose, but essentially. The soul is this striving for being, i.e. in Platonic terms, the word 'soul' simply *means* striving for being. After our earlier considerations, the thesis must run as follows: striving for being co-constitutes the relationship of perceiving to what is perceived.

§ 30. Having and Striving

a) Apparent Incompatibility between Striving and Perception

What does 'striving' mean? This is the important question here. What is this *relationship* of man to being which we call 'striving for' being?

Perception is a receiving *having-before-oneself* of something given. But if in perception the soul's relationship to being is supposed to be a striving, the object of perception cannot be *possessed* in such a relationship, the perception cannot be a *having*-before-oneself of the perceived! Further, in seeing the blue of the sky and in hearing the song of the lark, we do not *strive* after these beings! On the contrary, while lying in the meadow we simply encounter these kinds of things. In no sense do we strive for them, but we allow them to sway gently over us. Perceiving is accepting, and, in such accepting, *having*, but it is not a striving. In its essential nature, striving is such that we strive only for what we do *not yet* have. Thus the relationship to being in perception cannot be seen as a striving. Is Schleiermacher, therefore, ultimately correct when he translates ὀρέγεσθαι as the *conceiving* [*Erfassen*] of being? But Plato says ἐπορέγεσθαι, which means striving for somethings. This, however, does not fit with the essence of perceptual *having*-before-oneself. Each seems to exclude the other. How can we discover the right way forward?

Or is there indeed a way of reconciling the striving comportment with perceptual having-before-oneself? We can say we strive *for* 'perceptions', i.e. for what is perceptible in perception, for *beings* in other words. So in this way we strive for beings. But two objections can be made against this.

First, not every perception is necessarily *striven* for by us; on the contrary, most simply happen to us and rule over us.

Second and most importantly, Plato does not say that perception is *preceded* by and originates from striving, but that the relationship of perception to the perceived in part consists in the relationship to being, and that this latter is a striving.

So the reconciliation does not work, and the problem returns in all its difficulty: on the one hand Plato speaks (there can be no quibbling on this point) of a 'striving' relationship to being, on the other hand our understanding of the essence of perception as accepting and having-before- oneself excludes any striving. But is our understanding of the essence of perception really fitting and adequate? We are just beginning to gain some insight into the *essence* of αἴσθησις through dialogue with Plato. And the same goes for 'striving': so what is this? Have we as yet attempted to clarify its essence? Not at all. With no grounding in the relevant phenomena, all we have done is to 'argue' that accepting is different to striving, and that the latter therefore cannot constitute the relational character of the former.

b) Losing Oneself in Immediate Perception

So we must look once again at what is meant here, or better, we must for the first time actually *look*. Let us bring to mind the example we mentioned earlier, imagining ourselves as lost in perception of the blue sky and the lark's song. We encounter them and they show themselves to us as beings. We perceive, therefore, these beings themselves: the blue that is, the singing that is. Is *everything* in perception an *accepting*? *What* is it that is accepted? What does it *mean* that we perceive these beings which we encounter? Do we occupy ourselves with the fact that they are beings? No; for in our situation, lying in the meadow, we are not at all disposed to *occupy* ourselves with anything. On the contrary, we *lose* ourselves in the blue, in what gives itself; we follow the song along; we let ourselves *be taken*, as it were, by these beings, such that they *surround* us. To be sure, *beings* surround us, and not nothing, neither anything imaginary. But we do not occupy ourselves with them as beings.

What would happen were we to do that? We would have to bring the blue of the sky and the song of the lark closer to us *as* beings, *as* present things. In that case, we couldn't lose ourselves in the blue and in the song, but would have to *dis*-regard [*ab-sehen*] the blue as blue and the song as song, so as to look at them both as *beings*. We can indeed do this at any time, i.e. we can take up a relationship to the given such that we are aware only that *something* and not nothing is present, that something stands over against us. But in this way we have already left immediate perception behind. The latter, on the other hand, loses itself in the perceived beings and does not stand itself over against anything. Precisely this lost and self-losing perception gains the beings in their immediacy, the blue that is and the song that is. This immediate, i.e. self-losing perceiving takes [*nimmt*] and per-ceives [*ver-nimmt*] *in as much as* it lets itself be taken along. In this way it perceives beings, but not in respect of the fact that they are. The beings do not stand under this kind of *regard* [*Hinsicht*]. This kind of regard is *lacking*. In immediate perception, beings are perceived, as we say, in a manner which is *non-regarding* [*hinsichtlos*].

c) Non-regarding and Non-conceptual Perceiving

But is something perceived *as* a being when we do not perceive it *with respect* to the fact that it is? This is indeed a tricky question, which cannot be decided by the everyday logic of healthy common sense. We must allow the matter itself to speak. Let us look at what essentially occurs in such perceiving.

How do things stand in the situation when we do *not* perceive what we encounter in a non-regarding way, but rather occupy ourselves with the fact that it is? We can only do this by taking it as an existing being, i.e. by having regard to the fact that being belongs to it. We can pay regard to being, so-and-so-being, being-different and so forth, only if we know *in general what* being *means*. Do we know this?

'Being' is the nominalization of the verb 'to be'. The latter's most familiar form is 'is'. 'The door is closed': everyone understands the 'is'. We know without further ado what 'is' means. We are quite confident in our use of 'is' and 'being' and cognate expressions. In a particular case it can be doubtful whether the door is or is not closed; but we know and must know what 'is' means, for otherwise we could not even doubt whether the door 'is', or 'is' not, closed. We *understand* the word 'is' ('being'), we know the meaning; but we are unable to say what we 'really' mean by it. We understand it, but we do not *grasp* it. We do not have a concept of 'is'. We understand 'is' and 'being', but in a *non-conceptual* way.

When we perceive what is encountered as something that is, we take it in *respect* of the being that belongs to it. In so doing, however, already and in advance, we understand this being of the being [*dieses Sein des Seienden*] in a *non-conceptual* way. Precisely because we do not grasp being (most people never obtain a concept of being and yet they live at every moment in the understanding of being) we also cannot say how this being *belongs* to the being to which we attribute it. We are unable to specify the manner in which the being stands in its being. But despite this non-conceptual mode of understanding, we can accept, take in, and intend the beings in diverse aspects of their being and so-being.

Immediate self-losing perception, carried along by what is perceived, is both non-conceptual (in respect of the being understood therein) and non-regarding. By paying no explicit attention to being, nor grasping it conceptually, we are free to lose ourselves in what we encounter. But all this does not mean we lack an understanding of being. On the contrary, our understanding of 'is' and 'being' is not in the least diminished by the fact that we do not occupy ourselves with their meaning. Instead, this understanding of being is always already there with our Dasein; only for this reason is it possible for us to perceive a being *as* a being and make it into an object. A being does not first become a being due to our occupying ourselves with it as such. How could we ever occupy ourselves with a being as such, if beings were not already given in advance and familiar to us? Yet this familiarity of beings occurs in a non-conceptual and nonregarding understanding of being.

To be sure, this familiarity of beings in the Dasein of man has its own *history*. It is never just simply present, as neutral and constant throughout the history of humanity, but is itself rooted in what we call the *ground-stance* of man: in what nature, history, and reality as a whole *are* to man, and *how* they are this. This groundstance of man's Dasein can be lost, and for contemporary man not only is it largely lost, it is already no longer comprehensible. The familiarity of beings is itself uprooted, but this rootlessness itself is not just something negative: it has organized itself as it were, and has now gained domination, i.e. it has taken over the regulation and legislation for the relationship of man to being and beings. Whether something 'is something', whether there is 'anything in it' as we say, is no longer decided by the being itself and the power with which it can immediately speak to man, but something only *is* something, or is nothing, depending on whether one *talks* about it or not, depending on whether people *take an interest* in it or not. So, in both great and small things, contemporary man lives according to what is prescribed by journalism in the broadest sense. There exist 'literary interests'. Works of art, irrespective of their inner association with cult and ritual, no longer have their own being and effectiveness, but exist for the interest of American tourists, visitors to museums, and historians of art (who explain how art can be 'appreciated'). It is the journalist who decides what 'nature' is, so that e.g. a literary midget from Berlin presumes to advise us on this. When the familiarity of beings in their immediate power is uprooted to this degree, it is certainly difficult to awaken a real understanding for the unmediated perception of beings and their immediacy.

And yet, precisely because this familiarity of beings can be destroyed, it can also be saved and re-established. This is what we are concerned with. Instead of undertaking an irrelevant analysis of experiences, everything is attack and decision. The much-praised 'objectivity' of the sciences remains a self-deception as long as it does not involve a proper fundamental relationship to the object. This can only grow from a groundstance of Dasein; it can be neither attained nor preserved through scholarly pedantry. It is only the groundstance and force of the Dasein of man that can decide the meaning of the objectivity of objects. The primordiality of the understanding of being, and the power of familiarity of beings, are one and the same, they belong together. The more primordially the understanding of being arises from the depth of

Dasein, the more grounded is the right to the concept of being, i.e. the necessity of philosophy to bring being to conceptual expression.

On the basis of what we have thus far shown, we can obtain a more precise inner view of the essence of the perceptual comportment. It is a non-regarding and non-conceptual perceiving of beings – which means that we *occupy* ourselves neither with beings as such (with the blue as existing, with the song as existing) nor do we grasp their being conceptually (e.g. being-different as a specific content of knowledge). Perception is not *con*ceiving of beings in their being. In perception, *beings* are perceived, but not being. The latter is not anything perceived, not anything accepted and *had*. The relationship to being in the immediate perception of *beings* is therefore not at all a *perceiving*. But if the relationship to being is definitely not perceiving, thus also not conceiving, the way is clear for the possibility of a *different kind* of characterization of this relationship. So what kind of relationship is it? If the relationship to being is not one of having, the possibility remains that it is something else – Plato says that it is an ἐπορέγεσθαι, a 'striving'.

d) Free Possession of Truth (Knowledge) Only in the Relationship of Striving towards What Is Striven for; Inauthentic and Authentic Having

What does 'striving for' mean here? What does *striving* mean as such? We have already discussed this in a general way. We said that we strive for what we *do not yet* have. Proof: if we already had it, we could not and would not strive for it. In that case striving would make no sense at all. On the vulgar conception, striving is intrinsically a not-having. Proceeding from this quite reasonable observation we must say that, assuming also that the relationship to being does not have the character of a perceiving having, it still cannot be a striving. For while the latter is indeed a not- having, the relationship to being (*qua* relationship *to* . . .) is still somehow a 'having' of something. So it appears. But instead of engaging in clever argumentation let us *look* at the essence of striving.

To strive *for* something: that for which we strive, that to which striving is directed, is the *object of striving*. Is not the object *there* in the striving? To be sure, I might think: not only is it simply there and present, but it makes itself felt, it pulls and draws us towards it. The object of striving holds us to itself. Seen the other way around: the object of striving is there in the striving and is absent precisely in non-striving. Only in the striving for it do we have it 'there'! But do we *have it*? We are indeed only striving for it! The whereto of the striving, the object of striving as such, is had in the striving; it is had *as* the object of striving – and yet still as something striven for, thus as not-had. A curious phenomenon this: had and yet not had! The striving relationship is intrinsically a having-before-oneself, a having that is at the same time a not-having. We already see that everything depends on clarifying what 'having' means here. Thus the problem of determining the essence of striving is not so much a question of what striving is, as of what *having* is, where having is understood as a human *comportment*.

The question concerning the essence of striving is therefore a question concerning the essence of *having*. What is 'having'? In the following we shall encounter this question again and be constantly occupied with it. At this point it is important not just for the question concerning the essence of striving for being. Let us recall that the dialogue deals with the essence of *knowledge*. We have conceived knowledge as the 'possession' of truth; possession is *one* mode of having. What possession is cannot be decided at one stroke. The clarification of the essence of having proceeds in a way designed to advance our question concerning the essence of striving, and will later serve to clarify the essence of knowledge as *one* mode of possessing truth.

Having something always has the character of being 'finished' or 'completed': 'I *have* seen', 'I *have* thrown'. The 'perfect' tense in grammar, i.e. over and done with! An activity that has come to rest, where the unrest of striving has been left behind. But then, having still somehow stands in the light of *in*-completion, of striving.

'Possessing' is *one* way of having, and *one* way of possessing (the most familiar to us) is having disposal over things. It is *this* kind of possessing that we wish to bring to mind (only for the purpose of emphasis, not for an exhaustive analysis of the phenomenon), paying special attention to the fact that what is had here stands ready for our arbitrary employment. Such possessing can (but need not) be seen as the *highest* mode of having, for it is marked precisely by immediacy of disposition and arbitrariness of employment, thus by a kind of freedom in having. Now we ask: what is the character of this having as comportment? That is, what is the character of human existence in such having and possessing? Whoever possesses in *this* way *can* do whatever he pleases with what he possesses. He is not subject to any other claim. He can employ what he possesses in any arbitrary way depending on his desires and needs. Precisely on the basis of this extensive freedom of action, such possessing can (but need not) become, in its genuine comportmental character, a self-losing amidst all kinds of needs. The genuine comportmental character of having becomes a self-losing of he who has. The autonomy of the self gives way to the contingency and arbitrariness of needs and desires to be immediately satisfied. Although this kind of having has the appearance of fulfilled possession, it is not an *authentic* having in the strict sense of authenticity. What we understand by authenticity [*Eigentlichkeit*] is *that* mode of human existence wherein man (authentically) appropriates himself, i.e. wherein he comes *to himself* and can be himself. The having which we have just described *in*authentic, because its apparent freedom of disposition fundamentally amounts to servitude under the arbitrary rule of needs. Every having is at bottom a becoming-had through that which lures its disposition.

From this we can easily see the one thing which now matters, i.e. that having and having are in no way the same. But if this is the case, to distinguish striving from having is not so straightforward. Indeed the way is now clear to the fundamental question of whether striving is not just itself a kind of having, but even necessarily belongs to the essence of authentic having.

§ 31. Inauthentic and Authentic Striving. The ἔρως as Striving for Being

Yet we are now faced by a new difficulty: striving can be an inauthentic comportment in just the same way that possessing can be this. Inauthentic possessing proved to be an unrestricted claim upon arbitrary needs. So also can striving be a mere chasing after what is striven for. Striving is then fixed in *one* direction, thereby consuming itself in its striving and mere self-abandonment. This self-consuming striving then leads to the destruction of the authentic self. Such striving, as we meet it in every kind of greed that takes hold of us, is no less inauthentic than the aforementioned having. What is striven for is not *had,* but on the contrary *has* the striver, in such a way that the latter is ensnared within his own striving and loses sight of his ownmost self. Such striving is all the more ensnaring for its appearance of activity, vitality, and diversity.

I mention in passing that this ensnarement does not pertain only to striving, but belongs primordially to the existence of man, prevailing in diverse forms within the most various comportments of Dasein.

But restricting ourselves for now to striving, must we not say that every striving is held fast by its object? To be sure! But does this mean that every striving must *lose* itself in its object? No. Every striving is indeed a striving toward (the object striven for), but this toward . . . is not necessarily an away-from-oneself. On the contrary, one can think of a striving wherein the object is held fast *as such*, but also thereby held fast to *oneself*, so that one finds oneself in this holding fast to the object, indeed such that one finds oneself not just as a point and thing and subject, but in the sense of the soul's essence, which is essentially a *relationship* – thus finding oneself precisely as this striving relationship to the object. This kind of striving (whose *possibility* alone we are now considering) does not strive to possess the object, but strives for it to *remain* as striven for, as held in the striving, in order that the striver finds himself *from* that for which he strives. Such striving would be authentic in so far as the striving self does not strive away from itself but rather back towards itself, i.e. in order that, in this striving, it may gain its own self. While the respective objects of authentic and inauthentic striving do not coincide, they certainly go together in the essence of authentic striving.

What must be the *object* of authentic striving? It must at any rate be such that, in returning to it, the Dasein of the striving human being genuinely comes to itself as existing. We heard that existence means to comport oneself as a being to beings as such. But something is a *being* for us only if we understand *being*, i.e. if we come back to beings from being (despite our initially non-regarding and non-conceptual understanding of being). Plato says nothing else but that being belongs to that which stands in authentic striving. Does this mean that striving for being is a particular kind of authentic striving? Absolutely not! It is rather the striving wherein we allow to prevail, as measure and law, what from the ground up and as such, makes possible and carries our Dasein. Plato also calls this striving ἔρως. The force of this word has long become lost to us (most recently, and among other ways, through psychoanalysis).

Erwin Rohde, the classical philologist and friend of Nietzsche's, once wrote (*Cogitata*, Diary of 11 May 1878; see O. Crusius, *Erwin Rohde*, Tübingen and Leipzig 1902, p. 255): 'One of the worst deficiencies of the German language is that ἔρως and ἀγάπη are both expressed by the *one* word "love" [*Liebe*]. Many misinterpretations and false estimations of ἔρως stem from this, including the curious sentimental German *self-deceptions* about the nature of ἐρωτικόν πάθος. It is easy to judge the importance of these deceptions for the culture and literature of the Germans. What one can see here is precisely the importance of *words*.' So we should not understand the Platonic and Greek ἔρως in terms of what is nowadays called the 'erotic', but nor should we think that the Greek ἔρως would be suitable for bigoted old aunties.

The understanding of being as striving for being, ἔρως, is not only the most authentic striving by which the Dasein of man is carried, but, as this latter, it is simultaneously authentic having. For firstly, instead of the object of this striving becoming a thing which as such can be taken into possession, it always remains *untaken* as something striven for. And secondly, he who thus strives is held fast in his own self by the object of his striving, such that this striving provides the measure and law for the striver's comportment to beings, enabling existence from the ground of beings in the whole. Thereby, however, i.e. in such authentic striving, man *holds himself* as an existing being in the midst of beings; man has the beings, and in these beings has himself, in the way he as man *can* have anything at all. But because we normally interpret 'having' in terms of 'possessing' things and perceiving objects, we take all *striving* as not-having, and because striving is a not-having, having in the thingly sense is put forward as goal and ideal of striving. On this common conception it is incomprehensible how authentic striving can simultaneously be authentic having. Only in so far as we exist out of this authentic striving are we at all able to estimate what we possess or do not possess of beings, and are we able to decide whether we 'have' something authentically or inauthentically. Indeed, only from authentic striving can it be decided what *having* and not-having can mean for man. At bottom, the authentically existing human being does not strive in order to have and possess, but the reverse: he 'has' and possesses, i.e. beings are referred to him in his Dasein, and he is referred to them, so that in authentic striving for being he strives for his own Dasein, wherein it occurs that beings come to be and not to be [*worin überhaupt geschieht, daβ Seiendes seiend und un-seiend wird*].

We have attempted to clarify 'striving for being' by *contrasting* authentic striving in its essential constitution with having (possessing) and also with inauthentic striving. Yet we still cannot get a steady view of what this striving is; it becomes blurred and ever farther withdrawn from us if we believe it can be observed like stomach pains and similar experiences. But we could presumably obtain a better understanding of authentic striving for being if we could clearly indicate the nature of what is thus striven for – just *being*. What is being? Plato does not pose this question, nor does anyone after him. But being is what it is really about, indeed precisely as that, ὧ̓ ἐπορέγεται αὐτὴ ἡ ψυχὴ καθ᾽αὐτήν, that, 'for which the soul itself strives through itself, for itself, and toward itself'. It is being which in all circumstances is already present and there, not as a thing or any kind of object, but as that which is striven for in authentic striving. Whether we are aware of this or not, it is being that is most primordially and comprehensively held in striving. This characteristic of striving for being does not help us with the question of what being and authentic striving are in themselves. Plato explains only what is involved in the striving of the soul. What is all-important for him is that we see that, and how, precisely being is what is most primordially striven for. This is best done by bringing other elements of striving into view, whereby, however, it is being that is at bottom striven for.

§ 32. More Determinate Conception of Striving for Being

In order to focus on and comprehend what is striven for in this striving, Socrates asks Theaetetus (186 a 5 ff.):

Ἦ καὶ τὸ ὅμοιον καὶ τὸ ἀνόμοιον καὶ τὸ ταὐτὸν καὶ ἕτερον;

Ναί.

Τί δέ; καλὸν καὶ αἰσχρὸν καὶ ἀγαθὸν καὶ κακὸν;

Καὶ τούτων μοι δοκεῖ ἐν τοῖς μάλιστα πρὸς ἄλληλα σκοπεῖσθαι τὴν οὐσίαν, ἀναλογιζομένη ἐν ἑαυτῇ τὰ γεγονότα καὶ τὰ παρόντα πρὸς τὰ μέλλοντα.

'[There is contained in authentic striving] being-similar and being-dissimilar, being-the-same and being-different?'

'Yes.'

'And what about being-beautiful and being-ugly, being-good and being- bad?'

'It [the soul] also appears to view the *being* of these, especially in their relations to one another, reckoning, within and for itself, upon the past and present in relation to the future.'

What is being spoken of here? In order to aid our understanding of the third step, we shall begin with a mere outward enumeration.

a. The previously indicated excess is expanded. *Being* is there in the striving – not only in being-similar and being-dissimilar, being-the-same and being-different, but now also in being-beautiful and being- ugly, being-good and being-bad. In these cases too the soul has its relationship to being.

b. This relationship to being is now expressed through σκοπεῖσθαι, taking-in-view, perceiving.

c. This perceiving is interpreted in a particular way: it is an ἀναλογίζεσθαι, a reckoning back and forth.

d. This reckoning reckons with the past, present, and future – thus with time.

We do not think of an exhaustive treatment of everything mentioned here, but must restrict ourselves to an elucidation within the framework of our guiding task, only so far as enables us to see the extent to which the relationship of the soul to being (i.e. striving for being) receives a more determinate conception. For to arrive at such is indeed the task of the third step.

a) More Essential Unfolding of the Determinations of Being in Attunedness

Firstly then the new expansion of the excess. It is precisely from this expansion that we can clarify the previous excess in its specific peculiarity. What is the situation in regard to this previous excess? In the perception of colour, sound, and the like, there is a co-perceiving of being, being-different, being-the-same, being-similar, being-dissimilar. What kind of determinations of being are these? Everything we encounter shows itself to us in these characters of being; everything whatsoever, whether coloured or audible, heavy or light, round or square, late or early, whether a natural thing or an historical event, whether living or dead, natural or artificial, whether man or god. Irrespective of what and how anything is, it is always *something*. To be something is to be *the same as itself*. As the same as itself, it is being-*different* to every other self-same thing, likewise being-similar, being-*dissimilar*, and being-*countable*. To be sure, these characters of being pertain to *all* beings, whether possible or actual, but they still do not exhaust what beings are to us, i.e. what is brought together under the usual headings of God, world, and man. For example, the nature which surrounds us, which carries us, which penetrates through us and discards us, is not *just* by virtue of its difference or dissimilarity to historical being. Being-different and being-dissimilar etc. belong to it necessarily, but they do not suffice to characterize the being of nature. On the other hand, the characters *now* referred to (beautiful, ugly, good, bad etc.), if we understand them *comprehensively* enough, present a more essential unfolding of being (cf. later in the Middle Ages, and in Kant the 'transcendentals' *verum, pulchrum, bonum*), and bring the beings in whose midst we pass our Dasein closer to us as the beings they *are*. For they do not belong to any arbitrary something, but pertain precisely to *the* being [*Sein*] with which we are immediately *concerned* as nature, history etc.

The *delightful* in the broadest sense is what arouses ἡδονή (delight); it raises our spirits and somehow puts us in good cheer, in contrast to the disagreeable, which depresses us. The *attunedness* [*Gestimmtheit*], which constantly and from the ground up penetrates [*durchstimmt*] our Dasein, could not be what it is had it not attuned [*abgestimmt*] our existence in advance to the delightfulness of the beings we encounter, and to delightfulness as such. Only in so far as our Dasein is attuned to this, and thus also attuned to the possibility of changes and shadings of attunement [*Stimmung*], thus only in so far as delight and non-delight stand in the authentic striving of the soul, can we encounter the delightful as such. It is not as if we first find beings as present, and *then* find that they delight us. The situation is the reverse: what we encounter is already attuned in respect of delight and non-delight, or hovers between these as indeterminate (which, however, is not nothing), and only on the basis of this situation can we then *disregard* the character of delight/non-delight in order to look at what we encounter as something *merely* present. Something can strike us as delightful only in so far as our Dasein is already attuned to the delightfulness/non-delightfulness of what is present. Delightfulness and non-delightfulness, taken in the broad sense, thus belong to the region of perceivability that surrounds us, i.e. in the sphere of our striving, just like sameness, difference etc. What the Greeks call ἀγαθόν and κακόν, good and bad, belong in this same region, provided that these words are understood in the broadest possible sense.

The *Philebus* dialogue shows how much the later Plato struggled to discover the inner primordial connection between the first mentioned characters of being, and those characters (delightfulness, goodness) which have just now been indicated. In the present context it is enough to see that Plato does not restrict the characters of being to the former (sameness, difference etc.). It is another question whether Plato really succeeded in demonstrating the inner connection between the various characters of being. No more than Aristotle, and later Kant, did Plato find his way through this problem. The reasons for this already lie hidden at the beginning of ancient philosophy; Plato himself was no longer able to master them. The superior strength of what had *already* determined the direction of the understanding of being remained in force.

b) The Taking-in-View of the Connections of Being

Secondly, this broadened conception of the excess is explained by a more precise account of the region in which the relationship of the soul to being is maintained, and where all these characteristics emerge. What kind of relationship does the soul have to being-beautiful, being-good etc.? This relationship is now conceived as a σκοπεῖσθαι:

as taking-in-view and making into something viewed. We came across a related expression earlier: ἐπισκοπεῖν, i.e. looking-at in the sense defined within our interpretation of the cave allegory;[10] only now more precisely in the middle voice, which means that what is taken up in the looking refers back to the looker. Not just looking in the sense of staring at something present, but looking that has the character of striving: seeing in the sense of attending to . . ., of being directed to . . . ; σκοπός is that which is looked at, something intended *in advance*: the intention, the goal. What we *properly* 'have in view' is precisely what we commonly do *not* look *at*, but *just* look to as *authoritative* for our comportment. So σκοπεῖσθαι is *goal-directed* seeing, striving seeing, and is for this reason fitting as a characterization of authentic striving. Striving for being is not blind impulse, but is a *seeing* striving which perceives, and has in view, that for which it strives. σκοπεῖσθαι does not actually mean looking at, being occupied with this looking, but being occupied with something else, thereby already having in view.

Again the question is: *what* is perceived and held in view in this way? Plato says: ἐν τοῖς μάλιστα πρὸς ἄλληλα (σκοπεῖσθαι) τὴν οὐσίαν; 'being' naturally, and indeed 'especially in regard to the *inter*-connection', thus the *connection* of the one with the other. *Why* does especially the connectivity in being come into view here? Why is the being-*connected* of the one to the other [*Zueinander*-sein] suddenly spoken of? Because new characters of being have been exhibited: goodness and delightfulness. Goodness e.g. is itself always the goodness *of* something *for* something, delightfulness likewise. Connectivity is not something additional, but belongs to the essential constitution of this being; it points to referential connections between the one and the other. The soul maintains such connections in view when it exists in its relationship to being. This πρὸς ἄλληλα, these referential connections, belong as such in the sphere of the εἰς ὅ, of striving for being, and are co-constitutive for the latter.

c) Interpretation of Connections of Being in the συλλογισμός

Thirdly, this perceiving of the connections of being receives a further decisive determination, i.e. it is characterized as ἀναλογίζεσθαι. This description pertains not so much to the connection itself as to the way this connection unfolds, corresponding to the characters of being itself. λόγος, λέγειν means to gather, to collect something in its connections, to bring together the one with the other, and indeed in such a way that both present themselves and come into view in this togetherness. But this becoming-viewed is not an objective grasping, nor is it any kind of logical- formal reflection or deduction. When we encounter the delightful and immerse ourselves in this, we do and must *understand* it (delightfulness), but this mode of being, while perceived, is not conceived. It is the connection to beings as beings, founded upon ἀλήθεια, the gathering of the selfshowing into the singular (ἕν), the one enduring constancy of presence. Here λόγος, does not mean 'thought' and on no account is to be grasped 'logically'; it must be understood from the context of οὐσία, ἀλήθεια, δόξα, νοεῖν. So λογίζεσθαι means to gather together several (things and) connections; to reckon with both in going from one to the other; more precisely: ἀνά, to go back-and-forth in collecting and in this way to reckon up the referential relations of things. Not reckoning as numerical calculation, but in the sense of reckoning with relationships and circumstances. This 'reckoning with' is another characteristic of striving. ἀναλογίσματα (186 c 2) can only occur in ἀναλογίζεσθαι. Thus ἀναλογίζεσθαι is the authentic form in which this viewing, and this object of striving, unfold themselves, a going-back-and-forth between these connections: from something to what it is good for. These connections of being are not as such *conceived* and made into objects, but are *there* only in so far as they are reckoned with – how so? By perceiving and experiencing and dealing (and so forth) with beings. They are unfolded by the soul in the form of ἀναλογίζεσθαι, and as thus illuminated they are thrown over against the soul. The ἀναλογίζεσθαι characterizes the way in which the object of authentic striving comes into play.

Shortly thereafter (186 d 3), Plato employs a further characteristic expression for this comportment of the soul: συλλογισμός, which stands for the way in which the relationship to being allows being, as the object of striving, to hold sway. So the same stem, but with σύν rather than ἀνά. It would be quite erroneous to translate συλλογισμός here by 'syllogism', i.e. by the technical term for a type of theoretical deduction as this occurs in later logic. Schleiermacher actually falls into this error.[11] Here the expression does not refer to deduction or derivation, nor indeed to any kind of logical activity or 'thinking'. The word λόγος (λογίζεσθαι) in ἀναλογίζεσθαι and συλλογισμός should not mislead us. For these words are here employed *prior* to any development of 'logic' as a formal- technical discipline, i.e. they are employed in the closest possible interrelation with the fundamental philosophical question of *being*.[12]

We must be careful here not to think of logic in the modern sense. What Plato has in mind is something much more primordial: how in respect of the question of 'knowledge' (i.e. truth, i.e. relation to unhidden beings, i.e. to beings as such, i.e. to being) the *connection* to being (ἰδέα) is grounded in letting-appear and fixed in the λόγος. To be sure, although it is not here a matter of the connection of being to logical thinking and the logical formation of thinking (forms of thought and judgement), it is important to notice how the λόγος is traced back to the soul and to man, so that in subsequent philosophy (in a certain sense already with Aristotle) the connection of the soul to being and its forms is brought into an essential relation with ratio, judgement, and forms of thought, such that Kant attempts to derive the determinations of being in general, the categories, from the table of judgements. However, we should not read this later and faulty development (λόγος as proposition) into Plato's initial conception, which aims in a quite different direction.

d) Initial Clarification of the Connection of Being to Time

The *fourth* thing which emerged was that in ἀναλογίζεσθαι, in this unfolding of what is perceived by the relation to being, the soul simultaneously reckons with the past, the present (what is present), and the future. More precisely, the soul reckons with the *connection* of the past and present to the future – i.e. all reckoning with being intrinsically refers to relations of *time*. The tracking hither and thither of the connections of being is directed to the future, and perceives the past and the present in their reference to the future. Or better: the past and the present are understood and appraised in relationship to the future, in that the soul itself brings the past, and the present in its connection to what is coming (i.e. the present in its connection with that upon which everything depends and wherein everything comes together) into correspondence. The relationship to being is intrinsically a reckoning with time.

To be sure, the time which is spoken of here is not the clock-time by which we measure the succession of things and fix events at particular points of time. Instead, the soul is prior to any relationship to individual things; since it is a relationship to being, it is intrinsically a relationship to time.

It must be admitted that this fundamental connection between 'being and *time*', upon which Plato here stumbles, only comes into a weak half- light – to immediately again (and for good) sink back and disappear into the night of that blind logic of understanding which had become dominant.

Aristotle too claims that the soul has an essential relationship to time. Characteristically, however, he makes this claim in his *Physics*, a context in which the relationship of the soul to being is not under consideration, but which studies the way in which knowledge of nature can define and measure natural processes in their movement. Time is included among the essential determining moments of a moving being, alongside infinity, place and the void. But Aristotle does not see an inner connection to the problem of being as such: he does not see an inner connection of being itself to time, and just as little does he *illuminate* the relationship of the soul to time. He says only that if there were no soul, neither would there be time.[13]

It was Augustine who, in Book 11 of his *Confessions*, made the first major (and solitary) attempt to demonstrate the essential connection between soul (*animus*) and time. But having theological purposes in mind he was a long way from treating the specific relationship of the soul to being, and was *still farther* from seeing the connection between *being and time* (although objectively speaking this connection cannot be evaded).

Plato's treatment of the relation between being and time is too brief and indefinite for us to force a great deal out of it. It is enough that the passage we have interpreted (under the four points) indicates how much Plato was concerned to more precisely delineate the relation of the soul to being (striving for being), and to elucidate this from various sides, without, however, expressly posing the question of the essence of being.

To what degree an explicit and autonomous insight into the relation of being to time is already present in Plato cannot be objectively established. It is enough that these connections of the present and past, and indeed with a *predominant* connection to the future, here already come into view.

Before we summarize and illuminate the character of striving for being in a more systematic form, we must follow the discussion of the third step to its conclusion, especially since we encounter here yet another new and important determination.

§ 33. The 'Excess': Not an Addition to What Is Sensed, but the Conceptual Highlighting of Distinct Characters of Being in the Sphere of Striving for Being

The following (186 b 2–10) is self-contained:

[Socrates] Ἔχε δή· ἄλλο τι τοῦ μὲν σκληροῦ τὴν σκληρότητα διὰ τῆς ἐπαφῆς αἰσθήσεται, καὶ τοῦ μαλακοῦ τὴν μαλακότητα ὡσαύτως;

[Theaetetus] Ναί.

Τὴν δέ γε οὐσίαν καὶ ὅτι ἐστὸν καὶ τὴν ἐναντιότητα πρὸς ἀλλήλω καὶ τὴν οὐσίαν αὖ τῆς ἐναντιότητος αὐτὴ ἡ ψυχὴ ἐπανιοῦσα καὶ συμβάλλουσα πρὸς ἄλληλα κρίνειν πειρᾶται ἡμῖν.

Πάνυ μὲν οὖν.

'Stop there! Does it [the soul] not perceive the hardness of the hard through the medium of touch, and likewise the softness of the soft?'

'Yes.'

'But being, the what-being and that-being and so-being, and the being- opposed-to-one-another, and again the what-being of this opposition, the soul tries to determine for us by reverting to them and comparing them with one another.'

That is so.'

What is said here and what is intended? Socrates carries the conversation further with Ἔχε δή: 'stop there!'; δή has the meaning of referring back to something previously said, from which something resulted that it is now a matter of properly assimilating. And indeed it concerns a contraposition (μὲν . . . δέ).

On the *one* hand there is mentioned the perception of hard and soft, whereby the same obviously applies to colours and sounds. We perceive the hardness, colour, odour of something, by means of touch, sight, smell. We touch something hard, but we *cannot touch hardness itself*, just as little as we can perceive colouredness (we only perceive colour, coloured things). Nevertheless, to perceive hard and likewise coloured things we must obviously *understand* what it *means* to be hard and coloured. The hard and the coloured are somehow *there*, and accordingly demand a comportment which takes them in as such.

On the *other* hand there is the possibility of having *being* in view, the *what-being* of the perceived (of the hard, coloured); likewise *that* the objects of perception are such and such (their that-being etc.). Further, not only does the soul already and on its own account have all such matters in view, but it can *direct* itself to any specific matter, e.g. it can directly focus on being-different, on the being-opposed of one to another by virtue of which the soul experiences *two* things (colour and sound), inquiring into the what-being of this being-opposed itself and highlighting the essence of oppositionality *as such*. This applies to every character of being that resides in the sphere of striving for being.

More precisely, the soul *attempts* this kind of thing (πειρᾶται) and can attempt it. Although these characters of being, and their essential interrelations and distinctions, are in a sense constantly in view, they are not simply and expressly *given*. Rather, the soul must on its own account distinguish the lines of essential connections from one another; κρίνειν means to make stand out against, to distinguish, not to judge (in the Kantian sense). This is what the soul is concerned to do (πειρᾶται): the distinguished elements get worked through and concentrated in the singularity, being (ὄρεξις: its attraction to and concern with being, and only *thus* with itself). Where these connections of being were previously faded, indefinite, indeed unknown, they must, through a division of their essence, be made plastic as it were. The soul enacts this procedure of dividing highlighting by moving back and forth within these connections and laying them out in their connectedness. It does this for itself and on its own account: this means that it does not necessarily need to experience a particular individual being and hold on to this. Instead, the dividing highlighting itself marks out and illuminates the sphere of striving for being, thus making possible its conceptual expression. What was previously a non-conceptual having-in-view of being now becomes a conceptual perceiving.

On the *one* hand there is the self-losing immediate perception of what is hard, coloured, audible etc. through our bodily organs, whereby (albeit in a non-regarding and non-conceptual way) hardness, colouredness etc. are understood. On the *other* hand there is the free possibility of *looking at* what has thus come into view and illuminating it in its structure. These two sides – that the soul perceives specific things by means of its sensory faculties, and thereby always already has the connections of being in view – are no longer just distinguished, but are shown to *belong together*. Both are one and the same. The soul of man, one and the same soul, can and must perform *both* operations.

We thus come to the decisive result of the third step. It consists in the revision of the relationship between what is perceived through the senses and what we initially grasped as the 'excess'. We can perceive specific things as coloured, audible etc. only *on the basis* of the striving for being. Only because the soul strives is it able, in light of what is striven for, to have this or that before itself as given, i.e. to perceive it, to take it as true [wahr-*nehmen*]. All having-before-oneself, and having in general, is grounded in a striving for being. Thus being (what-being, being-different etc., but also colouredness, hardness) is always already perceived and in play when we perceive beings. Although not conceptually grasped, it is held and retained in the striving, and what is striven for in the striving is held up for us, such that this and that is made *have-able* as coloured and audible. Being in the unity of all its features is thus quite inadequately characterized if, as hitherto, we grasp it simply as the 'excess' over and above what is sensed and perceived. *Why* does Socrates describe this as excess? We encounter being, being-different etc. only if we *begin* our inquiry with colour, sound etc. and *then* establish that therein something more is perceived. Thus, in the order of the inquiry, we can say that this excess is an *addition* to what is sensed. However, what we subsequently find here is in its nature and essence not 'more' in the sense of addition, but on the contrary it is the *pregiven* (however not apprehended and interrogated as such).

More precisely, in so far as it is not given in the *looking*, it is *held up* in advance (*a priori*) for us in striving perceiving, as what must already be understood in order that something sensory can be perceived as a being, indeed as nothing else but that which co-constitutes the region of possible perceivability.

We can now more clearly understand the character Plato attributes to the soul at the very beginning. The soul is what holds up a region of sight within which everything sensorily perceivable is extended. It is not an excess or addition, but the holder [*Verhalt*] by which we are always already *en-held* [*umhalten*]. This *en-holding* of the region of perceivability *occurs* in striving. It is only striving, in which region alone something reachable and reached (had) is possible, that can up-hold and en-hold such an upholding and en-holding region. This region is filled up and constituted by the indicated connections of being. Striving is the way in which the soul holds being up before itself. Striving for being, qua striving, is in its from- itself an away-from-itself and a towards-which . . . However, as authentic striving it does not lose itself in the object of striving as something only striven for, but holds the object *in the strive [in der Strebe]*, in such a way that the striving at the same time finds its way back from the object to itself, to the striving soul itself.

Thus perception through the individual organs is not restricted by these to *their respective* fields, sight to colour, hearing to sound etc. A sense restricted in this way could never, within its field, perceive anything at all (i.e. could never have a specific being before it) were it not for the underlying striving. For such having-before-oneself of something is always a reaching, i.e. an inward having founded on striving, whereby the latter does not disappear but fulfils itself in its characteristic way.

That the soul is as such striving for being means that man as existing has always already stepped out beyond himself in his directedness to the all- embracing region of being. At the same time, striving for being is the way the soul *is* in its own self. For it *is* primordially the relationship to . . ., the relationship of striving that in itself strives back to itself, and therefore it is what it genuinely is only in so far as it maintains itself in this striving. What it means for a human being to be *himself*, or to be *a self*, can be understood only from this phenomenon of striving for being.

The third step has thus been concluded. Its aim was to give a positive characterization of the soul's relation to being.

D. Step Four: Being-Human as Historical in Staking and Stance (παιδεία)

§ 34. The Rooting of 'Abstract' Characters of Being in the Unity of Bodily Existence. Their Difference from 'Self-less' Nature. Being out Beyond Oneself in Primordial Yearning

Let us recall what all these steps are meant to serve! The undecided question is what organ comes into play when we perceive something in respect of both colour *and* sound. Answering this question requires the investigation of what in general is perceived on such occasions, and of how this perceiving (of the perceived) itself must be. The first step exhibited what we then called, but are no longer entitled to call, the 'excess'. The second step conceived this excess in a more concrete manner, showing how it is perceived: the perceiving can occur only through the soul itself, and only the soul can take up a relationship to being. The third step showed how this relationship to being is to be understood, namely as striving for being. But does this not bring us into difficulty and confusion? If we review everything that has gone before and do not deceive ourselves, we must admit that these considerations on being and striving for being are anything but transparent and comprehensible. Quite the contrary, they are odd, bewildering, ambiguous, and, as the common understanding says, they are also 'abstract'.

This is and remains the initial situation. We cannot claim to have clarified and made comprehensible, within a few hours, something which for centuries has been allowed to slip away in an uncomprehending manner. Indeed, perhaps the essence of what we are speaking about is such that it cannot be grasped like arbitrary propositions from some arbitrary science, or in the manner of everyday understanding. Perhaps there is a specific precondition for understanding striving for being, without which our whole reflection must remain incomplete.

This is not just 'perhaps', but is certainly the case. Despite the many- sided clarification of the essence of the understanding of being we must bear in mind that we cannot grasp this as a thing. Instead, understanding in this case is subject to specific conditions. So there follows a *fourth* step (186 b 11 – c 6). Socrates takes up his question, which is at the same time an answer, and Theaetetus agrees without reservation:

Οὐκοῦν τὰ μὲν εὐθὺς γενομένοις πάρεστι φύσει αἰσθάνεσθαι ἀνθρώποις τε καὶ θηρίοις, ὅσα διὰ τοῦ σώματος παθήματα ἐπὶ τὴν ψυχὴν τείνει. τὰ δὲ περὶ τούτων ἀναλογίσματα πρός τε οὐσίαν καὶ ὠφέλειαν μόγις καὶ ἐν χρόνῳ διὰ πολλῶν πραγμάτων καὶ παιδείας παραγίγνεται οἷς ἂν καὶ παραγίγνηται;

Παντάπασι μὲν οὖν.

'Is it not true that human beings, as well as animals, from the moment of birth receive sensations through the body, and that these sensations are concentrated in the soul; whereas reflections about these, with reference to their being and usefulness, are only acquired slowly and with difficulty, and only by those capable of much exertion?'

'That is precisely the situation.'

The first thing we come across here is that double characterization of perception which we already know from the first step. On the one hand the object of perception contains something that strikes our individual *senses*, but we also encounter it (albeit in a non-regarding and non-conceptual way) as *existing* in the multifacetedness of its being. Now at this point of the argument it is no longer a matter of analysing this difference within the object of perception, nor of focusing on the co-belonging of these two aspects (in the sense of the understanding of being as presupposition for what is given to the senses), but something else is in question: how this co-belonging is *rooted* in the primordial unity of the Dasein of man, how both elements are *there* in and with this Dasein, and how this unity itself requires a specifically *split* mode of being of the human being. In this regard, sharply set off against each other are: what we perceive through the senses, which is there φύσει; that what we perceive as existing (in its being) is only unfolded in παιδεία, in the course of the *history* of Dasein (μόγις καὶ ἐν χρόνῳ).

Φύσει, 'from nature': this means without our doing, but at the same time essentially related to us and built into our activity. The αἴσθησις is *from* nature, but it is never there as nature. The αἴσθησις of man is from the start something different to nature, even when the understanding of being into which it is built is not yet awake, and remains indeterminate and initially unfolded. But this means that it is already there in its indeterminateness. This indeterminateness of the understanding of being does not mean nothing, but is something positive: something that the animal never arrives at, because it altogether lacks an understanding of being.

Here man and animal are mentioned together only in respect of the perceivable things which press upon them as passive subjects. But nothing is said about how these are concentrated in the region of perceivability, e.g. about the way animals remain bound within such a region. The αἴσθησις of man depends *essentially* on sense-organs and bodily constitution. But just for this reason the *bodily constitution* of man is fundamentally different to pure nature: it is primordially inserted in the striving for being. It is not the case that man is first an animal and then something else in addition. Man can never be an animal, i.e. can never be nature, but is always either over the animal, or, precisely as human, *under* it (whereupon we say that man becomes like an animal'). Since nature does not have the inner elevation of *existence* which belongs to being-human *as being out beyond oneself* [*Uber-sich-hinaus-sein*], it is incapable of *falling*.

The human body is pure nature neither in its mode of immediate givenness nor in its way of being. It is suspended, as it were, between its height and its abyss, as a *passage-way* from the one to the other and as an open dwelling-place for both, but it is never shut up to itself, it is never, in the manner of pure nature, altogether lacking in self. The body belongs to the Dasein of man. Being-there [*Da-sein*], in the sense of existence, is a fundamentally different way of being to that of nature. Only by *disregarding* the specifically human character of the human body can this become something analogous to nature (not nature as such, but working in like manner). This in turn can only occur on the basis of an understanding of being, i.e. if we already understand what nature means. The express idea of nature as nature itself presupposes a positive understanding of nature as such. *From where* does this understanding come? Never in subjective experience of our own bodily constitution (as something sensed, or on the basis of artificially construed sense-data of our body in the sense of psychology). Rather, we gain this understanding immediately (primarily) from experience of the world to which we comport ourselves as being-in-the-world, and in so far as we do this, nature *manifests* itself as natural *power*, as day and night, land and sea, generation, growth and decline, winter and summer, sky and earth. And *what* is it experienced *as*? 'Natural power' first manifests itself when it intervenes in the region of human powers, as that totality over which man is power-*less* but to which he is bound and by which he is borne along, as that which over-powers and which as such necessarily *tunes* man in his essence, i.e. in his striving for being. Nature is primordially present in attunedness. As soon as man exists he is exposed to the sensations received through his body. This means that he corporeally participates, although in *his own* way, as nature within the totality of nature. The overarching power of nature first reveals itself when man tests his own power and fails. The narrowness, helplessness and powerlessness of the proximate but open environment of man is the primordial scene of the appearance of the breadth, supreme power, and closedness of nature; the latter cannot exist without the former and vice versa. Nature as such is not older than the tools and artefacts of man. Nature as such only *holds* sway where *being* is understood. But being is understood in striving for being, or, as the Greeks say, in ἔρως. To this there belongs what we call the primordial attunedness of Dasein. Fundamental attunements [*Grund- stimmungen*] such as joy and cheerfulness, anxiety and misery, are primordial, indeed *the* primordial ways in which all-powerful nature 'determines' [*'bestimmt'*] man, i.e. tunes [*stimmt*] his primordial attunedness as such and such. As thus attuned, this fundamental attunedness announces itself primordially.

The corporeality of man, however, *is* not nature, not even when it torments man, rendering him powerless and groundless. Then too it is still the groundlessness of the *existing* human being in his Dasein that *seizes hold* of his bodily being, and, although powerless, *determines* it; i.e. striving for being is the ground of the essence for the total Dasein of man.

What is said here about striving for being and its ἀναλογίσματα the same time provides us with an initial understanding of human Dasein. This understanding of being does not happen by nature, independently of our own doing, but requires the *staking* [*Einsatz*] of man's most authentic self. This, says Plato, can only happen through effort and patience. The staking of the authentic self brings the latter into the midst of the diversity of beings within which the πράττειν of man has to assert itself. It is only the confrontation with beings that allows man to experience the structure and unfolding and fulfilment of what beings are and can be for him. Only thus does he come to take on the *stance* [*Haltung*] within which all comportment [*Ver-halten*] to beings, i.e. existing, is held and secured, i.e. authentically is. But this staking of the authentic self, and the stance arising therefrom, are not immediately available to every arbitrary human being, nor to all in the same way. The Greeks knew better than anyone else before and after them that every existence has its own law and rank. All levelling is at bottom an *impoverishment* of Dasein – not of these or those possessions and goods, but of being as such. But this history in every case *occurs* through man, as existing, claiming his own self (not his tiny 'I'), i.e. only on the basis of striving for being. So striving for being does not come over man like some kind of arbitrary condition. We never find it present before us like a thing, mental property, or present process. We can never occupy ourselves with it in the manner of a scientifically graspable object, but the genuine essence of striving for being is such that it can exist only *in* and as striving itself.

Because we overlook or forget this, we are in danger of searching for this striving in some place or other, of talking about it, and in this sense arriving at a concept of it. This danger is ever present, because the Dasein is constantly disposed to see authentic having as the possession of what is had, in *that* sense of possession we have discussed. Since man seldom, and only with difficulty, understands his authentic mode of having as striving, i.e. understands that only what is held in (as we say) the most primordial *yearning* [*ursprunglichste Sehnsucht*] is authentically there, the primordial staking and the genuine stance of full striving for being is seldom achieved. This in turn is the reason we find it so difficult to grasp what this word refers to; not because it is difficult or intrinsically complicated, but because it seldom becomes *actual*, i.e. *occurs* in its authentic, simple, and immediate illumination. For this reason man remains a stranger to this essential ground of his existence.

Whoever wants to understand striving for being, i.e. wants to know what this is, must at the same time know how alone it can *be*, i.e. he must *understand* himself in *relation to* his own proper self.

§ 35. Inadequacy of Theaetetus' First Answer. Perception Still More Than Perception. Broadened Experience Possibility of αἴσθησις as the Condition of the Possibility of Unhiddenness

Only with this peculiar result, i.e. with the reference to παιδεία, is the four-step preliminary investigation concluded. The result is peculiar because it does not provide us with knowledge of anything. Instead, it delivers us over to the unavoidability of staking our authentic self.

The undecided question has now been answered. It was the question of what organ the soul perceives with when it perceives something over and above colour and sound.

1   What does it thus perceive? Beings.

2   The soul can have a relationship to these only through itself.

3   This relationship is striving for being.

4   This only occurs in the staking and stance (παιδεία) of man's own proper self, according to the law and rank of its existence.

The investigation, which had to set all this forth in its rigorous inner connection, for its part stands in the service of the question of αἴσθησις. The latter was more precisely determined as the question of what, in the perception of the perceived, constitutes the *relationship* to the encountered objects. It must come down to this question because αἴσθησις was put forward as the *essence of knowledge*. However, knowledge is the possession of truth, i.e. the unhiddenness of beings. Accordingly, such possession of truth involves a relationship to beings.

Only where this exists is there the possibility of unhiddenness and thus of the possession of truth, i.e. knowledge. There can be knowledge only where there is a relationship to beings.

If we clearly analyse this unambiguous chain of questions, while keeping the result of the foregoing investigation firmly in view, we immediately see that the question of whether αἴσθησις is, or *could be*, the essence of knowledge, is now decided in the *negative*. The original unclarity of the concept (perceiving of beings) has now disappeared: in its narrower and strict sense, αἴσθησις refers to what is given to the *senses*, while in the wider *sense* (which was the one intended by Theaetetus) it refers also to *beings*.

We can now say *what* in the essence of perception constitutes the true and what belongs to the being-true of a perceiving. In an extremely concise sequence of questions and answers (186 c 7–187 a), the decision on Theaetetus' thesis is arrived at. The interpretation of the essence of truth through the cave allegory has taught us that when the unhidden becomes *more unhidden* (ἀληθέστερον), what is (ὄν) comes to be *more beingful* (μᾶλλου ὄν). The latter belongs together with the former and is not a consequence of it. In order that something can in any degree be unhidden it must previously be given as a being. Unhiddenness is intrinsically unhiddenness of beings; indeed we saw that the Greeks generally use the word 'unhiddenness' to mean nothing else but the beings themselves in their unhiddenness. In respect of this relation to beings in the essence of ἀλήθεια, Socrates now asks Theaetetus (186 c 7):

Οἷόν τε οὖν ἀληθείας τυχεῖν, ᾧ μηδὲ οὐσίας;

'Αδύνατον.

'Is it then possible for anyone to attain something in its unhiddenness who has not already encountered beings as such [the being of precisely that something]?'

'Impossible.'

Here we have ἀληθείας τυχεῖν together with οὐσίας τυχεῖν. The encounter with beings is the condition of the possibility of encountering unhiddenness. Schleiermacher has completely misunderstood this statement. He translates: 'Can anyone attain the true essence [Wesen] of something who has not even attained its existence [Dasein]?'[14] Here Schleiermacher opposes ἀλήθεια and οὐσία to one another in the sense of the later school-distinction between *essentia and existentia*, essence and existence. This has no sense at all here, where the meaning is unhiddenness (in every sense) and beings (in their what and how). (186c9-e 12):

[Socrates] Οὗ δὲ ἀληθείας τις ἀτυχήσει, ποτὲ τούτου ἐπιστήμων ἔσται;

[Theaetetus] Καὶ πῶς ἄν, ὦ Σώκρατες;

Ἐν μὲν ἄρα τοῖς παθήμασιν οὐκ ἔνι ἐπιστήμη, ἐν δὲ τῷ περὶ ἐκείνων συλλογισμῷ. οὐσίας γὰρ καὶ ἀληθείας ἐνταῦθα μέν, ὡς ἔοικε, δυνατὸν ἅψασθαι, ἐκεῖ δὲ ἀδύνατον.

Φαίνεται.

Ἦ οὖν ταὐτὸν ἐκεῖνό τε καὶ τοῦτο καλεῖς, τοσαύτας διαφορὰς ἔχοντε;

Οὔκουν δὴ δίκαιόν γε.

Τί οὖν δὴ ἐκείνῳ ἀποδίδως ὄνομα, τῷ ὁρᾶν, ἀκούειν, ὀσφραίνεσθαι, ψύχεσθαι, θερμαίνεσθαι;

Αἰσθάνεσθαι ἔγωγε τί γὰρ ἄλλο;

Σύμπαν ἄρ' αὐτὸ καλεῖς αἴσθησιν;

Ἀνάγκη.

Ὧι γε, φαμέν, οὐ μέτεστιν ἀληθείας ἅψασθαι. οὐδὲ γὰρ οὐσίας.

Οὐ γὰρ οὖν.

Οὐδ' ἄρ' ἐπιστήμης.

Οὐ γάρ.

Οὐκ ἄρ' ἂν εἴη ποτέ, ὦ Φεαίτητε, αἴσθησίς τε καὶ ἐπιστήμη ταὐτόν.

Οὐ φαίνεται, ὦ Σώκρατες. καὶ μάλιστά γε νῦν καταφανέστατον γέγονεν ἄλλο ὂν αἰσθήσεως ἐπιστήμη.

I now simply give the translation, which after all the previous explanations speaks for itself:

'Can someone have knowledge of anything without attaining its unhiddenness?'

'How could they, Socrates?'

'Then knowledge does not reside in what we encounter through our senses [ἐν τοῖς παθήμασιν] but rather in what is gathered together in respect of them and presented as such [ἐν συλλογισμῷ]. For it is possible, apparently, to possess being and unhiddenness in this latter way, but not in the former way [through mere παθήματα].'

'So it seems.'

'Then will you call the two [παθήματα and συλλογισμός] by the same name, when there are such great differences between them?'

'No, that would certainly not be correct.'

'What name will you give, then, to the first one, which includes seeing, hearing, smelling, being cold and being warm?'

'Αἴσθησις, αἰσθάνεσθαι, perception. What else?'

'Taking it all together, then, you call this perception?'

'Of course.'

'By which, as we said, we are quite unable to possess being or unhiddenness?'

'No.'

'Not knowledge either, then?'

'No.'

'Then, Theaetetus, perception and knowledge could never be the same?'

'Evidently not, Socrates. And indeed now at last it has become perfectly clear that perception is something different to knowledge [ἄλλο ὂν αἰσθήσεως ἐπιστήμη].'

If we understand αἴσθησις as sensory sensation, it cannot be knowledge, therefore it has no ἀλήθεια, ἀληθές no. The first attempted answer to the dialogue's leading question of what knowledge is (namely that it is perception) is thus refuted. In perception (in the sense of seeing colours, hearing sounds) there is no relation to *beings*, therefore not even the *possibility* of unhiddenness. Nevertheless, what Theaetetus initially had in mind with the word αἴσθησις; remains in view as the immediate having- before-oneself of beings. But in so far as beings *are* perceived, αἴσθησις is already, at bottom and quite naturally for man, something different. Perception is always already more than perception. Thus 'perception' is *ambiguous* in respect of what is *perceived*; in the natural understanding it is two things: firstly perceiving of beings, secondly the seeing of colours, hearing of sounds etc.

This thesis of Plato's is surprising if we at once think of Aristotle, who says exactly the opposite about what is given by sense. Aristotle's fundamental thesis (*De anima* III, 427 b 12) is: αἴσθησις τῶν ἰδίων ἀληθής. Aristotle describes colour, sound etc. as the ἴδια, i.e. that which is unique to every individual sense and is perceived by it alone. 'The perceiving of what is given by the various senses is always true.' But Plato says that the αἴσθησις has no truth whatever. I cannot discuss here how these two theses, while representing different conceptions of the essence of ἀλήθεια, might nevertheless belong together. Aristotle's counter-thesis is only mentioned to indicate that the path taken by Plato in our dialogue is not the only possible one. But the influence of Plato's method and results proved so great that Aristotle too was not able to reverse the direction which the problem had taken.

The Platonic thesis that αἴσθησις καὶ ἐπιστήμη οὐ ταὐτόν (are not the same) does not necessarily mean that αἴσθησις plays no role whatever in knowledge. On the contrary, the possibility remains that it does indeed, and necessarily so, belong to knowledge, but without originally constituting knowledge on its own account. It would be tempting and instructive to follow the way in which *Kant*, after a long interval, encounters this same problem in the fundamental sections of his main work, The *Critique of Pure Reason*, admittedly in a quite different form, determined by the intervening Western philosophical tradition. I must forgo entering into these matters (see my book *Kant and the Problem of Metaphysics*). What concerns us here lies in a different direction.

Notes

1 Francis Cornford (Routledge & Kegan Paul) translates 'ask yourself whether'; Harold Fowler (Loeb) translates 'observe'. [Trans.].

2 See Supplement 15.

3 Both Cornford and Fowler also render the sentence as a question. [Trans.].

4 See below p. 146.

5 See p. 135 above and Supplement 16.

6 οἱ καλοί, cf. *Laws* XII, 966 d.

7 See Supplement 17.

8 Cornford translates as 'apprehends'; Fowler as 'grasps'. [Trans.].

9 See Supplement 18.

10 See above pp. 36 ff., 52 ff.

11 Fowler translates as 'process of reasoning'; Cornford as 'reflection'. [Trans.].

12 See Supplement 19.

13 *Physics*, Book 4, Ch. 14.

14 Fowler translates: 'Is it, then, possible for one to attain "truth" who cannot even get as far as "being"?'; Cornford translates: 'Is it possible, then, to reach truth when one cannot reach existence?'. [Trans.]

4

Towards a Discussion of Theaetetus' Second Answer: ἐπιστήμη Is ἀληθὴς δόξα. The Various Meanings of δόξα

§ 36. The Emergence of the Second Answer out of the Question of Untruth

It is important for us that the question of αἴσθησις (and therefore the question of knowledge) is closely connected to the question of being and the relationship to beings. We were able to see how the ground for handling and deciding on the leading question (whether the essence of knowledge consists in perception) resides in the essential connection between unhiddenness and being. From the interpretation of the cave allegory it emerged that truth *qua* unhiddenness never abides in and of itself, but that its nature is such that it is only as an occurrence, indeed as a fundamental occurrence in man as an existing being. That which occurs in man as primordial letting-become-unhidden is what we called *deconcealment*. However, in our interpretation of the *Theaetetus* we likewise encounter something that must occur in the ground of man's Dasein, and that we called striving for being. We have thus come across a fundamental event in the Dasein of man from two quite different starting points and problem constellations: deconcealment and *striving for being*. We discovered in each case that these are not simply passing events which man can register or fail to register, but that they make a claim upon man's essential nature. Each must be seized and made normative by man as he holds himself within the essence of his ownmost self, i.e. within the positioning stance of his Dasein. It is therefore no accident that παιδεία, i.e. the comportment of man by virtue of which he takes up his ownmost stance to beings and the true, is treated at decisive points in both these Platonic inquiries.

We conclude that the question of being (likewise the question of truth as unhiddenness, therefore simultaneously the question of the inner unity of striving for being *and* deconcealment) is directed to man himself, and makes a claim upon man himself, in a quite specific way. It is a question that does not bind man to his own tiny ego in its chance features, inadequacies and needs, but through which the breadth and primordiality of his grounding essence (i.e. of his Dasein) opens up to the relationship to beings in the whole, and wherein something can be intimated of the uncanniness of these beings: πολλὰ τὰ δεινά κοὐδὲν ἀνθρώπου δεινότερον πέλει.[1]

What is it that occurs here as striving for being? Is this striving itself also the power of deconcealing? We can only *pose* this question, because we know how far we are from comprehending the essence of truth, let alone the essence of being – how far indeed, so long as we understand nothing of *un*-truth and especially of un-beings [*Un-seienden*].

So where are we with this question concerning the essence of untruth? We will have long been impatiently asking this, provided that our detailed considerations have not in the meantime made us lose sight of the total context of the lecture course. It was in order to enter into this question of the essence of untruth, and into Plato's resolution of it (the only one which has yet been given), that we have taken up the interpretation of precisely this *Theaetetus* dialogue!

The question concerning untruth did not arise during the discussion of the first answer to the question of the essence of knowledge. It comes up during the discussion of the *second* answer, which is now given in the *Theaetetus*. Therefore, since we are in any case not going through the entire dialogue from beginning to end but are starting somewhere in the middle, couldn't we have spared ourselves the above investigation of αἴσθησις? So it appears, especially if we grant for the moment that 'sparing' ourselves this or that has sense and justification in philosophy. Why did we not just begin with the second answer? There are fundamental reasons for this, which will become clear when we are more familiar with the second answer to the question of what knowledge is.

We are not yet at our goal. We wanted to see how Plato sets about discussing the problem of untruth. First of all and quite generally: we did not begin at once with the second answer, for the simple reason that this would make it impossible to understand the passages following it; indeed we would not even be able to understand *why* the second answer to the leading question takes the form it does. One might ask, however, whether it is necessary to know this. This is indeed necessary, for it is within the framework of the second answer that the problem of untruth *arises*, and it is decisive that we see the kind of *context of inquiry* in which this problem is set. It is not a matter of seeing how Plato *defines* untruth (he does not define it at all) but of seeing how this problem is here posed for the first time in the history of philosophy. Only when this is clear can we be confident of reaching the ground of the essence of untruth. In fact it is our sole intention to awaken an understanding for where the *question* of the essence of untruth is *situated*, i.e. within *which* sphere of questions Plato *places* it, and how he thereby takes a decisive step towards the *problem* – but also a step that makes it possible for the question to be derailed and degenerate into a harmless triviality or disagreeable side issue, such that untruth, as the unwelcome opposite of truth, is regarded as a property of the assertion.

The second answer to the guiding question by no means follows from the first in an accidental or arbitrary way, just as little as the first answer arose like this. We said that the first answer arises not from a superficial whim or mood on the part of Theaetetus but from a perfectly natural experience. We must, therefore, above all clarify the manner in which the second answer is driven by the first, and unfolded from it within the *framework* of the Greek understanding of this proposition. From this it already becomes clear that the rejection of the first answer, although negative in its bare result, obtains a *positive* meaning for the further unfolding of the problem, and quite apart from the inquiry concerning the relationship to being, which stands *in itself* irrespective of how the question of ἐπιστήμη may be decided.

Socrates himself indicates (187 a 3 ff.) that the result of the investigation is not purely negative. The discussion has in fact been driven so far forward that now a whole region remains excluded from interrogation by the question of the essence of knowledge. We see that Socrates gives a methodological twist to the result, and this gathers force when we reflect how natural it is to claim precisely αἴσθησις as the essence of knowledge, in so far as it is αἴσθησις, obscurely understood, which the beings themselves in their presence offer to us. Yet what makes possible this offering of beings themselves in their presence is not αἴσθησις as given through the senses, but αἴσθησις only in so far as it is already borne and illuminated by striving for being. αἴσθησις and ἐπιστήμη are not the same if αἴσθησις is sensation. Nevertheless, the determination of knowledge as αἴσθησις provides an essential due, if αἴσθησις is understood as the perceiving of beings, indeed this secures the ground from which the question of the essence of knowledge can be posed anew (connection to being). And *that* is our proximal intention, i.e. to ask how the soul comports itself when it occupies itself (πραγματεύηται, 187 a 5) with what we call beings. Only where this relationship to being obtains is there a primordial possibility of the presence of beings and thus of unhiddenness (truth). Only in this case can we speak of the possession of truth, i.e. knowledge. The methodological guideline for everything that follows is therefore: what knowledge is, thus the essence of knowledge and its inner possibility, must from the outset be sought in the domain where the relationship to being as such occurs. In short, *the question concerning the essence of knowledge and its truth is a question concerning the essence of being* – rather than the reverse situation of the question of the essence of being *following on* from the question of the essence of truth or even of thought. However, since truth is specifically bound up with being, the former can, indeed must, present the *passage-way* to the latter.

Therefore Socrates/Plato very carefully says that the essence of knowledge is not to be sought in what *we call* αἴσθησις but in that autonomous comportment of the soul to beings whereby it αὐτὴ καθ' αὐτὴν πραγματεύηται περὶ τὰ ὄντα (187 a 5), 'it alone and by itself is engaged directly with beings'. It follows from our earlier results that only here can there be the possibility of truth and knowledge. However, Socrates is careful not to tie down this comportment of the soul by any kind of rigid definition, and instead gives substantive guidelines for the question; for it is only in the course of inquiry that definitions receive their substantively grounded meaning (cf. αἴσθησις). Now the question is which human comportment exhibits this character of πραγματεύεσθαι concerning beings, of engaging directly with beings in relationship to them, and in such a way that precisely this comportment makes possible what we call possession of truth, i.e. unhiddenness of beings. For it is unquestionably the case that the unhiddenness of beings belongs to knowledge. Socrates gives only a general indication of the direction in which this essential comportment must be sought, leaving it to Theaetetus to quote a suitable case.

§ 37. Double-Meaning of δόξα (View): Look and Opinion

The question is now firmly aimed at defining the relationship to beings. Theaetetus answers (187 a 7):

'Αλλὰ μὴν τοῦτό γε καλεῖται, ὦ Σώκρατες, ὡς ἐγῷμαι, δοξάζειν.

'This comportment of the soul which you regard as knowledge [possession of truth] is, I believe, called δοξάζειν.'

Socrates agrees, and at once demands that Theaetetus dispense with the whole previous investigation concerning αἴσθησις, i.e. that he no longer make use of these earlier considerations. Theaetetus is not to *argue* on the basis of what has gone before by developing long speeches and clever proofs for new wide-ranging theories. This is not because the matter has been settled, or these earlier ideas refuted, but in order that Theaetetus should keep his mind open for the indicated field of phenomena – to consider, εἴ τι μᾶλλον καθορᾷς (187 b 1), whether in some way he now has a *clearer* vision of the essence of ἐπιστήμη.

The investigation begins anew, as if nothing had happened, and yet the previous results remain somehow in the *background*.

According to the second answer, the essence of knowledge consists in that comportment of the soul which is called δοξάζειν. This verb is usually translated as 'opine' [*meinen*], and the noun δόξα as 'opinion' [*Meinung*]. This translation only goes half-way to capturing the Greek meaning of the word, a half-measure which, as everywhere and particularly here, is more dangerous than complete error. With this translation, which is only conditionally fitting in certain cases, the fundamental meaning of the Greek word is obscured. The situation the Greeks have in mind is covered up and it is thus no wonder that this fitting/non-fitting translation of the word hinders the understanding of the problems lying concealed behind it. But these problems must be brought out if one wants to understand the way in which Plato's and Aristotle's treatment of the δόξα forces the *question* of the essence of truth, and thus the question of the essence of being, along a specific future track from which it has still not departed. For us who have long proceeded along this track, or rather, who have settled down comfortably upon it, its direction seems so self-evident that we cannot imagine any other way of questioning. On the other hand, the false translation is excused firstly by the fact that the word was also ambiguous for the Greeks, secondly by the fact that in a certain sense 'opinion' is a fitting translation, and thirdly by the circumstance that the German language apparently does not have a word that preserves the ambiguity and at the same time gives the total meaning of δόξα. After giving a general indication of their meaning, we shall initially leave δόξα and δοξάζειν untranslated.

As with ἀλήθεια, ψεῦδος, λανθάνω, ἐπιστήμη, we give a brief indication of the concrete meaning of the words δόξα and δοξάζειν. My purpose is to show, from the substantive context of the dialogue as we have followed it, why Theaetetus comes to precisely this second answer, namely that the essence of ἐπιστήμη must reside in the region of δόξα.

On the basis of the positive investigation prompted by the first answer, Socrates indicates the sphere in which the essence of knowledge must be sought. The essence of knowledge can be located only in that sphere where the soul itself has dealings with beings – in short, in the sphere of the soul's relationship to beings (striving for being), in the sphere of the possibility of the possession of the unhiddenness of beings. Looked at closely, this involves a *double* claim: the essence of knowledge is determined firstly through that which has the character of a *relationship* to beings, but also through that which gives and makes available these beings in their presence and manifestation, thus such that these beings can and do show themselves from themselves. To be sure, αἴσθησις is unable to do this, but the discussion of the first answer in no way disputes that αἴσθησις is relevant, indeed that something like a becoming-manifest and self-showing of beings is essential for the unhiddenness of beings; it is only said that αἴσθησις by itself and as such cannot do this.

The question remains as to *how* the self-showing of beings is and must be possible. In short, there now emerges the task of discovering a phenomenon whose essential constitution involves firstly a self-showing of the beings themselves, secondly the relationship to being as this occurs from the soul itself. It is precisely this double claim that Theaetetus intends by referring to δόξα (δοξάζειν). More accurately, just as the first answer had recourse to the immediately *obvious* αἴσθησις, so this second answer has recourse to the phenomenon of δόξα as this is familiar from unreflective life. Why can and must Theaetetus fall back upon the δόξα? What does δόξα mean for the Greeks?

Let us begin with the verbs δοκεῖν, δοκέω, i.e. I show myself, either to myself or to others. In a certain sense the word is the exact counterconcept to λανθάνω, I am hidden (hide myself) to others or to myself. I show myself to myself: I come before myself as such and such, I appear before myself and others. This appearing-before-my self-and-others has the meaning of offering an appearance. But this is a self-showing in *some way or another*. This self-showing leaves it *open* whether what shows itself is or is not that which it shows itself as. It shows itself, i.e. it *appears*, and in this appearing, in this stepping forth, it appears to be this or that. This appearance leaves it undecided whether it is mere *illusion* or whether it is indeed what it appears to be.

For the fundamental meaning of δοκέω (δόξα) it is important to keep firmly in mind that it involves the self-showing of something, above all the offering of a *look or view*. Instead of citing arbitrary examples we choose a passage from our dialogue (143 e 6) that we mentioned earlier in connection with Socrates calling Theaetetus beautiful while Theodorus calls him ugly.[2] At the beginning of the conversation Socrates asks Theodorus to name a young Athenian whom he believes to have a good future. Theodorus replies that he knows one such person:

Καὶ εἰ μὲν ἦν καλός, ἐφοβούμην ἂν σφόδρα λέγειν, μὴ καί τῳ δόξω ἐν ἐπιθυμίᾳ αὐτοῦ εἶναι.

'If he were beautiful, I would hesitate to call him such, lest I give the impression to anyone that I bear a passion for him.'

Schleiermacher translates, characteristically, 'lest someone believe [of me]';[3] the Greeks say, by contrast, 'lest I appear before someone as such and such', 'who gives the impression'. Thus precisely the same reversal of linguistic usage as with λανθάνω.[4] δοκέω: I appear to others or to myself as...; only from this does δοίκετυ obtain a further meaning: I seem to myself to be such and such. *Iliad* VII, 192: ἐπεὶ δοκέω νικησέμεν Ἕκτορα δῖον. 'I appear to myself as someone who -1 believe of myself, I have the opinion that, I shall defeat Hector.' This is a characteristic reversal of the meaning: the state of affairs is no longer seen from the standpoint of *that which* shows itself, from the object, but from those who are looking at it, i.e. from this comportment; from those to whom something is shown and presented (this is himself: he presents himself to himself, he holds himself for such and such) and who thus have a *view* of what shows itself.

This same ambiguity also pertains to δόξα. The word means on the one hand: the look and view that someone offers or wherein something stands; in the accentuated sense: public reputation, honour, fame; in the New Testament: δόξα θεοῦ, brilliance, magnificence. Thereupon: what one *represents to oneself* in such self-showing, the image and picture one makes of it, thus the opinion one has of it. But these meanings of δόξα also imply that what shows itself *gives off* an appearance, awakens an *impression*; thus that the picture one has of something could really be different. The picture, seemingly *such*, is indeed decided upon from one side, but the other is not ruled out.

I have already mentioned that it is not easy to find a corresponding German word, especially one that expresses and preserves the fundamental meaning of δοκέω and δόξα. The word I find most fitting is 'Ansicht' (view), because this brings out the Greek meaning of selfshowing, the look. We use the word with the same ambiguity as the Greeks:

1   'Ansicht' in the compound expression 'Ansichtskarte' (picture postcard): a card that does not *represent* an opinion or view, but *creates* an actual look, that presents something showing itself.

2   But we also say 'ich bin der Ansicht' ['I am of the view'] and thereby mean: I am of the opinion, I hold that so and so, I see the matter in such and such a way.

The word δόξα, 'view', thus obtains its meaning from two opposed directions, from the object and from the comportment. Both meanings, i.e. the look of something and the taking of something as such and such, are present in the one word. It is characteristic of the Greeks, however, that they did not see these two meanings simply as juxtaposed in an unconnected way but as essentially related to each other. Indeed it is precisely this relationship which is most essential to the substantive problem under consideration. Understanding the one meaning involves attending to the other; δοξάζειν: to have a view about something which shows itself in such and such a way, i.e. what a particular view or impression *offers*.

Positively speaking, what emerges from the whole discussion of the possible character of perception (αἴσθησις) as knowledge is the following. In order to adequately grasp the essence of knowledge as the possession of the unhiddenness of beings it is necessary to discover a phenomenon that contains firstly the moment of becoming-manifest (the self-showing of the object), and, at the same time, the relationship of being to the beings which the soul takes up into itself. At first sight this twofold requirement seems to be met by the δόξα, and indeed in its double meaning. On the one hand, view as the look of something, as what the thing offers (whether rightly or otherwise is a further question; it is always the inner claim of a view to present the thing itself); and on the other hand the *comportment*, a stance-taking that springs from the soul itself, i.e. to be of the view, to hold something for such and such. I am of the view: for my part I see the matter as so and so (ἡ ψυχὴ αὐτὴ καθ' αὑτήν). The first meaning concerns the *perceiving* of a view, the perceiving acceptance of a look as this presents itself; the second meaning concerns the *fore-taking* [*Sich-vornehmen*] of the same, the perceiving of something *by* us (thus seeing it and taking it as such and such).

In this way it should become clear how the unfolding of the problem of the first answer necessarily presses into the region indicated by the term δόξα. The identification of this region, and of the path towards it, is of special importance for us because it is precisely within this region of δόξα that there arises the phenomenon of the *distorted* view [*verkehrte Ansicht*]. The Greeks understand untruth as τὸ ψεῦδος, distortion. This phenomenon does not arise here by accident, but necessarily. The δόξα cannot be further understood without attending to this phenomenon of distortion.

§ 38. Two More Faces of δόξα: The Wavering between Letting-Appear (εἶδος) and Distorting (ψεῦδος)

But let us again follow the actual course of the dialogue (187 b ff.)! Theaetetus has only just named the new region for discovering the essence of knowledge when he makes a curious qualification (187 b 4 ff.):

Δόξαν μὲν πᾶσαν εἰπεῖν, ὦ Σώκρατες, ἀδύνατον, ἐπειδὴ καὶ ψευδής ἐστι δόξα. κινδυνεύει δὲ ἡ ἀληθὴς δόξα ἐπιστήμη εἶναι, καί μοι τοῦτο ἀποκεκρίσθω.

'To say that knowledge is only view [having a view] is impossible, for a view can often be false [distorted]. Only the *true* view could be knowledge. Let that be my answer.'

We see that with δόξα we are immediately in a region which is indifferent in respect of truth and falsity. As Socrates says (187 c 3 f.): δυοῖν ὄντοιν ἰδέαιν δόξης ('the δόξα has two faces'). To be noted, however, is that this is not the double-meaning we just discussed (the look of an object and the comportment of having-a-view), but that *each* of these two meanings of δόξα has two faces. A δόξα qua 'look of something': the look can present the being itself, the given thing, but it can also *make something out* to be what it is not. The look can reveal, but can also hide and distort. Likewise, δόξα *qua* 'having-a-view' can be either correct or incorrect.[5]

We thus see that with δόξα we find ourselves in a very complicated region where it is necessary to keep our eyes open and survey *the whole*. For the various meanings attaching to the essence of δόξα make it tempting to focus on just *one* side and thus miss the problem.

But even this is not the greatest difficulty. As we shall see, the δόξα becomes the framework wherein the question of the essence of ψεῦδος is taken up. By introducing this phenomenon, one immediately ventures into the region of this wavering between correctness and distortion. Socrates already has an understanding of this complex region, and he directs Theaetetus hither and thither within it; not, however, in order to confuse him, but because he wants to familiarize Theaetetus with what cannot be mastered by the crude and apparently clear proofs of sound common sense.

In order, in a stepwise manner, to make Theaetetus see the various characters, even if he does not grasp their connections (αἴσθησις – διάνοια), Socrates poses the question (187 c 7):

Ἆρ' οὖν ἔτ' ἄξιον περὶ δόξης ἀναλαβεῖν πάλιν–;

'Is it then still worthwhile, in regard to the δόξα, to take it up again –?' [Theaetetus, astonished, interrupts:] Τὸ ποῖον δὴ λέγεις; 'What do you mean?'

The δόξα was already touched on earlier (170 a f.) because it was unavoidable in the context of the whole theme of the dialogue. But it was only considered in passing, without in any way determining its essence. Socrates now proposes to make the δόξα as such explicitly thematic. Indeed, as Socrates' answer shows, he is intent on attacking the most difficult side of the problem of the δόξα. He admits to Theaetetus that he too has often been troubled by his inability to say what this experience is, and how it comes about. 'Which experience?' asks Theaetetus. Τὸ δοξάζειν τινὰ ψευδῆ (187 d 6). 'This: that someone can have a distorted view' (ψευδὴς δόξα).

We too are pressed by Plato into the role of Theaetetus; for like Theaetetus we too are astonished only by Socrates' astonishment and unease. What, then, is so remarkable about the fact that we have distorted as well as true views? This is a quite ordinary and everyday fact. With respect to the guiding question of the dialogue, namely 'What is knowledge?', and the answer now given, namely that it is true view, we shall ourselves think that we should treat just of *true* view and not of distorted view. Why should we, as Socrates now proceeds to do, give lengthy consideration to whether *distorted* view should be treated first?

But Theaetetus leaves Socrates to make the decision, and we too give Plato the lead, following with him the traces of this remarkable path whose necessity we are initially quite unable to grasp, and which brings us to a discussion of ψεῦδος (untruth). We thus ask, along with Plato, what kind of condition of the soul, i.e. of the essence of man, obtains in the case of distorted view, and how this comes about. The question concerning the γένεσις of this condition does not seek a psychological explanation of its origin, i.e. it is not concerned with the causes of human beings falling into error, but rather with the *possibility* of this phenomenon. It is directed to what makes possible the ψευδὴς δόξα *as such*, irrespective of whether and how this factually occurs. In short, the question of γένεσις here concerns the inner possibility, the essence.

Looking back, we now see with greater clarity the context of inquiry within which the problem of the ψεῦδος arises: in the question concerning a phenomenon, the δόξα-character, which contains that ambiguity which is itself the ground of the possibility of wavering between 'distorted' and 'not distorted'. This is the context. But we still do not see the authentic *rootedness* of the problem of untruth (distortion).

Notes

1 See above p. 143; Sophocles, *Antigone*, lines 332 f.

2 See above p. 143.

3 Fowler translates: 'lest someone should think I was in love with him'; Corn- ford translates: 'lest I should be suspected of being in love with him'. [Trans.]

4 See above pp. 100 ff.

5 See Supplement 20.

5

The Question Concerning the Possibility of the ψευδὴς δόξα

Socrates proposes inquiring into the distorted view. The investigation of the ψευδὴς δόξα begins at 187 c 5 and ends at 200 d, proceeding in two stages, a preliminary and a main investigation. This is followed by a discussion of the ἀληθής δόξα (200 d to 201 e). Disproportionately greater space is thus devoted to the distorted view. Yet if the dialogue concerns the essence of *knowledge*, and if this is to be understood as the possession of *truth*, then the true view should be the proper topic. For this reason people have always wondered why Plato does not discuss the 'true view' at greater length, especially since, at the end, Socrates says that the 'distorted view' cannot be apprehended in its essence until the essence of the true view is grasped. Just why, despite all this, the ψευδὴς δόξα is treated first, and at such great length, just why it occupies the greatest thematic space in the entire dialogue, all this is very puzzling.

A. Preparatory Investigation: Impossibility of the Phenomenon of the ψευδὴς δόξα

§ 39. The Horizon of the Preparatory Investigation as Excluding in Advance the Possibility of a ψευδὴς δόξα

The oddity of this whole section concerning the ψευδὴς δόξα increases if we take note of how this investigation sets out and the direction in which it proceeds. The discussion seeks to impress upon Theaetetus just how remarkable this phenomenon of the ψευδὴς δόξα really is. In this way, however, the unstated positive intention plays the *guiding* role; exhibiting the puzzling character of the phenomenon allows it to be more clearly laid bare in its various sides and levels, so that our understanding becomes sharpened for a more thorough treatment. By no means should we regard the preparatory discussion as less important than what is developed thematically; on the contrary, it is in the preparatory discussion that the framework for dealing with the problem is defined. It is here that we become acquainted with those directions within which Plato (and the Greeks) necessarily had to comprehend the phenomenon of the ψευδὴς δόξα and thus of the ψεῦδος. We are concerned with the way in which the question of the essence of untruth was first approached, such that this became determinative for all subsequent ages.

The preparatory investigation extends from 187 d to 191. The question is (187 d 3 f.):

Τί ποτ' ἐστὶ τοῦτο τὸ πάθος παρ' ἡμῖν καὶ τίνα τρόπον ἐγγιγνόμενον;

'To have a distorted view: what state of the soul is that, and how does it occur?'

What can we say about such a thing, and what (out of which component parts) does such a condition consist in? The answer to this question is initially sought in three directions, i.e. the phenomenon of the ψευδὴς δόξα is considered from three perspectives. The first discussion extends from 188 a to d, the second from 188 d to 189 b 9, the third from 189 b 10 to 190 e 4. All three discussions come to the conclusion that the distorted view is in its essence utterly null [*nichtig*], therefore cannot exist at all.

However, in order to give this remarkable result the full force of astonishment and wonder, the whole inquiry is preceded by a reference to facts and basic principles which initially appear not to be doubted, and to whose truth the interlocutor readily agrees. We immediately agree that distorted views occur, that one person will have a distorted view and another person a correct view – just as if all this belonged to our essence.[1]

So on the one hand the existence of distorted views is an indubitable *fact*, grounded in the nature of man; on the other hand the conclusion is reached that such a thing as a distorted view *cannot exist*. Socrates, who is naturally already aware of both the factuality and the impossibility of a distorted view, is thus quite justified in being troubled by this strange phenomenon, and in being utterly at a loss about it.

But what is going on? How are we to understand this? Let us follow the three perspectives! To be noted is that Socrates *leads* the discussion, i.e. guides the direction of questioning. Distorted view is not directly illuminated by Plato/Socrates in the manner of a description, but Socrates proceeds from definite *basic principles*, under which he places the ensuing discussion. Nevertheless, to make what follows easier to comprehend, we shall consider an *example*:

a) First Perspective: Alternatives of Knowing and Not-knowing

What is that – a distorted view? We find the answer by looking at what *properties* are exhibited by such a comportment (having a distorted view); and we shall do this by bringing to mind an *example* that Plato has already consciously prepared in the dialogue and which we earlier mentioned in passing. We remember that, right at the beginning, mention was made of the fact that Theaetetus is snub-nosed and goggle-eyed, but not to such a degree as Socrates. So it could easily happen that someone approaching Theaetetus from a distance would take him for Socrates; this person would then have a distorted view. Now we could, as stated, directly describe this phenomenon. But Socrates does not proceed in this way; instead, he begins with a general reflection. Human beings are such that they either *know* or do *not* know something; they always have this dual possibility before them: that something is known or not known. This is so obvious and self-evident that Theaetetus immediately agrees, saying οὐδὲν λείπεται, 'there are no other possibilities' besides *either* knowing *or* not knowing. Knowing and not-knowing are mutually exclusive. This consideration provides the *guiding principle* for the discussion that follows. At the same time, however, this guiding principle positively indicates the perspective through which the phenomenon of the ψευδὴς δόξα, i.e. the δόξα in general, is to be examined: as knowing, or, more precisely, as representing [*Vorstellen*]. Plato employs the colourless expression εἰδέναι, whose ambiguity and vagueness cannot be rendered in the German language.

Socrates lays down this consideration as the guiding principle by expressly remarking: there is indeed something *between* knowing and not- knowing, namely learning-to-know, coming-to-know, the *transition* from not-knowing to knowing; *un*-learning and forgetting is the transition from knowing to not-knowing. This μεταξύ, says Socrates, we are now leaving aside; it does not belong to the matter that is now being treated. We agree upon the unambiguous thesis: everything is either known or not known.[2] This perspective is completely appropriate and therefore justified. For from the outset it is necessary (ἤδη ἀνάγκη) that when someone has a view, whether distorted or correct, he in any case has a view on [über] something – thus something he knows or does not know. Thus, when someone has a view on something, he in some sense has knowledge of something. To have a view on something is to have *knowledge* of something or a representation of something in the broadest sense. Knowledge stands under the guiding principle that it excludes not- knowing (and vice versa). This principle immediately implies, as Socrates says (188 a 10 f.):

Καὶ μὴν εἰδότα γε μὴ εἰδέται τὸ αὐτὸ ἢ μὴ εἰδότα εἰδέναι ἀδύνατον.

'That one who knows a thing does not know it, or that one who does not know it knows it, is surely impossible.'

Naturally, for we either know something, or we do not know it.

Why is Socrates not content with this general principle? Why is the implication of the principle actually quoted here? Because it brings to expression the *possibility* or impossibility of a phenomenon that becomes a problem under the heading of ψευδὴς δόξα. Only now is the perspective for apprehending the ψευδὴς δόξα made sufficiently precise.

For what is the situation when someone has a distorted view? They do not simply know something, have knowledge of . . ., but since it is distorted, they at the same time do not know it. A distorted view is still a *view*; it is not simply that they know nothing at all, for something is indeed *represented*. They thus know something, but it is a *distorted* view, such that what is known is not known. It is therefore a view and at the same time not. So in the fact of the ψευδὴς δόξα there is already a *phenomenon* that contradicts the guiding principle of the entire discussion. Nevertheless, this guiding principle is for the moment still maintained. To be noted is that this guiding principle is apparently maintained as *self-evident*, against the fact of a ψευδὴς δόξα. To the Greeks of the time, and for the moment also to Plato, this is absolutely self-evident. That there is something between the two is precisely the great *discovery* of Plato. The discussion of the ψευδὴς δόξα is the only path to this.

Thus a distorted view, to which it now pertains that (as Socrates says, 188 b 3):

Ἆρ᾽ οὖν ὁ τὰ ψευδῆ δοξάζων, ἃ οἶδε, ταῦτα οἴεται οὐ ταῦτα εἶναι ἀλλὰ ἕτερα ἄττα ὧν οἶδε;

'Someone thinks the things he knows are *not* these things, but some other things he knows.'

An example: someone knows Theaetetus and Socrates; in the distance he sees a man (who is actually Theaetetus) coming towards him along the street; he takes this man to be Socrates. On the present interpretation this means that he *takes* Theaetetus, whom he knows, *as not* he whom he knows (as approaching him along the street) but as someone else. He therefore holds what he knows for something he does not know. For otherwise he would have taken the man as Theaetetus rather than as Socrates. So the remarkable circumstance emerges that someone who knows both Socrates and Theaetetus in this case also and simultaneously does not know them (188 b 4 f.):

ἀμφότερα εἰδὼς ἀγνοεῖ αὖ ἀμφότερα.

'He knows both [he knows who Socrates is, and who Theaetetus is] and yet is ignorant of both.'

For, as we say, he confuses them.

In the case of a distorted view, one knows, and does not know, one and the same thing! However, Theaetetus promptly says that such a thing is *impossible*, ἀδύνατον. If this is so, what remains? One might presume: he knows *neither*. Then having a distorted view would mean that one takes something one does not know for something else one likewise does not know. Then someone who knew *neither* Theaetetus nor Socrates could intend both while taking Socrates for Theaetetus or Theaetetus for Socrates. That is obviously impossible! The distorted view, consequently, cannot exist at all. The guiding principle, and what followed from it, remain valid: it is impossible that someone who knows something also does not know it, and vice versa.

Socrates now (188 c 2) gives this result a different and characteristic turn: it is not the case that someone takes what he knows as something he does not know. Theaetetus answers: τέρας γὰρ ἔσται, 'that would be a miracle'.

To anticipate, and thus to make visible the astonishing structure of the whole: this miracle does in fact exist. Especially in his later dialogues, Plato always employs this expression τέρας, miracle, when something initially appears as absolutely impossible and miraculous to the common understanding, but is later shown by philosophical reflection to be possible, i.e. *demonstrated* in its own inner possibility. For the moment, however, we have not yet come this far, but we remain with Theaetetus in his astonishment, as he becomes ever more conscious of the puzzling character of distorted view. Socrates summarizes this first examination of the ψευδὴς δόξα and again repeats the guiding principle under which the phenomenon is set, agreeing with Theaetetus that (188 c 6 f.):

Ἐπείπερ παντ' ἢ ἴσμεν ἢ οὐκ ἴσμεν ἐν, δὲ τούτοις οὐδαμοῦ φαίνεται δυνατὸν ψευδῆ δοξάσαι.

'Within the framework of the present perspective [either knowing or not knowing] it appears to be utterly impossible for someone to have a distorted view.'

And yet it does exist! They have already agreed upon the *fact* of the false view, indeed of many false views alternating with true and correct ones!

Let us pause for a moment! If, as stated, this miracle of a distorted view is supposed to be possible, and actual and demonstrable in its possibility, then it is clear that all the characteristics of the ψευδὴς δόξα must be somehow *rightly* involved; more precisely: they must be apprehended in a more fitting and originary manner, in order that the possibility of the phenomenon should come to light. It is thus important for the interpretation that we keep in mind what was already positively indicated about the ψευδὴς δόξα in the preliminary investigation (without Theaetetus noticing). We may then see how the *illumination* of the phenomenon, i.e. the transformation of the previous perspective, takes place.

The discussion departed from the 'knowing *and* not-knowing' of one and the same thing; 'knowing' in the broad sense: to have knowledge of something, representing, a view of something. That is quite in order; but why begin with knowing? Because what is at issue is 'distorted view', which clearly involves me *not* knowing something. View is knowing, distorted view not knowing. The question is how these two are compatible. Guiding principle: they exclude each other.

However, we further saw that with the introduction of the ψευδὴς δόξα, Socrates, as a result of a fundamental reflection, brings up a new phenomenon which did not occur with αἴσθησις or with the simple concept of knowledge. But Socrates does not go into the circumstance that *knowing* (which is how δόξα, having a view about something, is conceived) concerns something which has the character of ἀμφότερα, i.e., of the one and the other (Theaetetus and Socrates). To have a view means: to know something as something and to see this one thing as such and such, i.e. as *something else*. In Greek terms: to the object of δόξα there belongs ἕτερον – ἕτερον. The object to which a view relates is actually twofold: something (the one), which is taken for something else. In its essence, the δόξα has two objects. It is for this reason that Plato employs the term ἀμφότερα.

Hitherto, in the case of αἴσθησις (perceiving something), ἀμφότερα *meant both together*; now, on the contrary: both (ἀμφότερα) are known *and not* known.

This is why, suddenly and without further introduction, the οἴεσθαι crops up, to take something as something, or also ἡγεῖσθαι: previously undiscussed modes of comportment which even now are not at all emphasized, but which Socrates has to draw upon in order to treat of δόξα and distorted view.

Since Socrates leads Theaetetus through all these moments of the phenomenon, the latter's understanding is sharpened, even though he initially takes the ψευδὴς δόξα to be an utterly impossible phenomenon. Socrates even wants to awaken this insight in Theaetetus, so that the latter may understand why this phenomenon continues to disturb him (Socrates).

In investigating the phenomenon both have proceeded κατὰ τὸ εἰδέναι καὶ μὴ εἰδέναι (188 c 9 f.), on the presupposition that a false view is a knowing and a not-knowing. Since such impossibilities have emerged, since the first perspective (either knowing or not-knowing) has led to the impossibility of the phenomenon, while on the other hand the fact of distorted views cannot be denied, Socrates now asks whether the investigation should not instead proceed κατὰ τὸ εἶναι καὶ μή, in respect of being and non-being.

b) Second Perspective: Alternatives of Being and Non-being

So the second investigation (188 d to 189 b 9) begins. Yet Theaetetus does not initially understand how this perspective of being and non-being is supposed to reveal something about the essence and possibility of the ψευδὴς δόξα.

The second attempt to approach the phenomenon of the ψευδὴς δόξα proceeds in a different way to the first. To be sure, it proceeds from something self-evident and again aims at presenting the characteristic features of this phenomenon. But what is taken as self-evident is now no longer a universally acknowledged statement, but the commonplace and supposedly clear meaning of a *word*, namely the word ψευδής (ψεῦδος).

The ψευδὴς δόξα is to be investigated; so what does ψευδής mean? You will remember the explanation given earlier: ψεῦδος is distortion, the distorted, the twisted; something that looks like . . ., but behind which there is nothing, therefore the null [*das Nichtige*]; ψεύδειν, to annul, to thwart or foil.[3] It is this ordinary meaning of ψευδὴς (void, vain) that Socrates now takes up. A ψευδὴς δόξα is then itself a view that is null [*nichtige Ansicht*], a view wherein something null is assumed and intended; ψευδῆ δοξάζειν is to intend something null. But the null is what *is* not. To intend something null is to intend something non-existing. So we now see how the difference between being and non-being can and must be a guideline for investigating the ψευδὴς δόξα, i.e. that this second perspective is not at all artificial but has its valid grounding in the phenomenon of the δόξα.

The question must now be answered: what then *is* the ψευδὴς δόξα, if The ψευδῆ δοξάζειν is nothing else but to τὸ μὴ ὂν δοξάζειν (to intend something null)? Socrates asks: is it at all possible for someone περὶ τῶν ὄντων του (188 d 9), in respect of some being or other, to have a view of something that is not? Indeed, can anyone at all *intend* the non-existing in itself? Certainly, we will say: this happens whenever someone accepts something that is not true; not true, i.e. not manifest, not present, nonexisting. Thus, we will say, the intending of what is not, does indeed exist. Socrates asks whether anything of this sort occurs elsewhere. That someone intends something, thereby intending something non-existing? That *in* representing we represent the non-existing, so perhaps that in *seeing* something one sees *nothing*? To *mean* the non-existing: is there such a thing? How then! If I intend something that is distorted, I nevertheless intend *something*, thus something that is, ὄν τι. Then I cannot intend some non-being. An intention cannot relate to something non-existing, for in that case it would have no object. Therefore it is not possible for a ψευδὴς δόξα *itself* to *be*. Socrates reinforces Theaetetus' view that such a thing is quite impossible. For whoever sees *something*, τῶν ὄντων τι ὁρᾷ (188 e 7), sees an existing something. Whoever hears *something*, hears a something and thus an existing thing. (Cf. earlier: οὐσία πρῶτον μάλιστα ἐπὶ πάντων παρέπεται, 186 a 2 f.) Therefore does not whoever intends something *intend* a something, thus an existing thing?

With this awkward question, Socrates leads Theaetetus along a false path, for he puts every δοξάζειν μὴ ὄντα, the intending of non-existing things, in a correspondence with seeing, hearing and the like, i.e. with modes of comportment which are *simply* directed, which do not involve intending something *as* something. By showing that seeing is always the seeing of something (i.e. something that *is*), thus that there cannot be a seeing which sees *nothing*, and by transposing this situation to the case of intending (opining), Socrates argues: if I intend *nothing*, then my intending, which here means representing, is itself void and therefore impossible. So whoever intends something that is not, intends a non-entity, therefore *nothing*, οὐδέν; but whoever intends nothing does not *intend* at all. For intending would have no object, and that would not be intending at all. Whoever has a view that is null cannot have a view at all. Thus a ψευδὴς δόξα is quite impossible. Yet if such a thing is indeed possible (which must be the case, since, as we have admitted, it is found everywhere) then it cannot be defined in the manner we have attempted. So it is once again forcefully impressed upon Theaetetus how this phenomenon obstinately eludes comprehension, how it remains ungraspable and miraculous, and thus disturbing.

Interpreting the distorted view as the view that is null, i.e. as viewing nothing at all, results in its self-cancellation as null. This negative result of the second investigation is derived not from the first guideline of inquiry (either knowing or not-knowing), but from the principle that something either is or is not.

We shall see that also this alternative (being or non-being), which for centuries the Greeks had regarded as quite certain, is shaken: that there is an intermediate between being and non-being, likewise between knowing and not-knowing. This intermediate is the ground of the possibility of the ψεῦδος.

However, just as with the first attempt, we cannot rest content with simply accepting the lack of any result. Rather, we must reflect upon the fact that there are clear grounds in the phenomenon itself for investigating it in respect of the null and non-being. Measured against true insight, the distorted view is not only something that turns out as null, but, in its relation to the object, it *intends* something that *is not*. This is the puzzling thing about the distorted view as such. The question is only why, despite this valid observation, made necessary by the phenomenon itself, the attempt to grasp the essence of the ψευδὴς δόξα in this way fails. Clearly, this is because the phenomenon is not seen as a whole. And why is that? Because Theaetetus is not yet *free* to learn to see, because he is still too much under the influence of commonly accepted principles and concepts into which he forces the phenomenon and thus deforms it. More precisely, Socrates leads him into this error by emphasizing the vulgar meaning of ψευδής (as 'null') and allowing him to fall into the trap. But in this Theaetetus is only the representative, as it were, of healthy common sense – to be sure, the healthy common sense which speaks and thinks in *Greek*.

There are three factors here which determine the common understanding and make its view unfree: at bottom, the same as what already hindered the first attempt.

1. Just as there δοξάζειν was οἴεσθαι (to take something as something), so now, compelled by the phenomenon, it must again be conceived as δοξάζειν τι περί τινος believing something *about* something, having a view *about* something, seeing something as this *and* as something else. It is therefore not to be overlooked that the object of δόξα is as it were *two* objects (ἀμφότερα). To the phenomenon 'having a view of something' there belongs the 'whereof' and the view of it. But we call 'having a view' δοξάζειν, and this is always δοξάζειν τι, intending *something*. So the obvious thing is to equate δοξάζειν with such modes of comportment as ὁρᾶν τι, ἀκούειν τι, therefore with αἴσθησις; what holds for this (seeing and hearing) must also hold for δοξάζειν (opining). Theaetetus falls into this trap. At the moment when he embraces this correspondence and understands δοξάζειν in the manner of seeing, hearing and the like, he fails to pay due regard to the object of belief, taking it likewise as a *simple* object. The object is given up and sinks out of sight; i.e. the ἀμφότερα, the double-aspect of the object of δόξα, is not held on to, and so what is further said is groundless.

2. If ψευδὴς is the null, ψευδὴς δόξα null opinion, and the null the same as the non-existent, μὴ ὄν then the distorted view cannot have any object at all. What is not something is nothing (οὐδέν); the non-existent, which takes the lead here, is equated with the nothing. It is not at all asked whether the non-existent is also a being and can be

such. For how otherwise could a distorted view be *resisted*, if from the beginning it were nothing! Here also the *phenomenon* comes into view in a certain way, in that someone who has a distorted view *believes something* about the object (something which does not apply, thus a nothing); *therefore* the impossibility of the phenomenon.

3. Finally, and in connection with this, the equating of the non-existent and the nothing is strengthened by the fact that beings exclude the nonexistent, exactly as in the previous case knowing excluded not-knowing, i.e. there is nothing between them.

We would misunderstand the whole meaning and difficulty of this second attempt of Socrates and Theaetetus if we believed, as is the usual interpretation, that Theaetetus commits logical errors here, and that Socrates/Plato is engaged in a frivolous game of words. The opposite is the case. In the manner in which Socrates guides Theaetetus, the dialogue makes a tremendous effort to *combat* the domination of everyday talk and to resist the power of that healthy common sense that thinks in mere words and sentences. That the non-existing and the nothing, the μὴ ὄν and the οὐδέν, are not the same, is, until Plato, not at all self-evident. That ὁρᾶν τι and δοξάζειν τι are not equivalent in their comportmental character is even less self-evident. That there is something 'between' knowing and not-knowing, and between being and being-nothing, is certainly not self-evident. And that this intermediate is *more* than an intermediate: this is quite hidden to the self-evidence of the common understanding. In the interpretation of the domination of the self-evident we should not assume a posture of superiority, dismissing these attempts to grasp the phenomenon as erroneous and primitive. Both these attempts to grasp the essential constitution of the ψευδὴς δόξα fail because their guiding perspectives do not suffice, or, more precisely and carefully put, because these perspectives are not sufficiently worked through in regard to what is required by the phenomenon. The guiding fundamental principles do not prescribe how the phenomena must be, but the phenomena themselves come first, and it is they which prescribe how the guiding fundamental principles must be constructed.

Externally, nothing is attained, and yet this one thing is achieved: the *puzzling character* of the phenomenon is heightened and shows *itself* in its various aspects. To be sure, it seems as if the reflection only circles around the phenomenon; at bottom, however, this circling around is a constant narrowing of the circle, i.e. a coming closer. That the sequence of three attempts does proceed in this way can be easily seen from the beginning of the third attempt and its guiding perspective.

c) Third Perspective: The ψευδὴς δόξα as ἀλλοδοξία (Substitution instead of Confusion)

The third attempt (189 b 10 to 190 e 4) proceeds in a different way to the previous two. Without any further preparation, directly and as it were dogmatically, it gives a new conception of the essence of the ψευδὴς δόξα, and in addition a new name: a ψευδὴς δόξα is an ἀλλοδοξία This word cannot be translated, at any rate not by Schleiermacher's quite unsuitable expression 'verwechselte Meinung' [confused opinion].[4] If opinion, then at best to opine distortedly, to mean something else. But however difficult the translation, the substantive intention of this third proposal is quite clear.

The essence of a distorted view in the sense of an ἀλλοδοξία is, as Socrates says (189 b 12 ff.):

᾽Αλλοδοξίαν τινὰ οὖσαν ψευδῆ φαμεν εἶναι δόξαν, ὅταν τίς τι τῶν ὄντων ἄλλο αὖ τῶν ὄντων ἀνταλλαξάμενος τῇ διανοίᾳ φῇ εἶναι.

᾽Α ψευδὴς δόξα, in the sense of an ἀλλοδοξία, occurs when a person, in perceiving, takes one existing thing for another existing thing.'

Example: when someone takes an approaching person to be Socrates, when he is actually Theaetetus, i.e. *instead* of Theaetetus he takes him for Socrates. (But ἀνταλλάττεθαι does not mean confusion, rather a switching around of one *for* the other.) This conception of the essence of the ψευδὴς δόξα is immediately explained in terms of its adequacy to the guiding principles of the two previous attempts. More clearly stated: it is claimed that with this conception the previously discovered positive characteristics of the ψευδὴς δόξα find their place and inner connection. There are three moments:

1. The ψευδὴς δόξα (according to the second attempt) is an opining of nothing. Now it is shown that it is not an opining of nothing, but that in distorted opinion something *existing* is intended, only instead of one thing (Theaetetus, who it really is) another (Socrates, who it is not).

2. It is thereby already claimed (and thereafter held to) that a view is always such as to relate to one thing *and* to another thing (it has to do with two things) – in the case of the ψευδὴς δόξα to the one *instead* of the other. What Plato wants to emphasize is that an opinion really has two objects: the one *instead* of the other.

3. In this way the nature of the ψεῦδος is also indicated: that which is intended is *missed* (instead of Theaetetus, Socrates).

Theaetetus considers this new conception of the essence of the ψευδὴς δόξα to be highly suitable, and is so sure of it that he claims, as additional confirmation, that whoever comports himself in this way (in the sense of this ἀλλοδοξία), ὡς ἀληθῶς δοξάζει ψευδῆ is 'truly of a false view'. Socrates reminds him in passing of this daring statement, that something should be 'in truth false': that is like walking quickly in a slow manner. This is meant to indicate how far the two still are from a genuine clarification of truth and falsity, and of the connection between them. But Socrates goes easy on Theaetetus; he does not tie him down to this peculiar statement, but restricts himself to an *examination* of the third attempt.

The same procedure now occurs: 1. the phenomenon is lured out to some extent; 2. however, with the help of an accurately observed aspect of the phenomenon, the examination again diverts from the path and comes again 3. to results which assert the impossibility of this conception too, for the reason that it destroys the phenomenon itself. Since from this point onwards the course of the conversation is transparent, I give only brief explanations of the three points.

Firstly: what new characteristics emerge? The ἀλλοδοξία is a ἕτερόν τι ὡς ἕτερον. . .τῇ διανοίᾳ τίθεσθαι (189 d 7 f.), 'a positing of the one as the other, and indeed in the assimilating perceiving of something': no longer just observing (seeing or hearing), but the taking-in of something in regard to something. Again the one and the other; both (ἀμφότερα) are necessary, either both at the same time, or each on its own account, and now as the object of a positing (τίθεσθαι).[5]

Yet what do διάνοια and διανοεῖσθι now mean? We already encountered this concept, in a whole series of descriptions, during the elucidation of the essence of αἴσθησις. It is not yet immediately obvious whether exactly this same phenomenon is now intended or intended in the same way. That must be left open; we know that in the dialogue Plato attempts to arrive at a sharper conception of διάνοια. διανοεῖσθαι, as middle voice, further sharpens the meaning as the moment of essence of δόξα and is now specifically equated with διαλέγεσθαι (to talk through something for itself); thus διάνοια is a λόγος, a speech in which the soul goes through what it sees with itself. It would be a mistake to take this as a logical concept; we must beware here of bringing in the Platonic 'dialectic'. This speaking and saying has a quite specific character: it is a saying something to oneself, i.e. discussing some given thing with oneself, becoming clear about something and taking a stand towards it. This is what is meant by, οἴεσθαι, ἡγεῖσθαι, further πίστις, belief in the general sense of holding something to be such and such. This saying to itself of the soul is a saying and speaking without any linguistic manifestation; it occurs σιγῇ, what it says it says silently. If therefore one thing is posited instead of another thing, this means: in saying to oneself it is set forth as such and such, re-presented as it were.

In this description of διάνοια as λέγειν we have the essential character of re-presenting to oneself as a saying to oneself. From this we derive the broad meaning of λόγος also confirming that the Greeks did not define the primordial essence of saying and speaking, thus of language, in terms of its oral expression, nor in terms of its optical manifestations in signs and the like; at the same time we see that the essence of language is inwardly rooted in the essence of the soul. It cannot be surprising that the authentic comportment of the soul is defined as a saying, as a questioning and answering, as a yes- and no-saying, if, that is, the soul is what bears and determines the essence of man, and if, for the Greeks, man is the living being who has saying at his disposal, i.e. who strives sayingly to his own- most being.

Only now do we understand why διανοεῖσθαι, the relationship of the soul to being, was earlier conceived as ἀναλογίζεσθαι and συλλογισμός. The λόγος as the relation of gathering, of the gathered perceiving of something singular, is the original meaning of συλλογισμός. From this we clarify ἀλλοδοξία: the positing, the re-presenting to oneself of the one *instead* of the other, proves to be a saying of the one for the other. What the soul actually *says* is being. Irrespective of whether it occurs in the form of an assertion, saying is in each case a saying of being, a *saying* of is or is-not. To be of a view: this is a saying to oneself and a positing as such and such. What is posited *instead* of the other is always such and such. In the δόξα there always resides the saying and representing to oneself of being.

What we positively obtain from this discussion of the inner speech of the soul is that the δόξα involves a comportment in some sense similar to what we already know as the soul's relationship to beings – this is indeed necessary, in order that it should be at all possible for a comportment to be true or untrue.

Secondly: precisely this new characteristic now leads the examination of the ψευδὴς δόξα completely away from its path. To posit the one instead of the other would mean saying that the one is the other, e.g. that the beautiful thing is ugly, the fitting thing unfitting. This is quite impossible. It would never occur to us to say, not even in a dream, that the beautiful is ugly, the straight crooked. No one will ever say that an ox is a horse or that two are one. But if saying one for the other is ruled out, then the ἀλλοδοξία is in itself impossible.

Whoever, therefore, as is indeed the case with δόξα, re-presents the one *and* the other, cannot posit the one *in place of* the other. But should he represent only one of the two, then he would not have it as that which, or better, as that *instead* of which he posited the other.

So (thirdly) it is said in summary (190 d 11 ff.):

Οὔτ᾽ ἀρ᾽ ἀμφότερα οὔτε τὸ ἕτερον δοξάζοντι ἐγχωρεῖ ἀλλοδοξεῖν. ὥστ᾽ εἴ τις ὁριεῖται δόξαν εἶναι ψευδῆ τὸ ἑτεροδοξεῖν, οὐδὲν ἂν λέγοι· οὔτε γὰρ ταύτῃ οὔτε κατὰ τὰ πρότερα φαίνεται ψενδὴς ἐν ἡμῖν οὖσα δόξα.

'Then neither he who intends both, nor he who intends just one, can intend that one thing is something else [ἀλλοδοξεῖν]. And so anyone who sets out to define distorted view as τὸ ἑτεροδοξεῖν will be talking nonsense [for he assumes an impossible phenomenon]. So neither by this method nor by our previous method is a distorted view found to exist in us.'

How could we nevertheless maintain that this third attempt comes closer to the phenomenon than do the earlier attempts? Is it perhaps because here the διανοεῖν (the δόξα) is more forcefully presented as λόγος? No, for that would result in the examination coming off course, to seeing the phenomenon as impossible. Instead, we maintained this because the attempt is now made to seriously consider the fact that the ψευδὴς δόξα, i.e. the δόξα in general, relates to the one and the other. More precisely, the third explanation sees that what is puzzling about the phenomenon is that it has two objects, the one and the other. Holding fast to this insight, the attempt is made to understand, and to bring forth, how the one and the other are posited. The explanation runs: the one is posited *instead* of the other. This explanation does indeed see the task in the proper and decisive way, but it is not adequate as a solution. The dual object and its duality are explained in an erroneous manner. For if the ψευδὴς δόξα is a *distorted* view, which confuses something with another thing, this distortion is not adequately captured by saying that in such a view one thing is substituted for another. If the one is posited *instead* of the other, at bottom this means that *just one thing* is always posited, such that the other is disregarded or left aside; the one as the other, then *instead* of the other. In brief, interchanging is not the same as confusing; the essence of the latter cannot be grasped through the former. The two phenomena are mixed up, not only by Theaetetus but also by Schleiermacher. The guiding perspective of the third attempt (the substitution of one for the other) does not suffice. It leads precisely to the obfuscation of the phenomenon. When we clearly understand this, it is also not difficult to see how fundamentally erroneous is Schleiermacher's commonly accepted translation of ἀλλοδοξία as 'confused opinion' [*verwechselte Meinung*]. It is precisely *confusion* as such that this third explanation does not grasp. The misunderstanding is grounded in the faulty translation of the word ἀνταλλάττεσθαι; this does not mean confuse, but rather substitute, interchange.

From this you can see that the third attempt does get close to the peculiarity of the phenomenon of distorted view – which is indeed something like confusion – but on the other hand does not grasp the *structure* of confusion, only of substitution. This is not by accident, but there is a reason for it. In the background is the idea that opinion is the positing of the one and the other. Instead of seeing that the δόξα has only one object, which, however, possesses a complex rather than a simple unity, and that this complexity is the genuine problem, the prevailing view is always that the object of δόξα consists of two objects. We shall now see in what degree Plato succeeds in comprehending this complexity and its corresponding comportment, and in what points, and for which reasons, he fails.

§ 40. Result of the Preliminary Investigation: λόγος-Character of the δόξα; Its Aporia: Suppression of the Phenomenon through the Guiding Perspectives

Does the conversation remain without 'result'? We can recognize, without even coming to the end, that much 'results' to which subsequent philosophy and human knowledge could no longer measure up.

We are discussing the ψευδὴς δόξα. We have brought the preliminary investigation to a close. We have shown why the third attempt (ψευδὴς δόξα as ἀλλοδοξία) comes closer to the phenomenon than do the first and second attempts. What positively emerges from this third attempt, i.e. what is important for the main investigation, is that an attempt is made to grasp the δοξάζειν as a λόγος, λέγεσθαι, διαλέγεσθαι. The saying-something-to-oneself and the holding-of-oneself-to (to what is said) means simultaneously: to address something in a specific way. This demonstration of the λόγος-character of the δόξα is important in so far as it *alone* is retained in the later development of the δόξα concept, so that the primordial elements of the δόξα disappear behind this characteristic, and the δόξα, as 'opinion', is linked to *assertion* and the genuine phenomenon disappears.

Where do we stand at the conclusion of the preliminary investigation? It emerged that the guiding perspectives do not suffice, for they always lead to the assertion of the impossibility of anything like distorted view, i.e. to the *essential* impossibility of the phenomenon. Yet this phenomenon undeniably exists! We find ourselves confronted by the *phenomenon* of distorted view, and yet we nevertheless maintain the inner impossibility of the same. What must give way?

Our thesis of the impossibility of the phenomenon must give way to the fact that there *is* such a thing. This means that the guiding perspectives of the three attempts were inadequately grounded and also that the phenomenal state of affairs was for its part inadequately comprehended. A fact as such does not immediately have the priority of an essential insight, already for the reason that 'pure facts' do not exist for us at all. Every fact is already understood as this and this, i.e. it stands under the knowledge of essence. Where the knowledge of essence is grounded, then in respect of facts Hegel's statement holds: 'all the worse for the facts'. In our case the thesis must give way – not simply to give priority to the fact, but in order that we can ask *after it* in an unhindered manner. If we do not want to close our eyes, we must save the phenomenon, despite, indeed even because of, its 'miraculous' character. If the phenomenon itself has the first say, its clarification requires that the previous guiding perspectives be retracted.

B. Main Investigation: Saving the Phenomenon of the ψευδὴς δόξα

§ 41. Retracting the Guiding Perspectives of the Preliminary Investigation in Favour of Previously Denied Intermediate Phenomena

This retraction is admittedly only a negative step. We do not in this way arrive at those positive perspectives which allow the phenomenon itself to come forth. Or do we need no perspectives at all? Can we see the phenomenon directly, purely and simply for itself? No! From the interpretation of the cave allegory, and likewise from the discussion of αἴσθησις, we have learnt to understand that we always perceive what surrounds us in the light of, in regard to, an ἰδέα.

It was an error of phenomenology to believe that phenomena could be correctly seen merely through unprejudiced looking. But it is just as great an error to believe that, since perspectives are always necessary, the phenomena themselves can *never* be seen, and that everything amounts to contingent, subjective, anthropological standpoints. From these two impossibilities we obtain the necessary insight that our central task and methodological problem is to arrive at the *right* perspective. We need to take a precursory view of the phenomenon, but precisely for this reason it is of decisive importance whether the guiding perspective is adequate to the phenomenon, i.e. whether it is derived from its substantial content or not (or only construed). It is not because we must view it from some perspective or other that the phenomenon gets blocked off from us, but because the perspective adopted most often does not have a genuine origin in the phenomenon itself.

The task of the main investigation is now indicated, namely to arrive at more adequate perspectives for the ψευδὴς δόξα and to clarify the phenomenon in the light of these. The preliminary investigation is by no means unimportant for this task, especially since all three attempts, despite their ultimate inadequacy, did catch sight of certain moments of the phenomenon, thus bringing it closer to us, and now making it possible for the phenomenon, albeit as undetermined, to speak for itself.

The retraction of the previous inadequate perspectives is the step which completes the transition from the preliminary investigation to the main investigation. The same Socrates who earlier put forward these perspectives now undertakes their retraction, and indeed, in a so to speak holistic attack, he takes back the guiding principle of the first attempt, which also played a leading role in the two subsequent attempts. This is the principle that (188 a 2) 'either we have knowledge of something, or we have no knowledge of it'. Strictly speaking, this is only a modification of the principle that explicitly comes into play with the second attempt: 'either something *is* or it is *not*', alternatively, 'nothing can both be and not be at the same time', or 'the non-existent is not'. This principle, however, until Plato, and particularly until our dialogue, is the fundamental truth of all previous ancient philosophy. Western philosophy began precisely from this principle, *that what is, is, that the non-existent is not*.

Now if this fundamental principle of all being, and consequently of all knowledge, is retracted, the entire foundation of previous philosophy becomes unstable. From this we can get an idea of what a daring task Socrates/Plato undertakes. At the same time we can have an intimation of what power the phenomenon of the ψεῦδος (untruth) possesses to disturb and amaze, i.e. such that it forces this fundamental principle of all previous philosophy to be questioned. We can also appreciate the poverty of those later thinkers for whom untruth became a harmless self-evidency, the mere opposite of truth.

In his honourable role as pupil, Theaetetus does not suspect anything at all of Socrates' intentions. Neither is this necessary. But we must once again attempt to newly gauge what is actually happening in this conversation. Firstly, it seems outrageous, an infringement against the normal behaviour of human beings, to give up obvious and long-standing fundamental principles in favour of a likewise *familiar*, everyday, although uncomprehended and till then *miscomprehended* phenomenon. But secondly and more especially, the retraction concerns precisely those insights which, from the very beginning, inspired the whole power of seeing and questioning in ancient philosophy, and gave solidity to its foundations.

Now that the guiding principles have been given up, the way is clear for the interrogation of the phenomenon itself. The *inner turn* of the conversation occurs at 191 a 5 ff.:

[Socrates] ᾗ οὖν ἔτι πόρον τινὰ εὑρίσκω τοῦ ζητήματος ἡμίν, ἄκουε.

[Theaetetus] Λέγε μόνον.

[Socrates] Οὐ φήσω ἡμᾶς ὀρθῶς ὁμολογῆσαι, ἡνίκα ὡμολογήσαμεν, ἅ τις οἶδεν, ἀδύνατον δοξάσαι ἃ μὴ οἶδεν εἶναι αὐτὰ καὶ ψευσθῆναι· ἀλλά πῃ δυνατόν.

'Hear, then, by what means I still see a prospect of success for our investigation [of the ψευδὴς δόξα].'

'Do speak.'

'We were not really justified when we agreed that it is impossible for someone to think the things he does not know are the things he knows, and thus to be distorted. Rather, such a thing is somehow possible [ἀλλά πῃ δυνατόν].'

As soon as this possibility is opened up, and the obstacle of the previous guiding principle removed, Theaetetus too takes heart. He now ventures to reflect upon and articulate in an unprejudiced way what had initially, during the preliminary investigation, immediately impressed him as the givenness of the phenomenon, but which, owing to the rule of the guiding principle, he did not dare to assert. This is that he himself, who knows Socrates, sometimes takes a man approaching from a distance to be Socrates, who in truth is not Socrates. Consequently: he takes something he does not know (the approaching man) for something he knows (Socrates). Theaetetus assures himself of a phenomenal fact: its reality and at the same time its *possibility* and therefore the necessity of the *question* concerning this possibility, or as Plato says, concerning its γένεσις, its essence.

What does the retraction of the guiding principle *yield* for this question (concerning the possibility of a distorted view)? This retraction is not purely negative but at the same time positive, opening the way towards new possible perspectives on the phenomenon. Which? When it is said that the guiding principle ('either we know something or we do not know it') is not valid, it is at the same time conceded that there is still something between knowing and not-knowing, something which is neither knowing nor not-knowing, but a mixture as it were, of both ἀλλά πῃ δυνατὸν μεταξύ, 'somehow there is something in the middle'.

Now are there such intermediate phenomena? Indeed! Theaetetus must admit the facts of μάθησις, of learning, coming-to-know (191 c 3 f.): ἐστιν μὴ εἰδότα τι πρότερον ὕστερον μαθεῖν. 'It is possible for someone who does not know a thing at one time, to learn it later.'

This means, however, that in a certain sense one knows, yet also does not know, the same thing. In learning, one knows something and yet does not know it. Coming-to-know involves this *occurrence*, that one in a certain way *takes* cognizance of something without actually as yet knowing it. In the learning process there is always something that one knows and as yet does not know. Quite generally, this phenomenon between knowing and not-knowing does exist. Thus, in the wonderful composition of the dialogue, reference is now made to precisely the phenomenon which previously, in the preliminary investigation, was summarily dismissed (without Theaetetus noticing) from the inquiry (188 a): 'We hold to the phenomena; the μεταξύ, what lies in between, has no bearing on the matter'. Precisely this intermediate phenomenon is now brought in, so that new perspectives are opened up for the consideration of the phenomenon of the ψευδὴς δόξα.

But does not the main investigation now face the same danger as the preliminary investigation, namely that certain (albeit different) perspectives are assumed in advance and forced upon the phenomenon? This danger disappears if the phenomenon of 'distorted view', in and of itself, demands being seen in terms of such intermediate phenomena!

This is indeed the case. In what way? We now see the importance of the preliminary inquiry. During the whole preliminary investigation the phenomenon showed itself as a comportment directed to the one *and* the other in their characteristic unity and combination. As remarked, it has *two* objects as it were, which at bottom are just one, the one and the other combined. But if the object of δόξα is like this, there must be a corresponding *comportment* which is able to grasp this combined object as such. This must have the structure of a combined comportment, of knowing and at the same time not-knowing. So we see that the phenomenon itself requires attending to such intermediate phenomena. The task of the main investigation is to arrive at this new perspective (the possibility of a combined comportment) as demanded by the phenomenon itself.

The main investigation as a whole, of which one can say, without any exaggeration, that it has simply been misunderstood right up to the present day, only becomes comprehensible when this task has been actually seized hold of and realized. Only then do we see what dimension is opened up within which the possibility of the δόξα, thus the ψευδὴς δόξα and thus the ψεῦδος as such, i.e. its essence, can be secured. More precisely, only now can we properly situate the *question* of essence.

In view of this fundamental task, about which Plato was quite clear, it is of lesser importance whether the essence of ψεῦδος and δόξα receives a final determination or definition in the dialogue. We know that this does not happen. Furthermore, the dialogue never arrives at an answer to the guiding question τί ἐστιν ἐπιστήμη. And yet this (palpably result-less) dialogue is, for those who grasp philosophy, i.e. who can *question* in a philosophical way, inexhaustible in new insights. It is these which concern us, albeit with special reference to the ψεῦδος.

We shall now attempt to more closely comprehend this fundamental task of the main investigation: just that stretch of track upon which Plato travels (as the first and the last to do so) for the clarification of the essence of untruth. We can only really go along this stretch of track with open eyes if, as previously occurred, our view has been sharpened for the matter at hand, and if the direction and environs of this track, its landscape so to speak, has been reviewed in advance.

For this purpose, departing from the earlier procedure of interpretation, I give a precursory summarizing presentation of the fundamental task of the main investigation. In order for the specific course of the conversation to become accessible it is necessary: 1. to have in view the entirety of the lecture-course thus far; 2. in the interpretation of the passage which follows to go beyond Plato, i.e. in the way every interpretation must go beyond; 3. that we bring the phenomena in their interconnection into a more primordial dimension and thus outline them more clearly. The reflection proceeds by way of four questions.

1 What is the character of these newly presented phenomena (§ 42)?

2 What connection do they have to the earlier discussed αἴσθησις and διάνοια, perceiving, and the taking-in of something (§ 43)?

3 In what way can the positive clarification of the essence of δόξα now be undertaken (§ 44)?

4 What can we conclude from all this concerning the question of the essence of ψεῦδος, untruth (§ 45)?

§ 42. New Characteristics of the Soul: Two Similes

It is *first* a matter of bringing the phenomenon of distorted view under such guiding perspectives as are taken from the phenomenon itself. We are concerned, therefore, to comprehend the intermediate character of the ψευδὴς δόξα. The phenomenon of 'being of a distorted view' presents itself as a condition and comportment of man wherein he is somehow related to beings, albeit distortedly. However, the *relationship* to beings is the basic character of the *soul* (ψυχή). Thus the demonstration of the new phenomena leads to a renewed questioning concerning the soul.

If one understands the context of the problem it is not surprising that the main investigation's twofold approach to conceiving the phenomenon occurs by a new double characterization of the soul. The main investigation, we already see, has a quite different *style* to the preliminary investigation. The latter involved constant appeal to the presupposed guiding principles and argumentation *against* the phenomenon. Now it is a matter just of looking at new phenomena and of *drawing* the ψευδὴς δόξα *into* their context.

Further, this twofold characterization is in both cases realized through the elucidation of a simile and image. It is the same as in the case of the cave allegory: Plato stands before a task (of a new kind, but clear to him) in the face of which he does not venture to treat the new phenomena in a direct and unmediated manner. In particular, he does not attempt to seize hold of these new phenomena at the first attempt.

These are the two similes of the wax mass (κήρινον ἐκμαγεῖον) in the human soul and of the soul as aviary (περιστερεών).

a) Simile of the Wax; Keeping-in-Mind

The first simile is discussed at 191 c ff. ἐκμαγεῖον is not a 'slab' [*Tafel*], as it is usually translated, but simply a mass [Masse], into which something is imprinted. The second simile is discussed at 197 b ff.

Attempts have been made to show that Plato took over these images of the soul from earlier philosophers. In all such cases, professional historians of philosophy and philologists are immediately at hand to inquire into and demonstrate their origin. It has thus been discovered that Democritus 'already' knew the simile of the so-called 'wax slab'. The image of the aviary has likewise been traced back to the so-called 'primitive' conception of the soul as a bird. One now knows from where Plato obtained his material. *Against whom* the whole discussion of the dialogue is directed has also been worked out; the matter has been researched with historical exactitude. Just one thing is missing: one does not understand what Plato himself is asking and seeking. It would not be worthwhile to go into such methods here were they not characteristic of the general procedure of the history of philosophy and controversy with philosophers. If one has established where a philosopher has got something from and against whom he is philosophizing, then one is satisfied. What it is all about takes second place, i.e. is not even taken up. One is far from thinking that Plato, despite 'obtaining' these images from others, makes something different out of them, employing them to a quite different purpose and in a quite different problematic, that in the end this problematic opens up of *itself* and does not by any means need an *opponent*. Perhaps it is not too much to assume that a man of the stature of Plato could himself come across the phenomenon of untruth and the question of what it is.

We can assure ourselves from the beginning that Plato does indeed take a *great deal* from elsewhere. But we also wish to reflect that he takes this from *somewhere else* than those merely curious authors believe who cannot imagine anything except that a new book must arise from a dozen earlier ones (in the manner of opposing one or another). For us the question is not *from where* Plato obtains the images of the wax slab and aviary, but rather: to *what purpose* does he employ their analogical content, which phenomena of the soul does he wish, newly and for the first time, to indicate and make visible?

We have thus arrived at the point where the new field of the main investigation comes into view, the field within which we shall finally encounter the phenomenon of untruth, in order to see where it is itself rooted in its inner possibility.

From the preliminary investigation we know that it is a matter of finding those modes of comportment of the soul which enable it to relate to a complex object in the ψευδὴς δόξα. Socrates says (191 c 8 ff.):

Θὲς δή μοι λόγου ἔνεκα ἐν ταῖς ψυχαῖς ἡμῶν ἐνὸν κήρινον ἐκμαγεῖον, τῷ μὲν μεῖζον, τῷ δ᾽ ἔλαττον, καὶ τῷ μὲν καθαρωτέρου κηροῦ, τῷ δὲ κοπρωδεστέρου, καὶ σκληροτέρου, ἐνίοις δὲ ὑγροτέρου, ἔστι δ᾽ οἷς μετρίως ἔχοντος. . . Δῶρον τοίνυν αὐτὸ φῶμεν εἶναι τῆς τῶν Μονσῶν μητρὸς Μνημοσύνης.

'Assume then, by way of simile, that our souls contain something like a wax mass, sometimes larger, sometimes smaller, sometimes purer, sometimes more impure, sometimes harder, sometimes softer, and sometimes of just the right quality. [Everything that we immediately perceive, and also everything that we take in and comprehend, is imprinted upon it.] . . . This wax mass, we say, is a gift of the mother of the Muses.'

For the Greeks, the Muses enable the singer or artist to visualize and freely form his work in its entire fullness, *prior* to and without the help of any outline. Thus the mother of the Muses, i.e. what enables the Muses in their function, is said to be Μνημοσύωη, *keeping-in-mind* [*das*

Eingedenksein]. Through the simile, Socrates (Plato) wants to show that from the beginning this gift belongs to the essence of the soul as a primordial dowry. Along with this is given the faculty of μνημονεύειν; that is to say, neither recollection nor memory but keeping-in-mind. What is meant is that faculty and comportment in which we *think of*, keep thinking *of* something, e.g. a person, the situation *of* a nation, as in the saying: δέσποτα, μέμνησο τῶν Ἀθηναίων.[6] 'Lord, think of the Athenians.' This kind of thinking does not have to be recollecting or remembering, but is a holding-before-oneself of something, of a being, and indeed precisely when this being is absent, not present at hand in the immediate present; or, equivalently, to hold a being before us when we ourselves are no *longer present* with it.[7]

Through this simile we shall encounter a fundamental aspect of our (human) Dasein: once again a so to speak autonomous comportment of the soul whereby we are oriented to beings that are not at all bodily present.

b) An Example: the Feldberg Tower; Having-Present and Making-Present

We must, albeit briefly, further clarify this 'faculty of the soul', at this stage without reference to the Platonic simile. In so doing the most important thing to see is that this does not necessarily and in the first instance concern what we call 'recollection'. For this purpose we choose a trivial and quite uncontrived example.

On a walk in the Black Forest we come across the Feldberg Tower. It stands immediately before us, is vividly present. We see it and can think about it, e.g. about who built it, when, for what purpose it might have been built, etc.

Our comportment amounts to a having of the immediately present being in its presence. Our comportment is a having-present [*Gegenwärtig-haben*] of the encountered entity.

The same evening at home, or a few days later, we can come back (bring ourselves back) to what we saw and to what we thought about it. Then we no longer have the tower in our immediate presence. It is not, for example, present in this lecture room here. Our comportment towards this entity is no longer a having-present [*Gegenwärtigen*] in the indicated sense, but, as we say, we now *make*-present [*ver-gegenwärtigen*] the tower to ourselves.

What does this mean? One also says: now, at home or here in the lecture room, we no longer perceive the tower, but we 'only imagine it'. Therefore, it is said, we are relating to a mere representation, we have 'a mere image' of the tower. This description of our comportment (as making-present) is correct but also erroneous. Let us examine the matter, leaving aside all theories and psychologizing! What are we oriented towards when we now make-present the Feldberg Tower? To be sure, we are not oriented towards the tower as something bodily present in our sphere of perception. But are we *oriented* to a 'representation'? If I now picture to myself how it is snowing at Feldberg, and how the snow is falling on the tower, do I think that a representation is covered with snow, or that an image of the tower is snowed in? Towards what are we oriented when we make-present the tower to ourselves? Solely and precisely to the tower itself as an existing thing standing on the existing Feldberg. (This seems trivial but in the so-called science of psychology and also in epistemology you will find quite different things.) We mean this existing being and nothing else. We also do not need to imaginatively *remove* ourselves to the Feldberg, *as if* we were there, but from *here*, existing in this lecture room, we can orient ourselves to the thing in a quite natural way, intending and having before us *just this* thing and nothing else; admittedly, in such a way that the thing does not stand bodily before us but is in a certain sense removed, without, however, having disappeared.

Now this having-before-oneself of something not immediately present is not necessarily a recollecting. In making-present the tower we need not think of it as something *we* earlier observed, but we can simply make it present as it stands there, as a tower. Recollecting is a *specific* mode of making-present. But not every making-present is necessarily a recollection. In making-present we are not drawing upon memory as if we were searching around inside ourselves for representations. We are not inwardly directed. On the contrary, when we make-present the thing we are *outside* with it, oriented towards the tower, so that we can bring before ourselves all its properties, its full appearance. It can even happen that we can see the thing much more clearly and fully in making-present than in the having-present of immediate perception. Suddenly we have something before ourselves which, as we say, we 'did not notice' in immediate bodily seeing. But it is not representations, images, memory-traces and the like, that we have before ourselves; it is rather *that to which* this having-before-oneself is directed, and *solely* directed – the existing tower *itself*.

Making-present, therefore, is a specific mode of comportment to the beings themselves. Only when, without any psychology, we have assured ourselves of this fact of making-present from and in our *existing being*, only when we have come to comprehend it in an unprejudiced manner, can we *ask* what the simile of the wax mass means, and about the substantive grounds for explaining and depicting the fact of making-present in such a way.

We know that the Greeks grasp the immediate presence of a being in the look (εἶδος) it offers. In encountering a being in immediate presence, it is the εἶδος which is given to us: this is what we 'have' (having and possessing). Now when, instead of perceiving this same being, we only 'imagine' it (making-present), this still involves something like a look (εἶδος), but not such that the being itself, from itself, is given to us. Rather, we betake ourselves to it, without removing *ourselves* from our factual location. This phenomenon, that in making-present the look does not come to us from the thing itself, is immediately *explained* by saying that the look must therefore come from *ourselves*. But if this is so, it must be stored within ourselves, and we must be able to call it up. Since it is not the immediate full look (εἶδος) but only *looks like* this, the Greeks call the inwardly derived look εἴδωλον. Thus Plato says: ἔνεστιν ἐν τῇ ψυχῇ εἴδωλον αὐτοῦ;[8] in analogical terms: this εἴδωλον must be imprinted and preserved in the wax mass of the soul. The common and vulgar understanding now takes this simile as the real explanation, which is then adopted by science, psychology, and epistemology. This means that the fact of making-present is not clarified at all, so that the vulgar thesis is maintained that when we imagine something rather than perceiving it we can only be relating to representations, which, as is well known, are 'in ourselves' as something psychical. The fact that, contrary to all this, making-present is oriented to the beings themselves and not to anything psychical, is not sufficiently attended to.

To be sure, it cannot be overlooked that making-present, just like the perceiving having-present of αἴσθησις, has a *corporeal* aspect. But how this occurs can only be clarified, indeed can only be properly *inquired into*, when its enabling conditions have been adequately seen and grounded. It is for this purpose that Plato employs the simile: he is not attempting a psychological explanation of memory but wants to highlight and clarify the *essence* of making-present, i.e. what first makes something like memory necessary and possible.

We must now bring this phenomenon of making-present closer to us in a quite unprejudiced and natural way, simply from the existing comportment of human Dasein, and at the same time in an orientation which becomes important for the context of the Platonic problem.

In making-present we hold ourselves *before* beings by simultaneously holding ourselves *to* them. This kind of comportment can be seen in a modified form when we talk about holding to a person, not giving a person up. In this way, with various modifications, we constantly hold ourselves to all beings, also and precisely because not all beings are and can be bodily present. This making-present can be conceived as a mode of having-present, a way of holding beings in our presence, whereby the sphere of this presence broadens out in a particular way. When we come to know something, this means: we accept it into the sphere of what we hold-present in the broadest sense. We *retain* the thing we have come to know, and we maintain ourselves in such a relationship to it – to be sure, assuming that we learn in a *genuine* way and not *externally*, i.e. such that, *without* a relationship to the intended being, we have blindly imprinted ourselves with mere representations, words, and opinions.

We have, therefore, the faculty of *retention*. This does not mean a preservation of representations and images in memory, but a *holding* to beings that are not bodily given. What we can and do retain in this way we call *the retained*. This always means the beings themselves as they exist in and for making-present. Now everything that can enter into the retained is retainable in a different way. Retention and retainability can change in two fundamentally *different* ways, and thereby the mode of making-present also changes. Here we can only pursue the phenomenon in one specific direction.

One way in which what stands in the presence of our making-present can become more and more removed, is by we *ourselves* loosening up the connection to being – such that we are less, or are no longer at all, concerned with the beings to which we previously held ourselves. In this loosening of the retentive relationship to being, the *look* of the beings simultaneously (although not necessarily) becomes hazy: they become unclear, we allow them to slip out of our retention to such a degree that they are *forgotten*, that they become *hidden to us again*, that they disappear.

There are still further possibilities here: that we *experience* the changes of the beings and take this up into our retention; also, even if the beings have altogether disappeared, a kind of necessary *recollection* (how in this case making-present must necessarily be *recollection*).

However, changes in the retained can also be due to the beings themselves, without us overlooking or mistaking anything in making-present. To be sure, what we hold ourselves to, in accordance with the intention of making-present, is still those beings themselves. But by still being oriented to what we have retained, we *distort* the *beings*. We hold ourselves to what we have retained, and *intend* these beings, but in their own being they have become *different*.

Correspondingly, we can represent something, making it present in the *still* wider and novel sense, by simply 'imagining' it, freely creating a look of something, e.g. imagining that the Feldberg Tower lies next to a lake. Also in this case we are not occupied with 'inner' representations, but this imagining is a free *reconstruction* of the beings we know in the modes of having-present and making-present.

We can see, therefore, that this retaining holding-oneself-to-something, and thus the retained itself, can change in various ways. To repeat: on the one hand by we ourselves loosening the connection of being to beings [*Seinsbezug zum Seienden*] and removing ourselves from beings, on the other hand by the beings themselves, quite independently of our own doing, withdrawing from us and thus altering what we retain. Finally, we also retain what we (more or less) freely re-present in the manner of imagination. The μνημονεύειν, as depicted in the first simile, the retaining of what is retainable, is thus itself a compositely structured faculty of the soul. However, as we saw, the 'soul' is essentially the relationship of man to the being of beings. What is retained is in each case retain-able in a different way.

c) Simile of the Aviary; Modes of Retaining

It is one of these modes of retaining which Plato now attempts to bring to light in the second simile of the *aviary* (197 b 8 ff.). We shall briefly follow what he says, without going into its context within the dialogue.

[Socrates] Οὐ τοίνυν μοι ταὐτὸν φαίνεται τῷ κεκτῆσθαι τὸ ἔχειν. Οἷον ἱμάτιον πριάμενός τις καὶ ἐγκρατὴς ὢν μὴ φορῶν, ἔχειν μὲν οὐκ ἂν αὐτὸν αὐτό, κεκτῆσθαί γε μὴν φαῖμεν.

[Theaetetus] Ὀρθῶς γε.

"Ορα δὴ καὶ ἐπιστήμην εἰ δυνατὸν οὕτω κεκτημένον μὴ ἔχειν, ἀλλ᾽ ὥσπερ εἴ τις ὀρνιθας ἀγρίας, περιστερὰς ἤ τι ἄλλο, θηρεύσας οἴκοι κατασκευασάμενος περιστερεῶνα τρέφοι, τρόπον μὲν [γὰρ] ἄν πού τινα φαῖμεν αὐτὸν αὐτὰς ἀεὶ ἔχειν, ὅτι δὴ κέκτηται. ἦ γάρ;

Ναί.

Τρόπον δέ γ᾽ ἄλλον οὐδεμίαν ἔχειν, ἀλλὰ δύναμιν μὲν αὐτῷ περὶ αὐτὰς παραγεγονέναι, ἐπειδὴ ἐν οἰκείῳ περιβόλῳ ὑποχειρίους ἐποιήσατο, λαβεῖν καὶ σχεῖν ἐπειδὰν βούληται, θηρευσαμένῳ ἣν ἂν ἀεὶ ἐθέλῃ, καὶ πάλιν ἀφιέναι, καὶ τοῦτο ἐξεῖναι ποιεῖν ὁποσάκις ἂν δοκῇ αὐτῷ.

Ἔστι ταῦτα.

Πάλιν δή, ὥσπερ ἐν τοῖς πρόσθεν κήρινόν τι ἐν ταῖς ψυχαῖς κατεσκευάζομεν οὐκ οἶδ᾽ ὅτι πλάσμα, νῦν αὖ ἐν ἑκάστῃ ψυχῇ ποιήσωμεν περιστερεῶά τινα παντοδαπῶν ὀρνίθων, τὰς μὲν κατ᾽ ἀγέλας οὔσας χωρὶς τῶν ἄλλων, τὰς δὲ κατ᾽ ὀλίγας, ἐνίας δὲ μόνας διὰ πασῶν ὅπῃ ἂν τύχωσι πετομένας.

Πεποιήσθω δή. ἀλλά τί τοὐντεῦθεν;

Παιδίων μὲν ὄντων φάναι χρὴ εἶναι τοῦτο τὸ ἀγγεῖον κενόν, ἀντὶ δὲ τῶν ὀρνίθων ἐπιστήμας νοῆσαι· ἣν δ᾽ ἂν ἐπιστήμην κτησάμενος καθείρξῃ εἰς τὸν περίβολον, φάναι αὐτὸν μεμαθηκέναι ἤ ηὑρηκέναι τὸ πρᾶγμα οὗ ἦν αὕτη ἡ ἐπιστήμη, καὶ τὸ ἐπίστασθαι τοῦτ᾽ εἶναι.

Ἔστω.

'Well, having and possessing seem different things. If a man buys a cloak and in this sense brings it under his power, but does not wear it, we should certainly say, not that he has it on, but that he possesses it.'

'And rightly.'

'Now see whether it is possible in the same way for someone who possesses knowledge not to have it, in like manner, for instance, to a man who catches wild birds – pigeons or the like – and sets up an aviary at home in which to keep them. Might we assert that in a certain way he always has the birds, because he possesses them?'

'Yes.'

'And yet in another way he does not have any of the birds, but has acquired power over them, since he has brought them under his control within his own enclosure. He can take them and hold them whenever he likes, by catching whichsoever bird he pleases, and letting it go again; and he can do this as often as he likes.'

'That is true.'

'And again, just as a while ago we contrived some sort of waxen figment in the soul, so now let us make in each soul an aviary stocked with all sorts of birds, some in flocks apart from the rest, others in small groups, and some solitary, flying hither and thither among all the others.'

'Consider it done. What next?'

'We must assume that when we were children this receptacle was empty, and we must understand that the birds represent the varieties of knowledge. And whatsoever kind of knowledge a person acquires and shuts up within the enclosure, we must say that he has learned or discovered the thing of which this is the knowledge, and that precisely this is knowing.'

'So be it.'

In the soul there is an aviary (περιστερεών), or more generally, a container (ἀγγεῖον). Thus you already see the substantive relation and the meaning of *both* images, despite their complete disconnectedness and dissimilarity. At the beginning of every individual human Dasein this container is κενόν, still empty, there are no birds in it. Gradually the aviary becomes filled with birds of various kinds, i.e. we become familiar with beings and store them in the container. What goes into the container is κτῆσις, possession. But the captured birds behave in different ways in the aviary. Some separate themselves off in fixed groups, others cluster around in looser groups, still others are διά πασῶν, flying around anywhere and everywhere. Whoever keeps birds in an aviary 'has' them but yet has them not. In other words: besides this having in a container there is another 'having', namely when we *again* catch individual birds *within* the container, when for a second time we hunt them down and try to hold them in our hands. This kind of having (having immediately in hand) is what Plato calls ἕξις, as distinct from κτῆσις. In straightforward terms, this means that in the sphere of possible making-present we have many and varied beings, and of these we can make-present now this one, now that one, holding it expressly before us; we can also leave the content of the container to itself as it were, whereby we realize that at any time there remains the δύναμις τοῦ λαβεῖν καὶ σχεῖν. This means, says Plato, that the soul has in itself (besides this faculty of retention) the capacity of bringing into view what is retained in the sphere of making-present.

In this dialogue Plato does not further discuss the various ways in which the birds are arranged and distributed within the container. From the *Sophist*, however, which belongs to the *Theaetetus* both chronologically and substantively, we can and must conclude that the groupings correspond to specific characters of individual beings, but also to general characters pertaining to every kind of being (διὰ πασῶν). The birds that fly about everywhere (he speaks of these διὰ πασῶν also in the *Sophist*) are the determinations of being which we already know from the interpretation of αἴσθησις and διάνοια. Wherever we encounter beings, however they may differ from one another substantively, they are always encountered as beings, as beings that are different from other beings. Unity, difference, otherness etc., i.e. everything which, as we heard, immediately follows from being – in the present simile these determinations are the birds that (διὰ πασῶν) fly around everywhere and anywhere. This second simile thus wants to demonstrate that our making-present of beings can simply have these in the sphere of making-present (κτῆσις) without expressly conceiving them (the situation depicted in the first simile); however, from the sphere of making-present we can at any time select out a specific being and *bring this expressly to mind* (ἕξις). So we must say: the distinction between having-present and making-present again returns in a modified form within the sphere of making-present.

Yet despite the inner connection between the content of the two similes, we still do not at all see what Plato intends with them, i.e. what the presentation of the phenomenon 'making-present' and its modifications is supposed to mean in respect of the guiding problem, i.e. the question concerning the inner possibility of the ψευδὴς δόξα. We shall now attempt to bring out what is decisive by setting the new phenomena of retention over against the phenomena earlier discussed, αἴσθησις and διάνοια, at the same time indicating the connection with these latter.

§ 43. Confirmation of the Connection between αἴσθησις and διάνοια through Broadening the Field of the Present

We thus come to the second question of the main investigation. How are the indicated phenomena (of making-present) connected to αἴσθησις and διάνοια? Strictly speaking we need only repeat, somewhat more pointedly, what has already been said. The new phenomena of retention (making-present in the broadest sense) have already been set over against the immediate having-present of what is bodily present, i.e. perception (αἴσθησις) in the broadest sense. Now we see: the domain of beings to which we constantly comport ourselves is not at all exhausted by the region of *those* beings we hold in immediate presence, but is essentially wider. For this reason the usual starting point of epistemology, which asks after an object, after something given, is erroneous.

We are always comporting ourselves to beings, even when we do not immediately perceive them. However, there is something peculiar here: we can hold (comport) ourselves towards beings without actually perceiving them (or bringing them to mind), but precisely these merely retained beings can also, from time to time, be perceived in a having-present – just as every perceived being is retainable in the sense required for making-present. We thus arrive at the insight that there are two ways in which every being accessible to us can stand,

and be had, in our presence. At bottom it is this essential twofold possibility, pertaining to every accessible being, that Plato wants to bring out.

Correspondingly, the faculty of retention has the twofold possibility of explicit *apprehension* within making-present and mere awareness that such making-present is at any time *possible*. But all this immediately shows that the relationship to being (which is what constitutes the soul) not only goes beyond what is perceived, but that every accessible being can enter into this wider region of retainable beings. Thus Plato speaks of εὐρυχωρία and στενοχωρία τῆς ψυχῆς (194 d 5, 195 a 3), of the spaciousness and confinedness of the individual's soul. He does not mean a greater or less amount of memory, but differences in power and degree of familiarity with beings themselves.

From this demonstration of the interrelation between the making-present and the having-present of one and the same being it is now clear that the earlier thesis 'either we know something or we do not know it' ultimately says nothing useful. For we can know something by having it before us in immediate presence, but we can also know it through making-present, and the latter in turn can be either an actual *enactment* of making-present or a mere awareness of its possibility. Thus there are various modes of not-knowing. What we know in the mode of having-present we can also know in the mode of making-present, and what we know in this latter way we may in a given case also not know, because we do not have the possibility of having it bodily present, e.g. now the Feldberg Tower: I know it (making-present) and do not know it (in so far as I do not have it immediately before me in αἴσθησις).

There are thus modes of comportment between knowing and not-knowing, and indeed, which is decisive, in respect of one and the same being. The earlier guiding principle (in relation to the ψευδὴς δόξα) must now be rejected *not just because* it leads to impossible consequences, to the denial of the phenomenon, but because modes of comportment have now been *positively* exhibited which it is unable to grasp and which are ruled out by its own content. It is not the case that beings are either perceived in αἴσθησις or not perceived; neither is it the case that they are intended in reflection (διάνοια) or not intended, but *the same* being can be perceived in having-present as *well as* only intended in making-present. In this way a new prospect is opened up:

the same being can simultaneously stand in relationship to αἴσθησις and διάνοια, the two *go together* in a new way.

§ 44. Clarification of the Double-Meaning of δόξα: Its Forking into Having-Present and Making-Present

But we have not yet examined in what degree the new retentional modes of comportment are taken from the phenomenon of the ψευδὴς δόξα and δόξα; in other words, how far this connection is critical for the positive clarification of the essence of δόξα. We thus come to the *third* point.

Answering this question comes down to the following task: it is a matter of assessing in what degree the essence of δόξα can be made more comprehensible by attending to the phenomena of retention and making-present. For this it is necessary to once again bring forth those characteristics the preliminary investigation already presented as belonging to δόξα, but which were not fully comprehended. On the one hand there was the peculiarity that the δόξα has, as it were, two objects, which are given and yet not given (ἀμφότερα) – i.e. a *complex* object: one and the same object stands over against us for having-present *and* also for making-present. Also this, that δοξάζειν, being of a view, is not simply an acceptance of something, but is rather οἴεσθαι, ἡγεῖσθαι, a holding-for.

We shall now exhibit the essence of the δόξα from the example of a true view. The distorted view, the ψεῦδος, will be considered later, under the fourth point.

Theodorus takes somebody approaching from a distance, who in fact is Theaetetus, to be Theaetetus. What we have here is first the approaching man, and then him whom it is taken to be. We already know from the first attempt of the preliminary investigation that it is not really a matter of two objects, of which only the one ever comes into consideration, but of *both* – such that they are in some way related to each other, and such that precisely the unity of this relation constitutes the specific unity of the object of δόξα as such. This one object is itself complex, and thus the *comportment* to this complex object of δόξα, as δοξάζειν, must be correspondingly constituted, i.e. in order to grasp this complexity in its unity.

Now do the newly exhibited phenomena of retention, together with the phenomena earlier indicated, provide a way of clarifying the possibility of such a comportment, and for making comprehensible the possibility of the complex object of δόξα? The analysis clearly showed how one and the same being can be perceived in both immediate bodily presence (having-present) and through making-present. In principle, then, there is a twofold possibility in respect of one and the same object, with which the indicated complexity of the object of δόξα (and of the corresponding comportment, μνημονεύειν) is able to connect. Further, making-present lets something not bodily present be represented in advance, prior to it *again* coming into bodily presence, e.g. Theaetetus. Whether or not he is now present, we who know Theaetetus can make him present in advance.

Besides this newly indicated phenomenon of retention and making-present (μνημονεύειν) we know αἴσθησις in the wider sense of immediate perception, of bodily having-before-ourselves, wherein something immediately present is encountered as such; and finally διάνοια, which was ultimately explained as λόγος: a description of something, a claiming of something as something. With these *three* modes of comportment (μνημονεύειν, αἴσθησις, διάνοια) we have in fact *the* foundation stone from which the essence of δόξα can be constructed. In the example: the person approaching in the distance, perceived in αἴσθησις; this immediately and bodily present being is taken for Theaetetus, i.e. is represented and made-present (μνημονεύειν) in advance as Theaetetus; what is present and encountered is taken (λόγος) to be the same as what is made-present. Thus Plato (195 d) directly calls the δόξα a σύναψις αἰσθήσεως πρὸς διάνοιαν, 'a combination of what is encountered in immediate having-present with what is made-present in advance'. To be noted is that διάνοια has various meanings here: on the one hand non-perceptual representing, which does not have-present but rather makes-present; and at the same time a taking and holding of something as something, λόγος, i.e. what is accomplished through συνάπτειν.

Let us put this definition of the essence of δόξα to the test! If this explanation of the essence of δόξα is accurate, the σύναψις must be able to clarify what occupied us when the phenomenon of the δόξα was first introduced, i.e. when we translated this latter word as 'view' and δοξάζειν as 'being of a view about something', and when we emphasized that δόξα is necessarily ambiguous (translation is always interpretation). Can this ambiguity now be grasped and understood from the phenomenon we have just exhibited?

Yes indeed. Let us again follow the example of a man approaching from a distance. He presents a view, a look, indeed the look of Theaetetus; accordingly, on the basis of this look, we take him for Theaetetus. Another possibility: we know Theaetetus, we know in advance that at this time of day he usually comes along this road, we can already visualize him doing this, we can hold ourselves to him as this being who is not yet bodily present. And now a man appears in the distance, presenting a view to us, without our being able to see with sufficient clarity that it is Theaetetus; but we opine that it must be him: we now take the approaching person to be Theaetetus, not because of the look (having-present) but because of prior making-present.

We see that 'view' is on the one hand a having-present of what we encounter, and on the other hand a making-present holding-for. Since the two moments of having-present and making-present belong to the essence of every δόξα, we have the dual possibility: we can take a *first* footing either in what is presented in having-present, or in what is presented through making-present. Since the δόξα can always be conceived in either way, it is essentially ambiguous, as look or as opinion. So we see how the elucidation of the essence of the δόξα clarifies the primordial meaning of the word; further, we see in this the profound wisdom of language. The common linguistic ambiguity of the word δόξα is nothing else but the still uncomprehended reflection of a complexity of the comportment that belongs to δοξάζειν, of the primordial essence of the δόξα itself.

Going beyond Plato, we can now say that δοξάζειν is a comportment that is unitarily directed both to what is bodily present and to what making-present re-presents in advance. In brief, this comportment of the δόξα is in itself two-pronged or *forked*.

I shall provide a diagram, naturally with great reservation. It does not present the matter in a more exact way, but the reverse. It is nevertheless an aid for understanding, simply a scaffolding around the phenomenon, a scaffolding that must be torn down immediately.

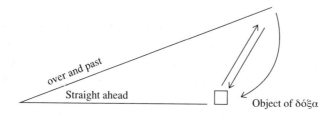

The fork has two prongs, of which the second reaches further than the first: making-present has a wider domain, leads further away from us. Now it is the nature of a fork to spike with *both* prongs. The *essence* of δόξα is neither the one prong nor the other, but rather: to see someone approaching in the distance as . . .; or e.g. to make-present this approaching person in advance as Theaetetus, who could very well be coming.

As building blocks for constructing the essence of δόξα there come into consideration αἴσθησις, μνημονεύειν, and διάνοια (λόγος): what holds the two prongs together and thus makes possible the fork itself. However, the construction only receives its possible *blueprint* when the new phenomena of μνημονεύειν, of retention, of making-present (i.e. of a comportment that is not only different, but *goes further*) become visible. These phenomena are thus of decisive importance, although by themselves they do not suffice for building the essential structure.

We immediately see how αἴσθησις and διάνοια, which in the earlier investigation apparently failed to provide what was needed, are enabled, by the phenomenon of making-present, to enter into interrelations which in their specific nature circumscribe the essence of δόξα as σύναψις αἰσθήσεως πρὸς διάνοιαν. Looking back, we now understand why the discussions of αἴσθησις and διάνοια were necessary, that therefore the result of the discussion of the first answer (ἐπιστήμη is αἴσθησις) is not at all merely negative, but is of decisive positive significance for the clarification of the essence of δόξα – but simultaneously for the question concerning the essence of ψεῦδος. For this latter question moves *in the framework* of the problem of δόξα. But if, as has just been shown, the phenomenon of making-present is decisive for the clarification of the essence of δόξα (proceeding from the true δόξα), the former must also be important for the inner possibility of ψεῦδος and thus for *untruth*. Nothing in a Platonic dialogue, however laughable and nonsensical it may appear, is without significance.

The *fork* is the condition of the possibility of untruth, but at the same time the condition of the possibility of truth; both are subject to the same conditions. What does the fork mean? It is the image of the fundamental constitution of human Dasein, of its essential construction.

We thus come to the *fourth* and final point.

§ 45. Enabling of Mis-taking through the Forking of the δόξα

At the conclusion of the preliminary investigation the question concerning the essence of ψεῦδος remained unanswered. The third attempt wanted to conceive the ψεῦδος as substitution of one for the other. When I erroneously take Theaetetus for Socrates, then, according to this interpretation, I take Socrates *instead* of Theaetetus. Accepting this interpretation led to impossible consequences, to the total denial of the phenomenon.

At most, however, the impossibility of the consequences was able to force the admission of the impossibility of the *assumption*. Thus no insight was obtained into how far this explanation necessarily remains inadequate to the phenomenon. This insight was lacking, because the phenomenon itself was still inadequately, or not at all, in view. Only the main investigation provided help here.

We now ask: can the inner possibility of the ψεῦδος be read off from the indicated essential structure of the δόξα? More precisely put: how does Plato now conceive the essence of ψεῦδος? I shall give its essential constitution only in its fundamental features and with respect to just one of the essential possibilities of distorted view.

Let us keep in mind the result of the main investigation: in the δόξα we view objects in a twofold way, in and through the *forking*. On the one hand we have the object as sighted in immediate bodily presence (αἴσθησις), on the other hand we have this same object seen as *something*, where the 'as something' is likewise *sighted*, but in the mode of making-present. If now the fact of a ψευδὴς δόξα is again brought forward, we shall initially interrogate it in respect of the indicated structures. In the example: someone takes the distant Theaetetus for Socrates. (We know that in some ways he looks like Socrates: he has a snub nose and is goggle-eyed.) In this total comportment there is something that is bodily encountered, the man in the distance, but he is not just given in general: rather he has a look, and indeed, he looks *like Theaetetus*. This means, however, since Theaetetus in some ways looks *like Socrates*, that the approaching person, in so far as he cannot be clearly discerned, *also* looks like *Socrates*.

Thus the approaching person is not simply given, but *seems*, looks like, and indeed looks like Theaetetus as well as like Socrates. The look does not provide a decision one way or another. This indeterminateness belongs to the seeming, to the givenness of the person who is bodily given in the distance. But what must be the case in order that this seeming of the approaching person, as this or that, becomes possible? Theaetetus and Socrates must already be known (otherwise there could be no looking like one or the other), but they are not bodily there, for then everything would be decided. Not bodily given and yet present – made present; only in a making-present can they be at all represented in the manner here necessary (in the ψευδὴς δόξα). If in the given case I have a *distorted* view, then I see what looks like Theaetetus (and *like* Socrates) as Socrates. In what, therefore, does the *distortedness* of the view consist? Looking at the approaching person in his specific character as appearing, I *look past* him (as looking like Theaetetus) and yet in doing this I still look at him (as Socrates). This looking-past [*Vorbei-sehen*] in the mode of seeing-as is a mis-taking [*Sich-versehen*], namely of him who is bodily seen, of him who seems like both Theaetetus and Socrates.

In order to further clarify this new and authentic definition of the essence of the ψεῦδος, we wish to set it off against the earlier explanation of the ψευδὴς δόξα as ἀλλοδοξία. There the same state of affairs was explained by saying that whoever has this distorted view simply posits Socrates *instead* of Theaetetus. In its result this explanation is in a sense correct, and yet it fails to understand what is essential (and prior to the main investigation could not understand this):

1 that both, Theaetetus and Socrates, must be known and represented in advance, in order that something seeming (in this double respect) can be encountered; that therefore making-present belongs to δόξα and ψευδὴς δόξα.

2 attention is not paid to the fact that the person bodily encountered seems like the one and the other in the light of the prior making-present of them both.

3 above all, however, it is not grasped that, in making a mistake, I cannot simply *look away* from Theaetetus, but I must precisely look at him who seems like Theaetetus, in order then that I can look *past* him. It is only possible to miss a target if one *aims* at it, not if one shoots just in any direction. In mere substitution, on the other hand, I necessarily look away and disregard the one. Simple disregarding does not permit mis-taking. The ψεῦδος, however, consists in a mis-taking. In mistaking something, I look past *it*, and *in* this looking-past it is precisely seen.

The ψευδὴς δόξα is not ἀλλοδοξία, not substitution of the one for the other, but in looking-past I must see both. Accordingly, Plato now no longer uses the expression ἀνταλλάττεσθαι, but the very sharp and precise παραλλάττειν; παρά means next to, past one to another. *What* is passed by is precisely *there*, is as such present.

In summary: the ψεῦδος of the δόξα, the distortedness of a view of something as something, is now grasped as a *mis-taking that looks past*. Plato therefore speaks (195 a) of παρορᾶν, παρακούειν, παρανοεῖν. But then: what does the *inner possibility* of mis-taking consist in? Answer: in the *forking* which belongs to the essence of δόξα. The longer prong represents both (Theaetetus and Socrates) in making-present; the shorter prong presents what seems, in the *light* of this making-present, to be this or that. What is bodily encountered, albeit in the distance, presents itself from the very beginning in a *sphere* of 'looking like' (like Theaetetus *and* like Socrates). The having-present looking at what is encountered is drawn now in this direction, now in that direction, by what seems. This looking-at can at any time mis-take and look past, because as a seeing of something as something it must *necessarily* look in one *direction*, either in the one or in the other.

Plato says (194 b 2 ff.) quite clearly:

περὶ δὲ ὧν ἴσμεν τε καὶ αἰσθανόμεθα, ἐν αὐτοῖς τούτοις στρέφεται καὶ ἑλίττεται ἡ δόξα ψευδὴς καὶ ἀληθὴς γιγνομένη.

'It is precisely in relation to what we perceive simultaneously through *making*-present *and* bodily *having*-present, that viewing something as something [the δόξα] twists and turns, becoming sometimes distorted, sometimes not.´

However, the essential forking of the δόξα not only creates the possibility of mis-taking, but promotes this possibility in a particular way, in that the δόξα according to its own nature *pre-pares* [*vor-bereitet*] the possibility of looking-past and must always assume this possibility, in so far as the forking involves a *doubling*, i.e. a *sphere of free-play* [*Spielraum*] for seeing something as something.

§ 46. The Shifting of Ontological Failure into the Incorrectness of the Proposition. What Remained Un-happened in the History of the Concept of Truth

But the *decisive* step in our interpretation of Plato's elucidation of the ψεῦδος is still outstanding. We must ask: what interpretation does Plato *himself* give to the phenomenon of mis-taking as looking-past?

In the mis-taking of something encountered, the latter is seen as what it is *not*. What it is 'mis-takenly' seen *as* (Socrates) must thereby be in *view* (the Socrates as co-represented in advance). But since Theaetetus must likewise be represented in advance (otherwise what is encountered would not seem like Socrates), it does *not* happen in mis-taking that the *represented* Theaetetus is encountered as the person who is coming towards the observer, and to whom the latter is actually turned. Instead, the holding-to Socrates is a passing-by of Theaetetus: οἷον τοξότης, says Plato (194 a 3), like an archer who misses the mark, here I hit Socrates instead of Theaetetus. So mis-taking does not hit what is made-present in advance. It is a missing of the mark, a failure of the intended *predicate*. Missing the mark is a failure of *direction*: a being-un-correct. The mis-taking look of the approaching person (as Socrates) is an un-correct *addressing*. Incorrectness in the *predicate* means incorrectness of the *proposition*. Thus Plato grasps the essence of the ψεῦδος as the un-correctness of the λόγος, of the proposition. In this way the λόγος becomes the seat and locus of the ψεῦδος The essence of un-truth is now un-correctness, so that the mis-taking which looks-past becomes a character of the λόγος, the proposition. But untruth is the opposite of truth; accordingly, *truth* also must have its seat in the λόγος. Thus *truth* is correctness of the proposition (cf. Aristotle, *Metaphysics* Θ 10, 1051 b 3-5).

The main investigation proceeds in four steps:

1   demonstration of making-present as distinct from having-present;
2   the possibility of the look of something as something;
3   the possibility of looking-past, of mis-taking: ψεῦδος;
4   this ψεῦδος interpreted as the failure of the intended predicate, as incorrect addressing.

This interpretation of the ψεῦδος as *incorrectness*, as the not-hitting of the object by the predicate, goes hand in hand with the conception of the δόξα as *proposition*; i.e. the *original* character of view as looking recedes. However, when truth becomes correctness, and untruth becomes incorrectness, correctness and incorrectness simply stand *alongside each other*, indeed they have opposing directions, they even *exclude* one another. What we saw at the end of the cave allegory, namely that untruth *belongs* to the essence of truth, is in this way obscured. We asked earlier about how the Greeks in general conceive of un-truth. We now see that Plato interprets the phenomenon of truth in terms of the λόγος, and not by reference to the *primordial* essence of truth, i.e. the unhiddenness of beings.

Why Plato and the Greeks 'failed' in this way is a further question. Now we ask only: *could* Plato have proceeded differently? Could Plato have seen that the essence of the ψεῦδος properly belongs to the essence of truth as ἀλήθεια, so that truth is not defined from ψεῦδος, but, on the contrary, ψεῦδος is defined from ἀλήθεια? Did Plato's own approach to the clarification of un-truth permit such a focus on ἀλήθεια? That would have been one possible way of proceeding. Why Plato did not proceed in this way cannot be discussed here; in the last resort it is a mystery of the spirit itself.[9]

The ψεῦδος is a mis-taking in the seeing of something as something. What is immediately perceived is 'mis-takenly' seen as something else. This something else, which determines the look of what is mistakenly seen, *distorts* precisely the *genuine* look of the thing. This distorting of the look is a kind of *hiding* of the thing. But the thing is *not completely* hidden, for it *shows itself*, offers a look, we have a view of it. This self-showing, however, is in itself precisely a self-hiding. This self-hiding in and *through* self-showing is seeming [*Scheinen*]. The latter, however, is a mode of being-manifest, i.e. of *unhiddenness*, which in itself is simultaneously, and indeed essentially, *hiddenness*; a truth to whose essence there belongs un-truth. If appearing is a self-showing wherein what shows itself hides itself, then self-hiding belongs to the essence of self-showing and vice versa. So there is an inner connection between ψεῦδος and ἀλήθεια, which, however, is unable to assert itself due to the domination of the λόγος (reinterpretation of δόξα as 'belief').[10] Thus 'appearing' is no longer seen together with unhiddenness *and* hiddenness.

Yet we must make an objection: this demonstrated essential cobelonging of untruth *qua* appearing and truth *qua* unhiddenness pertains only to the truth of the δόξα, not at all to the essence of truth as brought forth in the interpretation of the cave allegory, to *deconcealment*! The latter consists in the fact that the Dasein of man must from the outset have insight into the essence of *being*, must have freed itself to the ἰδέα, in whose light alone beings can be encountered as unhidden. In other words: being must originally be held in striving, in order that beings may become familiar to us.

What do we encounter with the phenomena of insight into essence and striving for being? We encounter what constitutes the essential structure of δόξα, and which we called the *forking*.

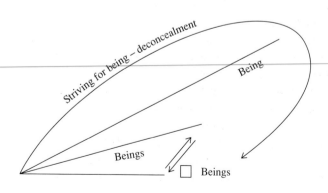

Only that now the forking pertains not only to beings, i.e. to the short prong (that which is bodily encountered) and the longer prong (the making-present of beings), but now we have an extension of essential insight to being and simultaneously a reception of *beings* of every kind. This *primordial* forking belongs to the essential constitution of our Dasein, i.e. our comportment to beings is always already oriented to being. However, with this forking there is given a primordial sphere and thus the possibility of mis-taking not only in regard to *beings* (as in the δόξα) but in regard to *being*. Anything which can be existent to us can [was uns ein Seiendes *sein*kann], in so far as it shows itself as unhidden, also *seem* (appear). So much being, so much seeming. Untruth belongs to the most primordial essence of truth as the hiddenness of being, i.e. to the inner possibility of truth. The question of being is thus thoroughly *ambiguous* – it is a question of the deepest truth and at the same time it is on the edge of, and in the zone of, the deepest untruth.

We attempted to answer the question concerning the essence of truth by looking at a piece from the history of the concept of truth, and at a piece from the history of the concept of untruth. But perhaps we have learnt to understand that it is precisely *here*, and *only* here, in such *history*, that we experience the presenting of truth. We cannot bring anything to the appearance of its essence through sheer cleverness and empty pedantry. For this reason we can reach what truth is, and how it presences, only by *interrogating* it in respect of its own *occurrence*; above all by asking after what remained *un-happened* in this history and which was closed off, so much closed off that ever since it has seemed as if in its primordiality it *never was*.

Notes

1 See Supplement 21.

2 Cf., however, 191 c 4 ff. (see below pp. 204 ff., 208 ff.).

3 See above pp. 98 f.

4 Fowler translates as 'interchanged opinion'; Cornford translates as 'mis-judgement, that occurs when a person interchanges in his mind two things'. [Trans.]

5 Concept of 'positing' [*Setzung*]: positio, pro-positio; cf. Baumgarten and Kant.

6   Herodotus, *History* V, 105.

7   Being is presence, non-being is absence; but: what is absent can *be*! Absence is complex-and presence too, depending on the *range* of ecstatic temporality.

8   Cf. 191 d.

9   See Supplement 22.

10   See Supplement 23.

Appendix
Supplementary Materials from Heidegger's Notes

1. (for p. 5)

The question concerning the *essence* of truth can easily seem like a *belated* question. It merely attempts to establish that wherein particular truths in particular regions of knowledge and action agree, precisely as truths – a *post-facto* verification of something, which is at bottom irrelevant, for we hold ourselves only to particular truths.

The appearance remains. And yet this opinion about the character of our question is erroneous. For if we are concerned simply with individual truths, this is because we have long been beholden to a quite definite customary fundamental conception of truth. And precisely this, the ground and foundation of *our* struggle for truth, becomes unstable. The essence of truth will change, and our questioning must bring this change into motion and give it the power of penetration. For our claims upon truths, our demands for proofs and ways of proof, our division of the burden of proof, can be transformed only from the changed *essence* of truth.

Our question concerning the essence of truth is not a superfluous addition, but is the *carrying forward* of our willing and existing into quite different regions and trajectories. However, this change of the essence of truth is not the mere modification of a conceptual definition, i.e. a matter of the scholarly critique of some theory or other, but is that comprehensive transformation of man's being in whose initial phase we now stand. Today, to be sure, it is only a few who can foresee and appraise the extent and inexorableness of this transformation of the being of man and world. But this assuredly does not prove that the transformation is *not* happening, that daily and hourly we are not rolling into a completely new history of human Dasein. Such profound transformation, however, is not mere release from the past, but is the sharpest and most comprehensive confrontation of the forces of Dasein and powers of being.

2. (for p. 11)

If it is necessary to go back to ἀλήθεια, then we must also inquire into the origin of *adaequatio*, its justification and limit.

But truth as correctness is *grounded* in truth as unhiddenness; the latter, however, is the unhiddenness of *beyng* [*Seyns*]! What is beyng? The question of being [Seinsfrage] is ambiguous. The first thing we must do is enter into the overcoming of metaphysics, whose *completion* must be experienced beforehand: this, however, as that which now and proximally 'is'. Not any escape into history, neither to Plato nor to Dante, neither to Kant nor to Goethe.

3. (for p. 35)

What does 'idea' mean? With this question we touch on the foundation and fundamental constitution of Western spiritual Dasein. For it was with the assistance of the Platonic doctrine of ideas that the Christian concept of God was unfolded, and thus the standard established for the governing conception of all other (non-divine) beings. The modern concept of reason, the age of Enlightenment and rule of rationality, thus also the movements of German Classicism and Romanticism, all unfolded with the help of the doctrine of ideas. The synthesis of these two forces, completed in Hegel, is the Christian completion of the Platonism of antiquity and a counter-thrust with the latter's own instruments and forces – the doctrine of ideology and the whole system of Marx and Marxism.[1] But also, in another direction, Kierkegaard; the watering down, mixing together, and domestication of all these powers of the nineteenth and early twentieth centuries. At the end of the nineteenth century Nietzsche against the three fronts of Humanity, Christianity and Enlightenment. There has since been no clear, no primordial, no decisive, and no creative, spiritual, historical standpoint and stance of man. And above all: despite all 'analysis' and 'typology' no insight and experience of the situation. This can only occur through circumspectively active [*handelnd-sorgenden*] controversy within a sphere of necessary decision; how completely it is governed by the doctrine of ideas, albeit as falsified and trivialized, thus also remains hidden.

4. (addition to Supplement 3)

The *doctrine of ideas* as the presupposition of Marxism and the *doctrine of ideology*. 'Worldview' as ideology, *abstractum*, reconstruction of the social relations of production.

Overcoming of Marxism?! K. Marx, *The Poverty of Philosophy*: 'The same people who form social relations in accordance with their material mode of production also form the principles, the ideas, and the categories according to their social relations.'

5. (for p. 38)

It is said of Theaetetus' father (144 c 7 f.): καὶ οὐσίαν μάλα πολλήν κατέλιπεν 'also left behind a great fortune'.

Why is οὐσία spoken of here?

6. (for p. 47)

But the allegory tells us that, if the liberation is to be authentic, looking into the light must ultimately become a looking into the sun itself, the source of light.

7. (for p. 77)

The image

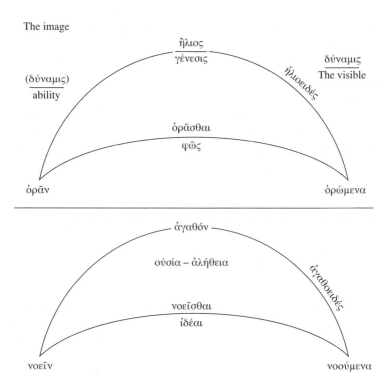

8. (for p. 105)

The driving force and restlessness of this history is the liberation of man to the essence of being: spirit, world-projection, worldview, a fundamental reality and mode of thought in which there is light and space for epic, development of the state, tragedy, cult architecture, sculpture, philosophy. Truth begins with the beginning of this history, and with this beginning man steps into un-truth in the most profound sense of not truth, i.e. hiddenness of beings. History is nothing in itself, but exists precisely and only where something is manifest; its limit and definiteness is precisely the hidden. *What* unhiddenness is can only be shown from *hiddenness*.

9. (for p. 109)

Theaetetus

Preliminary Conversation (Euclid and Terpsion in Megara).

Preliminary Reflection to the conversation proper (Socrates, Theaetetus, and Theodorus).

However, this conversation proper is already an account of Socrates' *recounting* of a prior conversation with Theaetetus.

Therefore: the actual conversation, the narration of Socrates, the record of Euclid, the reading of this record, the conversational introduction to this record. For what purpose all these complicated layers and levels?

10. (for p. 109)

This (*Theaetetus* 184 to 187) is the essential and decisive section. Here also the turning point is particularly clear, where Greek thought turns away from its origin to go over into 'metaphysics', i.e. to ground thought in the doctrine of being as ἰδέα and truth as ὁμοίωσις. Only now does 'philosophy' begin.

11. (for p. 109)

The hidden intention of the not fully mastered questioning (cf. 184 a) in this section only becomes clear when Plato himself, through Socrates, brings in train the decisive discussion about Theaetetus' assertion, and completes the 'overcoming' of the latter, i.e. provides a view of the ἰδέα. This occurs in section 27.

Chapters 29 and 30: 1. within the entirety of this conversation, 2. within the entirety of Plato's philosophy, 3. within the entirety of subsequent Western thought, of metaphysics.

12. (for p. 111)

The question put to Theaetetus, the question concerning the ἐπιστήμη 'is' the question concerning the ἀλήθεια, and the latter is the question concerning being (εἶναι). However, the Platonic-Socratic questioning is such that the question of being and truth *becomes* a question about ἐπιστήμη – without it being permissible to grasp this as 'epistemology'. Instead, the original Greek thinking gets lost, the origin withdraws into itself. For what is decisive is the *devastation of being* (in so far as this is only now actually *happening*): ἀλήθεια is no longer, or not at all and never, *that which is worthy of questioning*, but instead the mode of its appropriation and possession is this – whereby what ἀλήθεια is becomes slowly redefined from the question of appropriation: instead of ἀληθές the ἀψευδές (152 c 5).

13. (for p. Ill)

The significance of the conversation for the beginning of metaphysics consists in the way, guided by the question concerning 'knowledge' (i.e. truth, i.e. relationship to unhidden beings, i.e. to beings as such, i.e. to being) the relationship to being (ἰδέα) is grounded in the *letting-appear*, and this latter fixed in the λόγος.

14. (for p. 131)

Perceiving: 1. to receive something in its look (so-and-so-being), to have before oneself; 2. to take in, to interrogate in respect of something; 3. to *for*-take, to make into an 'object', to bring before oneself.

15. (for p. 135)

One misrecognizes the inner context of the genuine interpretation of the 'essence' of αἴσθησις in Theaetetus' statement, and in the Greek way of questioning, when one translates διανοεῖν as 'thinking' and αἴσθησις as 'sensation'. What remains decisive is that precisely so called 'thinking' is exhibited as the authentic ἐπισκοπεῖν; the σκοπεῖν of the ἰδέα is the immediate, genuine, and prior having-before-oneself. In modern times, αἴσθησις, νοῦς, and διάνοια have been interpreted subjectively in terms of the certainty of re-presenting, but simultaneously misinterpreted and falsified in a 'subjective' psychological manner, and this is read back into Greek thought.

This thinking as διανοεῖν is the name for the relation to the *being* of beings, thus precisely not to anything 'abstract' (to the stripped off essence), but to that wherein all beings *grow together* (concretely) and are gathered, thus firstly and exclusively the name for the relation to *beings*, as beings.

16. (for p. 142)

For διανοεῖν stands: 1. ἐπισκέψασθαι, 2. λαμβάνειν, 3. δηλοῦν, 4. ἐπισκοπεῖν, 5. σκοπεῖσθαι, 6. ἀναλογίζεσθαι (ἀναλόγισμα), 7. συλλογισμός.

17. (for p. 144)

What does 'beautiful' mean here? Beauty is what can be seen in you, Theaetetus, your intimation and knowledge of the connection to being. The beautiful is ἐκφανεστεστεῖον, enchanting, and ἐρασμώτατον, enrapturing. The beautiful holds fast and raises up, is something we can hold to, *and* at the same time it is the point of departure and inner impetus to further questioning. The beautiful is the emergence of differentiation (τὰ μέν – τὰ δέ).

To the Greek, to say 'beautiful' is the highest praise. To be sure, this does not mean stimulating, pleasant, for pleasure and enjoyment, also nothing 'aesthetic', although (again precisely here) with i8ea aesthetics is already *beginning*.

18. (for p. 147)

The pull [*Zug*] of the 'soul' is towards being; this pull grounds the connection [*Bezug*]. This connection is its *ground-pull* [*Grund-zug*]; the soul is nothing else but this *pull to being*, and indeed in such a way that this is not itself (or hardly and seldom) 'conceived'. The pure *proximity* to the essential is not the oft-mentioned seizing and taking-charge, but is the holding-to-oneself of *intimation*, a knowledge of the coming [*des Kommens*]; an echo of the fact that the *perceiving* relation surpasses everything and is more primordial and proximate than 'possession' in the sense of ordinary thingly grasping.

19. (for p. 161)

Συλλογισμός means: to perceive as gathered in a singularity (in being); to let something appear *as* something and thus have it before oneself (δόξα as λόγοζ) in the unity of its gathered presencing. λόγοζ as the relation of gathering, of the gathered perceiving of a singularity, is the primordial meaning of au συλλογισμός.

But the metaphysical rigidification of 'thinking' to the 'concept' and to the 'categories' begins straight away, then the 'logical' and 'psychological' misinterpretations of thinking as *ratio*, soul, 'spirit', reason. The impetus to this was precisely Plato's interpretation of being as ἰδέα. It was never recognized that this first essence of 'thought' is already rooted in a quite unique and specific interpretation of being (οὐσία) and of truth (ἀλήθεια).

20. (for p. 185)

The δόξα essentially wavers between view (look) as εἶδος ἀληθές, and view (looks like) as ψεῦδος. δοξάζειν has in each case to decide, it must *grasp* something as it 'looks'; it must let something appear *as what it is*; to *take* something as something and thus *to arrive* at the unhidden. ἀληθὴς δόξα means: to take something in its undistortedness and have it before oneself. But λόγος is necessary for this, λέγειν as relation to being *(qua* ἕν), the gathering into presencing, i.e. the δοξάζειν as λέγειν of beings, the addressing and gathering of beings with respect to the unity of their being.

21. (for p. 188)

With the δόξα we have now found a phenomenon which is sometimes distorted, sometimes correct; previously it was said that the αἴσθησις as such is *neither* distorted *nor* correct! In searching for the truth of αἴσθησις we therefore found too *little*; in the case of the δόξα it is equally *too much* and thus particularly confusing, especially if the view is not just *incidentally* distorted or correct, but *must* according to its own *essence* always waver between the one and the other.

22. (for p. 227)

The usual, traditional and firm opinion: *veritas per prius in intellectu* (medieval), *proprie in solo intellectu* (Descartes), truth as holding-for-true in thought and as 'value' (Nietzsche), is prepared through Aristotle and Plato: ἀλήθεια and ψεῦδος are ἐν διανοίᾳ.

23. (for p. 228)

The turning of the λόγος to the λέγειν of the ψυχή is grounded in the connection of being as ἰδέα to the ψυχή, above all in taking back this connection itself simply to the 'soul', which is then fully subject to the Christian interpretation of the soul as a *single* independently existing thing whose 'salvation' [*Heil*] is all-important. This is the *complete* burying of the origin. For this reason Plato and Aristotle are precursors of 'Christianity'.

Note

1 See Supplement 4.

Editor's Afterword

This volume provides the text of the *first lecture course* entitled 'Vom Wesen der Wahrheit' delivered by Heidegger at the University of Freiburg in the winter semester of 1931/32 (from 27 October 1931 to 26 February 1932). These lectures were preceded by a lecture of the same title, first given in 1930 and repeated on several occasions, published in 1943, and since 1967 also available in *Wegmarken* (now GA Vol. 9, pp. 177–202). The same theme was taken up in modified form, with an extensive new introduction, in the winter semester lectures of 1933/34, to be published as Volume 36/37 of the *Gesamtausgabe*. The train of thought of the 1940 essay 'Platons Lehre von der Wahrheit', first published in the yearbook *Geistige Überlieferung* in 1942, and then in 1947 together with the 'Brief über den Humanismus', also goes back to these lectures from winter semester 1931/32 (not 1930/31, cf. GA 9, p. 483), but is restricted to the cave allegory. To indicate these connections, the present text of the lectures appears with the sub-title 'Zu Platons Höhlensgleichnis und Theätet'. The logic lectures from Marburg winter semester 1925/26, which appeared in the *Gesamtausgabe* (Vol. 21) with the subtitle 'Die Frage nach der Wahrheit', already briefly alluded to Plato's significance for the history of the concept of truth, but were more extensively occupied with Aristotle, Hegel, and Kant. The first interpretations of the cave allegory and of the Theaetetus, different from the later ones, occur in the 1926 summer semester lectures *Grundbegriffe der antiken Philosophie*, [published in 1993] as Volume 22 of the *Gesamtausgabe*; cf. 1927 *Die Grundprobleme der Phänomenologie* (Vol. 24, pp. 400–5).

It is not the task of this Afterword to demonstrate that there are significant *differences* between these works, and in particular that the lectures given here are in no sense a mere broadening out of the 1930 lecture, but involve quite independent textual interpretations. Attention would thereby have to be paid also to the *continuity* of the questioning, and not prematurely assert a break from the truth-thematic of *Being and Time*. Indeed, it is the *one* constantly abiding fundamental question that drives these variations and that sets us the task of doing justice to their co-belonging. The prerequisite for this is the most complete possible presentation of this hitherto unpublished text.

I have had at my disposal photocopies of the manuscript, together with two typescript copies of a stenographic transcript the original of which is apparently no longer extant. One of these two typescripts (which do not significantly differ from each other) contains occasional corrections and short additions in Heidegger's hand, the content, form, and extent of which indicate that he went through the text soon after the lectures. Further, I have had access to photocopies of 192 note sheets, handwritten additions to the manuscript; many of these form coherent sequences; others are inserted between the pages of the manuscript, presumably as originally found.

The manuscript comprises 71 DIN A4 sheets, of which 64 are consecutively numbered. The wide right-hand margins of the pages contain numerous insertions, additions and corrections, which are often abbreviated or only formulated as keywords.

The editor had first to produce a faithful typescript of the manuscript text. With few exceptions, uncertainties in reading could be clarified by comparison with the transcript, with parallel passages of the manuscript, or with the corresponding note sheets. A comparison of the relatively good manuscript copy with the original in Marbach resulted in only minor corrections.

The typescript was compared with the copy of the *transcript* which Heidegger had gone through. Often, particularly in the Plato translations, the texts correspond precisely. But the wording of most sentences differs in greater or lesser degree. The comparison showed that in his oral presentation Heidegger frequently provided nuances, additions and more precise formulations, occasionally also short excursuses which went beyond the manuscript text. The transcript also contains the recapitulations of preceding material, sometimes only brief, that Heidegger gave at the beginning of the lecture hour; these are not to be found in the manuscript, only seldom in the additional materials. Passages of the manuscript missing from the transcript were probably omitted from the oral presentation; it emerged, however, that square brackets in the manuscript do not always indicate an omission, for these passages are sometimes also found in the transcript.

That we possess a copy of the transcript as corrected by Heidegger accords with the six lecture courses for which he gave special instructions, because copies of the stenographic transcripts of Simon Moser, as corrected by Heidegger himself, were available. For this reason the production of the printed text proceeded in corresponding fashion.

I have striven, accordingly, to reproduce the *delivered* text as completely as possible. It would not have been a responsible procedure simply to dispense with everything missing from the handwritten manuscript. However, the basis had to be the text of the manuscript, including some passages which were perhaps not delivered, and excluding those which Heidegger immediately rejected during composition. The insertions and marginal comments have been added according to marks given in the text. When such marks are missing insertions have been made within the continuous text depending on their sense, or otherwise given as footnotes. Incomplete marginal notes of a keyword character had to be expanded, if possible according to the context or formulations of the transcript; otherwise the editor had to restrict himself to the indispensable form-words. The residual material from the oral presentation was then worked into the complete manuscript from the transcript corrected by Heidegger. For what was taken over in particular cases, the more clear, precise and better-formed version of the thought was decisive. In cases of mere variations in expression the manuscript text was preferred; in cases of nuances of no substantive relevance both versions were retained, supplementing each other. The recapitulations in the transcript were only taken up into the edited text where they contain new, additional, clarifying or summarizing material, or where they provide an overview. To bridge gaps in meaning, and for the sake of clarification, I occasionally had recourse to short passages from sketches in the handwritten materials. A selection of relevant but undelivered thoughts from the additional materials is provided in the Appendix. Footnotes, which refer to these additions, stem from the editor. The numbering of the additions follows their place in the manuscript text; it does not wish to pre-empt an archival registration of the manuscript additions.

Idiosyncrasies in Heidegger's spelling, sentence construction, and expression were retained if possible; in doubtful cases clarity and authenticity had priority over stylistic smoothness. Smaller obvious oversights in manuscript and transcript were corrected without notice, while the rudimentary punctuation of the manuscript was brought into conformity with normal punctuation.

With few exceptions, bibliographical references and citations were checked against copies used by Heidegger and where necessary made complete. Bibliographical information is given in the footnotes, on the occasion of first mention of a title or edition. Heidegger cites the Greek Plato text according to the second Oxford edition (cf. above, p. 17; in the few cases where he diverges from Burnet's reading, I have indicated this in a footnote). Where Heidegger quotes or critically comments on Schleiermacher's translation, this usually refers to the third edition, of which he possessed a copy (cf. above p. 23). He also refers to the (at that time readily available) Reclam edition of the *Theaetetus* translation (cf. above p. 94), but only by way of exception does he quote from this. Since neither text is easily accessible today, I have given additional references to the Rowohlt edition (cf. above p. 94), also indicating discrepancies between the editions. Anything I have given in the footnotes which might be confused with Heidegger's own marginal comments has been marked with 'Ed.'.

To the extent that divisional headings (the main headings of Part One and Two, and of the stages of the cave allegory) are to be found in the manuscript, or steps of the inquiry mentioned, they were drawn into the differentiated division produced by the editor. Additional headings were, when possible, taken from the language of the relevant portion of text. Formally speaking, the division of this text, as is also the case with nearly all other lecture courses published in the *Gesamtausgabe*, follows Heidegger's own practice in his main work *Sein und Zeit*.

I am especially grateful to Dr Hartmut Tietjen for his critical advice, collation of the transcripts, and bibliographical references. Dr Tietjen, along with Dr Hermann Heidegger, Professor Friedrich-Wilhelm von Hermann, and Professor Walter Biemel, provided much appreciated assistance in deciphering difficult passages of the manuscript. Thanks are also due to Dr Hans-Wolfgang Krautz for locating the source of several quotations, and to Dr Franz-Karl Blust for proof corrections.

Hermann Mörchen

Frankfurt a. M., May 1988

English–German Glossary

ability-to-be: *Sein-können*
absence: *Abwesenheit*
accept: *hinnehmen*
accessible: *zugänglich*
accomplish: *leisten; accomplishment: Leistung*
actual: *wirklich;* the actual: *das Wirkliche; actuality: Wirklichkeit*
addressing: *Ansprechen*
anticipatory: *vorgreifend*
appear: *scheinen, erscheinen*
appearance: *Schein, Erscheinung*
apprehend (grasp): *fassen, erfassen*
appropriate: *sich zueignen*
appropriation: *Aneignung*
assertion: *Aussage*
assess: *beurteilen*
assessment: *Beurteilung*
assimilating accepting: *durchnehmendes Hinnehmen*
assimilating perceiving: *durchnehmendes Vernehmen*
attack: *Angriff*
attunedness: *Gestimmtheit; attunement: Stimmung; attuned: abgestimmt*
authentic: *eigentlich*
authenticate: *bewahrheiten*
authenticity: *Eigentlichkeit*
avoid: *ausweichen*
awaken: *erwecken*

basic word: *Grundwort*
becoming: *Werden*

being: Sein; (the) being (s): *das Seiende*
being gone: *Weg-sein*
blueprint: *Bauplan*
bond: *Bindung*
brightness: *Helle*

care: *Sorge*
character: *Charakter*; characteristic: *Charahteristik*; characterize:
   charakterisieren
claim: *Anspruch*
co-belonging: *Zusammengehödrigkeit*
co-constitute: *mit ausmachen*
commanding: *beherrschend*
completion: *Vollendung*
comport: *sich verhalten*; comportment: *Verhalten, Verhaltung*
concealing: *Verbergen;* concealment: *Verbergung*
conceive: *erfassen, begriefen, fassen*; conceiving: *Erfassen*
concept: *Begriff*
conception: *Erfassung*
conceptual: *begrifflich*
confuse: *verwechseln*
connectedness: *Bezogenheit*
connection: *Bezug; connection of being: Bezug des Seins, Seinsbezug*
connectivity: *das Bezughafte*
constitute: *ausmachen*
context: *Zusammenhang*
controversy (confrontation): *Auseinandersetzung*
corporeality: *Leiblichkeit*
correctness: *Richtigkeit*
correspondence: *Übereinstimmung*
cover up: *verdecken*
create: *schaffen*

dangerousness: *Gefährlichkeit*
dark: *Dunkel*
darkness: *Dunkelheit*
decision: *Entscheidung*
deconceal: *entbergen*

deconcealment: *Entbergsamkeit, Entbergung*; the deconcealed: *das Entborgene*

definition: *Definition*

delight (joy): *Freude*; the delightful: *das Erfreuliche*

delusion: *Einsichtlosigkeit*

depress: *herabstimmen*

determination: *Bestimmung*; determined: *bestimmt*; determine: *bestimmen*

devastation of Being: *Seinsverlassenheit*

difference: *Verschiedenheit*

differentiation: *Unterscheidbarkeit*

disclose: *erschliessen*; disclosedness: *Aufgeschlossenheit*

dispersion: *Zerstreuung*

disposal, *disposing* over: *Verfügen*

disregard: *absehen*

distort: *verkehren*; distorted: *verkehrt*; distorted view: *verkehrte* Ansicht

distress: *Not*

dividing highlighting: *gliedernde Abhebung*

division: *Gliederung*

divorce: *Scheidung*

empower: *ermächtigen*; what empowers: das *Ermächtigende*; empowerment: *Ermächtigung*

enable (make possible): *ermöglichen*; enablement: *Ermöglichung*

enact (realize): *vollziehen*; enactment: *Vollzug*

encounter: *begegnen*; what is encountered: *das Begegnende*

endangerment: *Gefährdung*

en-hold: *umhalten*

ensnare: *verfangen*; ensnarement: *Verfänglichkeit*; ensnaring: *verfänglich*

enthusiasm: *Begeisterung*

envisability: *Sichtsamkeit*; the envisible: *das Sichtsame*

epistemology: *Erkenntnistheorie*

essence: *Wesen*; essence-hood: *Wesenheit*

essential connection: *Wesensbezug, Wesensbeziehung*

essential construction: *Wesensbau*

essential lawfulness: *Wesensgesetzlichkeit*

essential view: *Wesensblick*

everydayness: *Alltäglichkeit*
excess: *Mehrbestand*
exemplary: *ausgezeichnet*
exhibit (demonstrate): *aufweisen*, *erweisen*; that which is exhibited:
  das Aufgewiesene
existence: *Existenz*; ex-istence: *Ex-sistenz*
experience: *erfahren*; Erfahrung: *lived* experience: *Erlebnis*
extend: *sich erstrecken*; extension: *Erstreckung*

faculty (power): *Vermögen*
familiar: *vertraut*; familiarity: *Vertrautheit*
footing: *Halt*
foresee: *ahnen*
fore-take: *sich vornehmen*
forgetting: *Vergessenheit*
forking: *Gabelung*
form: *bilden*
fulfil: *vollenden*
fundamental attunement: *Grundstimmung*
fundamental experience: *Grunderfahrung*
fundamental occurrence: *Grundgeschehnis*
fundamental stance: *Grundhaltung*
future: *Zukunft*; futurity: *Zukünftigkeit*

gather (collect): *sammeln*
give: *geben*; what is given: *das Gegebene*
goal-directed: *zielend*
God: *Gott*
godhead: *Gottheit*
gone-ness: *Weg-heit*
grant: *gewähren*
groundlessness: *Bodenlosigkeit*
groundstance: *Bodenständigkeit*

harnessed together: *zusammengespannt*
have: *haben*
have-present: *gegenwärtigen*
having-before-oneself: *Vor-sich-haben*

having-in-view: *Im-Auge-haben*
hidden: *versteckt*
hiddenness: *Verborgenheit*
highlight (emphasize): *Abhebung*
history: *Geschichte*
hold oneself: *sich halten*
hold sway: *walten*

illuminate (light up): *lichten*
illuminating view: *Lichtblick*
illusion (illusory appearance, seeming): *Schein*
image (picture): *Bild, Abbild, Sinnbild*
imagine: *einbilden*
immediacy: *Unmittelbarkeit*
immediately (immediate, unmediated): *unmittelbar*
impression: *Anschein*
inquire into: *nachforschen*
intangible (ungraspable): *unfaβlich*
intelligible: *verständlich*
interchange: *austauschen*
intermediate: *das Zwischen*
interpretation: *Auslegung*
interrelation: *Zusammenhang*
interrogate: *abfragen*
intimation: *Ahnung*
intrusiveness: *Vordringlichkeit*

judgement: *Urteil*

keeping-in-mind: *das Eingedenk-sein*
know-how: *sich-verstehen*
knowing one's way around: *sich auskennen*
knowledge: *Erkenntnis*, *Wissen*

law-giving: *Gesetzgebung*
let-through: *durchlassen*; the letting-through: *das Durchlaβ*; what
    lets-through: *das Durchlassende*; what does not let-through: *das
    Undurchlässige*; the not-letting-through: *das Undurchlässigkeit*

liberation: *Befreiung*
light: *Licht*
lived experience: *Erlebnis*
look: *Anblick*
look at: *anblicken*
looking past: *Vorbeisehen*

make possible: *ermöglichen*
make-present: *vergegenwärtigen*
manifest: *offenbar*; manifestness: *Offenbarkeit*
mistaking: *sich versehen*; mistaking that looks past: *vorbeisehendes
    sichversehen*
more beingful: *seiender*
mystery: *Geheimnis*

non-conceptual: *begrifflos*
non-regarding: *hinsichtlos*
nothingness: *Nichts*
null: *nichtig*; the null: *das Nichtige*

object: *Gegenstand*
occupy oneself with: *sich befassen mit*
occur (happen): *geschehen;* occurrence: *Geschehen*;
    occurrence-character: *Geschehenscharakter*
offer: *bieten*
ontological failure: *Seinsverfehlung*
open: *eröffnen*
opinion: *Meinung*
order: *Auftrag*
originary: *anfänglich*
overcome: *aufheben*; overcoming: *Aufhebung, Überwindung*
ownmost: *eigen*

paradigmatic: *vorbildlich*
passage-way: *Durchgang*
penetrate through: *hindurchdringen*
perceivability: *Vernehmbarkeit*; perceivable: *vernehmbar*

perceivable, the: *das Vernehmbare, das Erblickbare*

perceive: *vernehmen, erblicken, wahrnehmen*

perceived, the: *das Vernommene, das Erblickte, das Wahrgenommene*

perceivedness: *Vernommenheit, Wahrgenommenheit*

perceptible: *wahrnehmbar*; perceptibility: *Wahrnehmbarkeit;* the
    perceptible: *das Wahrnehmbare*

perception: *Wahrnehmung*

positing: *das Setzen*

positionedness: *Gehaltenheit*

possess: *besitzen*; possessing: *Besitzen*; possession: *Besitz*

power: *Macht*

preconception: *Vormeinung*

predominance: *Übermacht*

pre-form (pre-model): *vor-bilden*

pre-modelling (pre-forming): *vorbildlich*

presence: *Anwesenheit, Gegenwart, Anwesung*

preserve: *erhalten*

presupposition: *Voraussetzung*

primordial: *ursprünglich*

prisoner: *Gefangene*

production: *Herstellen*

projection: *Entwurf*; projection of Being: *Seinsentwurf*

projective: *vorausgreifend*

property: *Eigenschaft*

proposition: *Aussage*

proximity: *Nähe*

question: *Frage*

questionworthiness: *Fragwürdigkeit*

reason: *Vernunft*

recognition: *An-sehen*

referential connections: *Bezüge der Verweisung, Verweisungsbezüge*

relatedness: *Angewiesenheit*

relation: *Bezug, Beziehung, Verhältnis, Zusammenhang*

relation to being: *Seinsverhältnis, Seinsbezug*

relational: *das Verhältnishafte*

relationship: *Verhältnis*

represent: *vorstellen; representation: Vorstellung*

retain: *behalten; retainable: behaltbar*; the retained: *das Behalt;*
   retention: das Behalten

rootedness: *Verwurzelung*

rule: *herrschen*

scholar: *Gelehrte*

science: *Wissenschaft*

secured: *gesichert*

see: *sehen*

seem: *anmuten, scheinen*

self-evidences: *Selbstverstandlichkeiten*

self-evident: *selbstverständlich*

self-less: *selbst-los*

self-understanding: *Selbstverständnis*

sensation: *Empfindung*

sense: *empfinden, Sinn*

sense of sight: *Gesichtssinn*

sensory image: *Sinnbild*

shackled: *gefesselt*

show: *zeigen*; show itself: *sich zeigen*; what shows itself: *das*
   Sich-Zeigende

sighted: *gesichtet*; what is sighted: *das Gesichtete*

singularity: *Eines*

situation: *Lage*

solitary: *einsam*

solitude: *Einsamkeit*

spirit: *Geist*

spiritual: *geistig*

so-being: *Sosein*

soul: *Seele*

staking: *Einsatz*

stance, bearing: *Haltung*

strive: *streben*; the striven-for (the object of striving): *das Bestrebte*

striving: *Streben, Strebnis, Erstreben, Erstrebnis*

striving for Being: *Seinserstrebnis*

substantial content: *Sachgehalt*

substitute: *auswechseln*
surpass: *überragen*

take: *nehmen*
take in, accept: *hinnehmen; durchnehmen*
take-in-view: *in den Blick nehmen*
take up: *aufnehmen*
theory of knowledge: *Erkenntnistheorie*
theory of science: *Wissenschaftstheorie*
thinking: *Denken*
throw over against: *entgegenwerfen*
thrownness: *Geworfenheit*
transparent: *durchsichtig*; transparency: *Durchsichtigkeit*; the
    transparent: *das Durchsichtige*; the untransparent: *das*
    Undurchsichtige
true, the: *das Wahre*
truth: *Wahrheit*
tune: *stimmen*

uncanniness: *Unheimlichkeit*
underdetermined: *unterbestimmt*
understand: *verstehen*
understanding of being: *Seinsverständnis*
unfolding: *Entfaltung*
unhidden, the: *das Unverborgene*
unhiddenness: *Unverborgenheit*
unintelligible: *unverständlich*
universal: *das Allgemeine*
uphold, hold up: *vorhalten; vor-halten*

value: *Wert*
view: *Ansicht*
violence: *Gewalt*
visible: *sichtbar*, the visible: *das Sichtbare*
void: *Leere*

waning: *Schwinden*
what-being: *Was-sein*

willing: *Wollen*
withdrawing: *Entziehen*
withstanding: *Standhaltung*
worthy of questioning: *frag-würdig*; what is worthy of questioning: *das
  Frag-wüdige*
yearning: *Sehnsucht*
yoke: *Joch*

Greek–English Glossary

ἀγαθοειδές: like the good
ἀγαθόν: good
αἴσθησις: perception
ἀλήθεια: unhiddenness, truth
ἀληθής: unhidden, true
ἀλλοδοξία: substitution
ἀναλογίζεσθαι: to reckon

γένεσις: origination, genesis
γένος: genus
γνῶσις: knowledge

δηλοῦν: to reveal
διά: through
διαλέγειν: to discuss, to talk through
διανοεῖν: to perceive (through the soul)
διάνοια: perceiving (through the soul)
δοκεῖν: to show itself, to appear
δόξα: view, opinion
δοξάζειν: to have a view
δύναμις: potentiality for
δύναται: be capable of

εἰδέναι: to see
εἶδος: what-being, look
εἴδωλον: image
εἶναι: being
ἐπισκοπεῖν: to look upon

ἐπιστήμη: knowledge, knowing one's way around
ἐπορέγεσθαι: to strive for
ἔρως: desire, striving

ζυγόν: yoke
ζῷον λόγον ἔχον: the living being possessed of speech

ἡλιοειδές: like the sun
ἥλιος: sun

ἰδέα: idea, form, look

κοινόν: the common

λαμβάνειν: to take
λέγειν: to gather, to say
λήθη: forgetting
λογίζεσθαι: to gather together
λόγος: speech, discourse

μαθήματα: things we can learn
μεταξύ: intermediate, something between
μὴ ὄν: non-being, non-entity
μνημοσύνη: keeping-in-mind, memory

νοεῖν: perceiving (by reason, νοῦς)
νοεῖσθαι: to be perceived (in νοεῖν)
νοούμενα: what is perceived (in νοεῖν)
νοῦς: reason

ὁμοίωσις: correspondence
ὄν: being (thing), beings
ὁρᾶν: to see, to look at
ὁρᾶσθαι: to be seen
ὀρθότης: correctness
ὁρώμενα: what is accessible to the eyes
οὐδέν: nothing
οὐσία: being

παιδεία: positionedness, education

σοφός: someone who understands
συλλογισμός: process of reasoning

τέλος: end, goal

φαντασία: what appears
φιλομαθής: the person who has the drive to really learn
φίλος: friend
φιλοσοφεῖν: to philosophize
φύσις: nature
φῶς: illumination, light

ψευδὴς δόξα: distorted view
ψεῦδος: distortion, untruth
ψυχή: soul